SENSATION, THE INTUITIVE SYSTEM, AND DESIGNED EXPERIENCE

THE MISSING LINKS TO LEARNING FOR HUMAN FLOURISHING

SENSATION, THE INTUITIVE SYSTEM, AND DESIGNED EXPERIENCE

THE MISSING LINKS TO LEARNING FOR HUMAN FLOURISHING

QING ARCHER ZHANG AND JAMES PAUL GEE

First published in 2023
as part of the Interdisciplinary Social Sciences Book Imprint
doi: 10.18848/78-1-957792-70-5/CGP (Full Book)

Common Ground Research Networks
2001 South First St, Suite 201 L
Champaign, IL 61820 USA
Ph: +1-217-328-0405

Library of Congress Cataloging-in-Publication Data

Names: Zhang, Qing Archer, author. | Gee, James Paul, author.
Title: Sensation, the intuitive system, and designed experience : the
   missing links to learning for human flourishing / Qing Archer Zhang,
   James Paul Gee.
Description: Champaign, IL : Common Ground Research Networks, [2023] |
   Includes bibliographical references and index. | Summary: "This
   groundbreaking book redefines human learning in the context of human
   flourishing. By examining what "experience" really means when we say
   "humans learn from experience," the authors propose a more holistic
   approach to education that goes beyond talk, texts, and analytical
   reasoning. This book highlights aspects of learning that are often
   overlooked in school, such as empathy, intuition, and balance. Drawing
   on insights from evolutionary biology, neuroscience, learning science,
   and the arts, the authors weave together a rich tapestry of ideas that
   challenge traditional approaches to education and the nature of human
   learning in and out of school. The book argues that good teaching is
   always a form of experience design and that not just school teachers but
   artists, architects, and good media designers are teachers as well. Its
   ideas about experience design are illustrated through examples from
   various media, including the widely revered Japanese anime series
   "Attack on Titan""-- Provided by publisher.
Identifiers: LCCN 2023027022 (print) | LCCN 2023027023 (ebook) | ISBN
   9781957792682 (hardback) | ISBN 9781957792699 (paperback) | ISBN
   9781957792705 (pdf)
Subjects: LCSH: Learning, Psychology of. | Experiential learning. |
   Intuition. | Holistic education.
Classification: LCC LB1060 .Z434 2023 (print) | LCC LB1060 (ebook) | DDC
   370.117--dc23/eng/20230712
LC record available at https://lccn.loc.gov/2023027022
LC ebook record available at https://lccn.loc.gov/2023027023

TABLE OF CONTENTS

INTRODUCTION

What is a Human?

We are interested in how humans learn and learn in a way that they flourish in life. Learning is not just about school. It is not even primarily about school. Learning is ubiquitous in life. We humans can potentially learn new things in any experience we have. The real issue with learning is not that people have learned—they almost always do learn something—but what they learned and whether it was good for them or not. And, yes, "good" requires a judgement; it requires we take a position on what is good and what is not. We will take and defend such a position in this book.

In mathematics classes at school, a student may have learned to pass math tests, but not learned why mathematics matters and is important. The student may have also learned that mathematics is not something she wants to engage with deeply. Even with good grades, she may have developed no capacity to think with mathematics in a fluid way. She will be like a dancer that can do dance steps correctly, one after another, but cannot really dance fluidly. The same thing can happen in any area, whether it be science or art.

We will argue that deep and useful learning should be like learning to dance fluidly. Deep and useful learning is a matter of performance. If you want to know art, this does not mean you have to be an artist (though that is an admirable goal and, by no means, requires you to be a "professional"). It means, at the least, that you can encounter a work of art with real engagement.

Many a person who has taken an art history class still stands mute and lifeless before a painting. It does not come alive to them. It does not really matter to them. Of course, not everything can matter to us. But here is the problem: Humans only learn well—in terms of placing what they have learned firmly in their mind for future use—if what they are learning matters to them, if they care about it in some meaningful and deep way (Damasio 2018; Immordino-Yang &

Damasio 2007). That is why so much of what we learn in school is not retained much past our school years. Too much of it mattered too little, perhaps only for grades or avoiding conflicts with parents and teachers. What is true of art is true of physics, gardening, cooking, civics, and anything else.

We mentioned at the start that humans usually learn something in any new experience they have. Experiences change people's brains and such changes are learning. What matters is what they learned, whether it was good or not. After all, a student could learn in math or art class that math or art is only for "gifted students," something that is both false and unhelpful to that student's life. We are interested in how learning can lead to human flourishing, but flourishing that is not achieved at the cost of others or the planet. This is what we count as good. Of course, this is a value judgment. However, we will see later that there are ways to measure the wellbeing of a human (or other sort of living creature) and, so, we can test whether the learner or those around the learner are flourishing as humans or not.

We cannot understand how humans learn and flourish unless we know what type of creature a human is. The same thing would be true if we were studying or caring for donkeys or dolphins. It is obvious that we could not take good care of a donkey or a dolphin if we did not know deeply what sort of creature they are. Yet, educational research spends far too little time thinking about what sort of creature a human is. Schools, we will argue, spend too much time teaching a creature that does not exist, a creature that is certainly not a human being. For example, they spend too much teaching a creature that will learn well what they do not care about. No such creature exists, for reasons we will make clear in this book.

If one had a teacher training program for teachers of donkeys or dolphins, surely there would be a good deal of discussion about what sorts of creatures donkeys or dolphins are, how they evolved, how their bodies and minds work, and how they sense the world. No such discussion is a part of teacher education, as far as we know. Perhaps, this is because, since we are humans, we presume we know ourselves—know what a human is. But this, we will see, is not true. Humans have a great many misconceptions about themselves.

In this book, we will use recent work on biology, evolution, human development, and neuroscience—as well as insights from art—to get at the questions: What is a human? How and when do humans learn well? When are they flourishing? This recent work is giving rise to new and important insights that we feel need to be seen as central to education, especially in our times of great change and peril, where human flourishing is hard indeed and will be even more so in the future. And, by "education" we mean in and out of school. Most of what constitutes an education in the broad sense happens outside school, though school can and should be a crucial guide for out of school learning. Perhaps, that should be, in the end, the main point of schooling.

Humans Learn from Experience

It is pretty much taken for granted that humans learn from experience (Barnett 2020; Eagleman 2020). Experience, for humans (and many other creatures), is composed of sensations, that is, interactions between the world and our sense organs (outer ones like vision and inner ones like the internal states we sense as feelings and emotions). When these sensations have mattered enough to us—have made us care enough about them to want to retain them—we "store" them (keep a "record" of them) in our brain. We do this so that we can make use of them in the future (Seligman, Railton, Baumeister, Sripada 2016).

The brain "stores" sensations in the sense that it represents all the stored associations—all the patterns, regularities, and connections—we have discovered in experience as connections among neurons. So, if I have an experience in which I have sensed an association (relationship) among the green of forest trees, the sound of a babbling brook, the feel on my skin of cool mist coming off the brook in the early morning, and an inner feeling of peace, all these elements will be represented by connections among ensembles of neurons in my brain, connections that represent the way all these elements are associated (connected) in my experience (Barnett 2020; Eagleman 2020).

When I remember the babbling brook in the forest, this means I have activated the set of neurons that represent this element of my experience. In turn, these neurons can set off activations of the sets of neurons that represent some or all of the rest of the elements in my experience (the green of the trees, the feel of the mist, the peace I felt).

The whole set of associations/connections in my brain represent all the elements of the world that I have sensed when interacting with the world with enough caring to have retained them. We can activate these associations to remember. We can mix and match them to create fantasies. We can replay them in different ways and sequences to plan our actions or futures before we act.

It is much as if we can record an experience while we are having it, record it as a sort of mental "video" (but one that captures all senses, not just vision) and then store this video in our head. Then we can replay all the videos we have recorded as a form of memory or slice and edit them to create new videos that work as imagination or scenario planning. This is, at base, just what learning is (Seligman, Railton, Baumeister, Sripada 2016). Learning is the effects of our former experiences—as they are activated and edited—on our futures. The fact that humans can use experiences (composed of sensations) to make "media" in their heads, media they can edit and use for different purposes, means humans were in the media business long before media was invented. It has always been a capacity of their brains.

It is interesting to note that the first media humans ever invented—starting about 60,000 years ago—were paintings on rocks and cave walls (Curtis 2006). These paintings were not just realistic pictures of animals that humans had experienced in their daily lives (some of which they hunted), but also pictures of half human/half animal creatures, imaginary beings. Reality and fantasy have been with us from the beginning of our becoming recognizably modern humans, as were these painters, though they lived long ago.

There is ample evidence, especially from Australia (David 2017), that these paintings often represented spirits or creator gods or priests/shamans (spiritual leaders). So, too, religion in the form of spirituality has been with us humans from the beginning. It is interesting that many Schools of Education celebrate diversity, but assiduously avoid religion and spirituality, major sources of historical, cultural, and social diversity today and across human history.

The human brain has the capacity to reorganize aspects of experience into new combinations—into possibilities, paradoxes, imaginary beings, even impossible things and happenings—beyond what any other animal can do. This capacity, in its evolutionary origins, is probably deeply connected to the form of communication (human language) that evolved in humans. No other form of animal communication is like human language, what linguists call "natural language," (Chomsky 2016). Animal communication systems can make limited messages about the here and now or the near future. Human language can make a limitless number of messages about the past and future—near or far—as well as the here and now. The limitless of the human mind and human language may well have arisen together in human evolutionary history.

Language

Human language can communicate an infinite number of messages about the real, the fictional, and the impossible. This is thanks to the "recursive" syntax of human language (Chomsky 2016). There is no longest sentence in a human language because one can always embed another phrase or clause into whatever sentence one produces (e.g., "Mary thinks her sister left" → "Joe knows Mary thinks her sister left" → "Sue hopes Joe knows Mary thinks her sister left"). Furthermore, any human can say something that has never been said before (e.g., "White wontons dream of black noodles").

When we use the world "sensation," we mean the things we sense (see, taste, smell, hear, and feel) coming from the outside world and the feelings and emotions that we get when we interact with the world. But, of course, we also hear and read words, a very special sort of sensory experience. As we have just seen, human language is quite different from the communication system of any other animal. Human language can be both much more general and abstract and can communicate many more messages than any other animal communication system.

When you sense (hear or see) the word "tree," you sense sounds or letters that have nothing to do with trees. The word "tree" is a completely arbitrary way to label trees. Other languages use different sounds or letters (if they use letters). When you hear or read the word, it contains no sensory properties or any details relevant to trees. Of course, sensing a real tree is replete with details and even a picture of a tree has many more details connected to trees than does the word "tree" (or "arbor" in Latin and "mti" in Swahili).

Language and sensation (of real things, images, or media) are very different ways of experiencing and learning. Language is abstract in a way other sorts of sensation never is. The word "tree" displays no features of trees at all. It lets us talk about them in a quite general way. Of course, we can add modifiers, but we will never arrive at anything as specific, full-featured, and replete as experiencing a tree. While I can say "a large green tree," any actual tree is a specific shade of green and a specific size.

Hearing or reading about trees—though often privileged in school—is a quite different way of learning about trees than being among them. We will see that one is not better than the other. Each has distinctive strengths and weaknesses. However, they work poorly when they are not connected and mutually informing. Here, again, we see an area where much formal schooling fails to represent the way humans actually work. Some schooling borders on sensory deprivation and, as we will show in this book, in such a situation neither people nor words can breathe.

Teaching as Designing Experience

Humans are, like many other animal species, social animals. This means not only that they learn from others, but, in many cases, that these others "teach" them. They teach them by designing experiences for them so that what they learn is not just left to chance as they encounter the world. In the animal world, by the way, teaching is much more common than most people realize (Kline 2014).

We will argue that learning, at its most fundamental level, is based on "designed experience," which means designing sensations (sensations integrated with words or not) for others. The people who design experiences for others to learn by—and this includes parents, social groups, artists, architects, media designers, and school teachers, among others—can be teaching good or bad things. They can seek to indoctrinate and manipulate or empower and free others from limitations that are undermining their flourishing as humans. We are, of course, interested in good teaching and good learning. We will later offer an objective measurement of flourishing (the absence of allostatic overload) and use this as our standard by which to judge good and bad teaching and learning.

Because we believe that humans learn from experience and that the most pervasive and powerful form of this learning in social animals is based on designed experiences—thus, the design of sensation—we are interested, as well, in how experience designers do their work, especially when they are doing good work. This book offers both a theory (a perspective, a viewpoint) and analyses of examples of experience design for learning. While we will deal with various artists and poets as examples of designers of experience, our primary example, when we apply our ideas to understanding how good media design works, will come from the Japanese anime series *Attack on Titan* (AOT). AOT—like a good deal of other anime—is a massively popular and widely respected worldwide phenomenon among the young and young adults.

Why Japanese anime? We chose anime because it is a form of media highly popular across many cultures among young people today. It is a worldwide phenomenon loved by a quite diverse array of people. It is "popular culture" (for the most part), but, more than any other popular media we know, it deals with important ideas in innovative and aesthetic ways. These are ideas of the sort that many (at least used to) consider core to a good education. They are ideas like freedom and responsibility; what we owe family, kin, and strangers; the nature of living beings and humans; individuality and society; violence, war, and government; the nature of good and evil; the risks and possibilities of science and technology; compassion, trauma, spirituality, death, and more.

Good anime often deals with these issues in ways that lead to questions, discussion, paradoxes, complexities, nuances, and dilemmas, not certainty and indoctrination. These are the sorts of "big ideas" that, we believe, should compose the curriculum for an education, in or out of school, for citizens as members of society and for humans who see themselves as kin to all other humans and part of life as a whole.

Japanese anime is often much more dramatic, "in your face," imaginative, and over the top than other forms of media. Characters cry, scream, go berserk, transform into other beings, and face massive challenges where they often lose, but never give up. They live in worlds where anything might happen and strange creatures might appear at any time. Creatures that look unhuman, even robotic, or ugly, often behave more humanely than humans. Bad people do good things, good people do bad ones, and often neither we, nor they, know whether they are "really" good or bad or somewhere in-between.

Characters in anime worry constantly about friends and friendship, but will sacrifice themselves for strangers. Characters in anime even sometimes stop and discuss deep issues and the nature of good and bad with each other in quite didactic ways. Anime does not shy away from violence, trauma, ugliness, controversy, or strangeness, though it can find great beauty in nature, friendship, or life, even in their most mundane aspects.

Because of these features—which are, of course, not as extreme in all anime—anime is often not something that would ever be used in school, though it can be a great force for learning, discovery, discussion, and reflection out of school. The trouble is, of course, that "real" life is a lot more like anime, as we humans experience it when we are awake to experience, than it is like school. And life, too, in that sense, often cannot go to school either. Nonetheless, the students bring it with them.

Where We are Going

We will deal in this book with the human mind/brain as an integral part of the human body. Brain and body are not separate. We will deal with the brain-body as an integral part of its environment. A creature and its environment are not separate. We will deal with language and thinking, on the one hand, and with sensing and feeling, on the other, as reciprocal forces, each informing the other. They are not separate either. But we will argue that sensation and feeling are prior to language and thinking in the order of life, in human existence, and when we humans act in the world for our survival and flourishing. This, too, is not the view of school or much educational research.

We will deal, as well, with social groups and society. And we will deal with spirits and spirituality. We will see that humans treat experiences they have had in virtual worlds in much the same way as they treat experiences they have had in the real world. They form mental associations represented in neural connections pretty much in the same way from both and sometimes cannot remember which is which.

And, too, we will see that humans can compose and live in virtual worlds inside their own heads via simulation (playing media inside their own heads). Humans can even design virtual experiences in their own heads to teach themselves, to be their own experience designers. We will also see that we can learn a good deal about teaching as experience design from artists, old famous dead ones and new emerging young ones.

We will find that there are two sides to each human (McGilchrist 2019). We have already touched on this when we contrasted language and sensation above. One side is linguistic, rational, thinks in categories and seeks solutions to specific well-defined problems. The other side is rooted in sensation, specifics, nuances, connections, and the perception of integrated wholes. One side is good at getting a part of the picture clear and right and the other is good at putting that part back into the bigger picture where it becomes part of a whole that is more than the sum of its parts. When these two sides operate well together, humans can be smart. When they do not operate well together, humans can be strikingly stupid, as we are seeing in our current world where humans are jeopardizing human life and much of the rest of life on earth.

We will be using relatively new work from a variety of different disciplines. This work is teaching us a good deal about the nature of life, the sorts of creatures humans are, the way humans learn, and what they need to flourish. It comes from biology, evolutionary biology, neuroscience, learning science, developmental psychology, animal studies, and work on sensation in science and in art. As with any new and cutting-edge research, there are many disagreements, terminological differences, and cases where ordinary language becomes misleading, but jargon gets cloying. However, we are interested in the big picture that is emerging and some of the details are less crucial at this level. We will do our best to be clear and consistent in how we use words and fair to the controversies without losing our path through a very thick forest.

Of course, there are dangers at getting out of academic silos and looking at connections across them. However, we believe that today, as we face a great many interacting crises in our world, there is grave danger in staying in our silos and doing "business as usual." What life is, what a human is, what learning is, what makes for flourishing, and how we can design experiences to help people and society flourish are not issues that could possibly be dealt with in any one silo. These issues are too important to be left as bits and pieces spread across silos that do not interact with each other enough. If we get some details wrong in the big picture, we believe that, as is the way with pictures, the basic pattern will still emerge and even show us where revisions are most needed.

A major paradox will arise from this book. As we take a tour of what is most central to making a human a human (in the way that a different tour could tell us what was most central to making a donkey a donkey or a dolphin a dolphin), we will see that the great majority of what is on our tour plays next to no role in school or only a very minor one.

This is odd, indeed. School is where we should be learning to be social (humans are social animals) and participants in social and cultural groups, small and large, including citizenship. It is as if we were to send donkeys or dolphins to schools that paid little attention to what is known about donkeys and dolphins. Of course, donkeys and dolphins do not usually go to school (though sometimes they do). For better or worse, humans do go to school, though, like donkeys and dolphins, most of what they learn and retain is learned out of school.

Nonetheless, it surely would be good—especially now in a time of change and crisis—for school to make more vital contact with life. After all, this is just to ask that school make vital contact with sensation and experience that make up the ever essence of learning and living.

We will see that what school mostly offers—talk, texts, and analytic reasoning—are profoundly impoverished when they are not integrated with core human capacities that must be developed to fully function for flourishing. These capacities are: empathy, intuition, balance (homeostasis), atmosphere, emotions, personhood, immersion in landscapes, simulation (imagination), action, situating language in experience, and what we will call "sensuous constructions." All of these are configurations of sensations. So, how sensation makes humans a specific type of living being and makes them as social animals is at the core of our story. What this can tell us about school and society—and why we face so many crises in both today—is also a central part of our story.

CHAPTER 1

ATTACK ON TITAN

In this book, we will use examples from a highly popular and highly regarded anime series *Attack on Titan* (AOT) to exemplify some of the points we want to make about designing good experiences for learning. "Anime," as we use the term here, means a Japanese form of animated film or video, not animation in general. AOT is a series with many episodes each of which is about 25 minutes. It started in 2013 and will conclude in 2023. Like many other anime series, AOT is based on a manga series. "Manga" is a term for wide variety of comic books and graphic novels originating in Japan. They are about a much wider array of topics, and written and illustrated for a much wider audience, than are comic books in the United States.

As of September 2022, the AOT manga had over 110 million copies in print. It is one of the best-selling manga series of all time and has won a number of major awards. As an anime series, AOT was the world's most in-demand TV show and anime of 2021 (Parrot Analytics). In 2022 it was the fourth most popular television show in the world. The AOT anime series was a massive worldwide hit. As one source says: "It's come to represent the anime industry itself, a business currently swelling and gaining more worldwide notoriety than ever before (https://www.polygon.com/23012210/attack-on-titan-biggest-anime)."

Why do we use anime for examples here when we could have used examples from other types of media? We do so because anime is today a widely popular form of media with young people across the world. Some of this anime deals with deep issues about morality, freedom, justice, death, government, history, friendship, love, social ties, responsibility, the health of the natural world we humans live in, and the nature of human beings. These are issues central not just to a real education but to living an aware, examined, and humane life as a person.

Educators largely ignore anime and yet it is today one of the deepest sources of out of school learning, especially around issues central to our complex, fast changing, and dangerous times. School, in our view, does a poor job, for the most part, in dealing with such issues. Anime deals with them in ways grounded in drama, sensation, feelings and emotions and yet, over time, leads viewers to reflection, analysis, discussion, argumentation, theorizing, and personal commitments to reasoned beliefs and values, at both the individual level and on a myriad of internet spaces where fans of AOT gather.

Much good anime—of course, not all anime is good anime and not all anime deals with the issues we have mentioned—gives viewers well designed experiences for learning and reflection. Such anime often reflects in dramatic and interesting ways the principles we will discuss in this book.

AOT, like much good anime, shows things about people and the world that cannot go to the antiseptic world of school where even references to evolution, the age of the universe, vaccines, climate change, and cultural diversity can upset people. Representations of violence are, of course, taboo in school, yet gun violence is an everyday occurrence in the news and fear of such violence is prevalent in many schools. Anime shows the world in imaginative terms that allow viewers to see the real world in new ways. It is about the world young people live in, in ways school rarely is; it is about the world young people must eventually change if they are to flourish.

When we were writing this book there were widespread protests in China over the strict COVID lockdown policies of the government and over the authoritarian nature of the government in general. Such protestors needed great courage to go into the streets in the face of a force that seemed so overwhelmingly more powerful than them, namely government, its police, and army. One protestor wrote the following on a Chinese media platform:

> When I was watching Attack on Titan the first time, I did not quite understand it. Now [in the midst of the protests] I'm watching it the second time and I realize I am in it. (Anonymous, Weibo)

In the summary below, readers will encounter some strange and magical things. Such things are commonplace in mythologies across the world and, indeed, in the Old Testament, a book that many a Western adult has read (much of the Old Testament could not go to school either). As we will point out below, AOT takes some of its inspiration from mythology.

Summary of AOT

Both viewers of AOT and the characters in it operate with very limited knowledge until well into the story when both viewers and characters make major discoveries. In fact, an important aspect—and demand—of viewing AOT is being able to live, for a while, sometimes a long while, with partial understandings. In AOT, later episodes "unlock" secrets in earlier ones. This encourages viewers to watch earlier episodes again to notice and make sense of details they missed the first time around.

In our summary, we will explicate some of what is unknown to viewers and characters for a good deal of AOT. This will, hopefully, create enough background for readers who have not watched AOT to understand our analyses. However, readers need not have watched AOT to get the point of our examples. With a bit of summary, the examples can stand on their own.

The Rise of Eldia: Ymir and the Founding Titan

Though it takes many episodes for viewers to discover, the AOT story has at its origin a spiritual figure named Ymir. Ymir was a slave to a man named Fritz, a leader of an insignificant tribe of people called Eldians. One day Ymir offended Fritz and he had his soldiers pursue her to kill her. As Ymir was running away from the soldiers, she came upon a giant tree with a hole at its base. She jumped into the hole to hide, but fell through a sinkhole beneath it into a deep pool of water. A strange shining creature came up from the depths of the pool and fused with her. The creature transformed Ymir into something not previously seen on the earth, a Titan. She became, at that moment, the Founding Titan, a human who can transform into an enormous humanoid creature with immense powers and then return to normal human form.

For reasons viewers can only surmise—but have to do with a recuring theme in AOT of freedom versus subjection—Ymir returns to Fritz. When she returns, Fritz uses her immense powers, together with his army, to build his tribe into a conquering empire, the Eldian empire. In the act, he destroys—and earns the hatred of—other nations including the then very powerful nation of Marley.

The Nine Titans

Ymir and Fritz eventually have three daughters. When Ymir dies, she goes to a spiritual place called "the Coordinate," a place that connects all Eldians through history. Ymir's daughters inherit her Titan powers and over time pass those powers down to their descendants. Eventually, there come to be Nine Titians each one inherited and passed down by an elite Eldian family. The royal family is ruled by the Founding Titan and the other families by the other Titans with their own unique powers.

The Fall of Eldia

Eldia ruled the world with its Titans until, eventually, the elite families that controlled the nine Titans, began to bicker and fight for power among themselves. Civil war erupted. This dissension opened the way for Marley, Eldia's most bitter enemy, to undermine the Eldian empire. Collaborating with some of the conflicting Eldian families and gaining their loyalty for Marley, Marley acquired for itself seven of the nine Titans, Titians who then fought for Marley. This deprived Eldia of its main source of power and, thereby, Marley began its return to prominence in the world.

As war weakened Eldia and the defeat of Eldia appeared inevitable, the Eldian king, Karl Fritz (a later king than the original Fritz)—who has the Founding Titan powers—decided to exile himself to remote Paradis Island. Other Eldians, fearing Marley's coming victory, flock to join him. Karl Fritz then brings the war to an end with a proclamation that he and the Eldians in Paradis will confine themselves within three giant walls. Fritz also makes a vow that is meant to bind him and his successors forever, a vow to never again start a war or use Titan powers to destroy others. In exchange, the rest of the world should let him and his people enjoy peace inside their walls.

To prevent his fellow Eldians in Paradis from knowing how they used to rule the world with Titan powers and how the rest of the world hates them, King Karl Fritz (using his Titan powers) erases the memories of everyone living behind the walls. This is why, when viewers begin their AOT journey, neither they, nor the characters they are coming to know, know this history.

When the truce was made official, some Eldians had failed to reach Paradis Island and were stranded on the now Marley-controlled mainland. Since Marley views the Eldians as their former conquerors and oppressors, these left-behind Eldians are treated as disdained second-class citizens, forced to live in a ghetto surrounded by a wall. However, a select few of these Eldians gain a better life in exchange for inheriting the powers of one of the Titans Marley acquired from Eldia and using their Titan powers to fight as part of the Marleyan military.

If any non-Titan Eldian in Marley commits a crime or violates the restrictions placed upon them, they are injected with a serum that turns them into a new type of Titan, a mindless one, called Pure Titans (to be distinguished from the nine intelligent Titans). When they transform, their bodies turn into oversized caricatures of their former selves, developing exaggerated facial features and disproportionate anatomy. Their heights vary, with some being around 16 feet tall, while others 50 feet tall or more. They are left to roam outside Paradis's walls and will eat any Eldian that ventures outside. They can, however, be controlled by some intelligent Titans who can use them as battle forces. Marley has placed them outside the walls of Paradis to be sure the Eldians never rise again to threaten Marley.

Marley's Attack on Paradis

The peace between Paradis Island and the rest of the world continued for a century. However, as Marley continues military expeditions around the world, it eventually begins to run out of natural resources and has left itself vulnerable to new military technologies being developed by their enemies across the world. So, Marley decides to invade Paradis Island, which sits on a huge reserve of valuable fossil fuels and other natural resources. It also hopes to capture the Founding Titan and co-opt his powers for themselves. Thus, Marley sends a secret team of its Titans to Paradis Island as spies. They hide their Titan powers (appearing only as humans) until the time is ripe to lead the Marleyan army in a takeover of Paradis Island. This team consists of Annie Leonhart (the Female Titan), Reiner Braun (the Armored Titan), and Bertholdt Hoover (the Colossus Titan)—each a major character in AOT—and directly leads to the events seen in the very first episode of AOT.

The Three Walls

When AOT starts, viewers see humans living on Paradis Island behind its three high walls, one inside the other: Wall Sina, Wall Rose, and Wall Maria. These walls exist to protect the people from the Titans outside the walls. The people of Paradis do not know why they live as they do, since, as we saw, King Karl Fritz erased their memories. The richest people live inside all three walls, the poorest live behind the outer wall only, and the people in the middle leave in-between. The rich are safest from an attack on the walls and the poor are most vulnerable.

Figure 1. The Three Walls (WIT Studio)

One day, two massive Titans (two of the Marleyan spies in their Titan form) tear a huge hole in Wall Maria and they, together with countless Pure (unintelligent) Titans, enter the town and begin to kill and feed on the helpless townspeople. A young boy, Eren Jaeger, watches in horror as his mother is devoured. This event makes Eren determined, when he is old enough, to join the Survey Corps, the part of the Paradis army whose mission it is to venture outside the walls to battle the Titans and fight for human freedom. Unfortunately, the Survey Corps has never been the least bit successful against the Titans and is considered a suicide mission.

Eren Jaeger

Eren Jaeger is the main character of AOT. He appears at the outset to be the "hero," but his status as a hero becomes problematic and complex as AOT proceeds. Eren grew up in the Shiganshina district of Paradis Island, a poor part of Paradis where the initial Titan breech of the walls occurred. Paradis Island is a deeply class-based society and, so, it is the poorer citizens who initially face the Titan assault.

Eren lives with his mother, Carla, his father, Grisha, and his adopted sister, Mikasa, and he spends a good deal of time with his childhood friend, Armin. Eren and Armin, even as children, have a deep desire to flee the walls of Paradis and see the wider outside world, whatever might be in it. They feel trapped behind the walls and see escape from the walls as the ultimate freedom. Many others in Paradis see the walls as a source of security and safety and look at everything outside the walls as alien and fearsome.

Amidst the chaos that ensues when Wall Maria is breached and after Eren's house is destroyed by a Titan, Eren's father finds him in a shelter and leads him into a forest. There he gives Eren a key to the basement under their home and tells him to do whatever he can to return there when and if he can, though this will involve fighting the Titans that now inhabit the area. The basement contains documents that detail the secrets about who and what the Titans really are and tell the true history of the world Eren lives in. This is all the knowledge that King Karl Fritz had wiped from his people's minds.

Eren's father also injects Eren with a special serum and forces his son to consume him. This process gives Eren Titan powers—the Attack Titan powers and eventually the Founding Titan powers—because Eren's father is much more significant than he and viewers know until much later in AOT. Thanks to the serum he has been injected with, Eren will not know or remember what has happened to him until much later either. Only later will he discover, to his amazement, that he has Titan powers. As one internet site says: "And here begins the tale of one of the most messed up families in manga and anime." Eren will enter the Survey Corps with his friends enraged by Titans and committed to killing them all, thanks to having seen his mother killed by a Titan, only to discover later he is himself a Titan.

There follows in AOT a great many other dramatic plot points. As Eren and his friends fight Titans, they discover there are spies in their midst who happen to be their friends. After Eren discovers he is a Titan, the Survey Corps does not know whether to fear him or view him as a reliable super weapon for Eldia. When Eldia comes to face an all-out attack from Marley and its allies across the world, the Survey Corps finds out that their current Eldian king is a fake and, eventually, discovers, from the documents in Eren's basement, the truth about the world they live in. Marley eventually overwhelms Paradis and threatens it with total destruction. At this point, Eren, now with the full powers of the Founding Titan, faces a profound choice: Should he destroy Marley and much of the rest of the known world (who are Marley's allies) using his Founding Titan powers or should he let Marley destroy Paradis and its people and, in the act, finally close the chapter on the Eldians' past history of conquest using Titans? Eren sees no path to a possible peace, but his friends Mikasa and Armin, in desperation, seek such a path, even if it means losing their best friend, Eren.

A rough plot summary of AOT can make it sound like a soap opera. However, as many fans of AOT know, AOT draws on a good deal of mythology and on the ancient history of humans here on earth. For example, Rachel Troung (2018) had this to say in her undergraduate honors thesis:

> … as the plot moves forward, the reader is introduced to a Titan, the primary monstrous antagonists of the graphic novel, named Ymir. All other Titans descend from her bloodline. The latter immediately draws a parallel with the primordial frost giant of Norse mythology, also named Ymir, from whom all frost giants descend. The parallel of the Titan Ymir to the primordial frost giant of Norse mythology is not simply isolated to the character. Throughout the graphic novel, Isayama draws strong parallels between his characters and the gods and stories found in Norse mythology. This, I argue, thus sets Attack on Titan apart from other manga that achieved large volumes of international sales and critical acclaim, such as Dragon Ball and Naruto. In the case of Dragon Ball, "it is strongly influenced by the two main religions in Japan (Shinto and Buddhism)" (Mínguez-López 28). As for Naruto, its "outstanding popularity… in the west can probably be traced back to the fact that it is a ninja tale" (Yukari 174). Both Mínguez-López and Yukari indicate that a large part of the identity of Dragon Ball and Naruto comes from their strong roots in Eastern folklore and myth. However, they are matched in popularity by Attack on Titan, which draws much more inspiration from a Western standpoint. It is through using Western mythology as a source of inspiration that Attack on Titan allows itself to stand out from other internationally successful manga. (p. 2)

In a 2017 article in *The Comics Grid: A Journal of Comics Scholarship*, Francesco Ursini has this to say about the walls in AOT (*Shingeki no Kyojin* in Japanese):

> *Shingeki no Kyojin*'s world is modelled on a dichotomy of Norse culture: ingards and utangards (Lindow 2001: 30–40; see also Yamazaki 2015). Ingards (i.e. 'inside') was a space where the laws of a community held, opposed to utangards, an outer space of lawlessness. Fences and walls symbolically separated the two spaces. In *Shingeki no Kyojin*'s world, the external world of the Titans and the internal world of the world of humans indicates this separation.

David Frye's important 2018 book *Walls: A History of Civilization in Blood and Brick* argues that this inside/outside is, in fact, central to the history of humans on earth. It is the dynamic between walled cities where "civilization" flourishes and the "barbarians" that always reside beyond them and threaten them, barbarians that betoken both freedom and risk in life beyond walls.

AOT constitutes a "curriculum" for the study of humans, their ideologies, human history, and deep philosophical issues about human nature. At the same time, it is "one hell" of a story.

CHAPTER 2

EMPATHY

We will begin our discussion of humans, learning, and flourishing with a capacity that is necessary for human flourishing that is not at the cost of others. This capacity is empathy. The word "empathy" is used for two different things. One is perspective taking, that is, being able to take the perspective of another person. The other is what we will use the term "empathy" here to mean: going beyond perspective taking to see and feel the world as if we were the other person.

Both perspective taking and empathy are capacities most humans are capable of, though there are disorders that make them hard or impossible for certain people. However, these capacities must be activated by use and people can learn to get better at them. Good experience designers can design experiences where people can learn about and practice empathy and move beyond factors like bias, fear, and othering those who are not "like us."

Before getting to an analytic discussion of empathy we are going to look at one example of how the designers of the anime *Attack on Titan* (AOT) create experiences that encourage and help viewers engage in empathy. This is a good example of designing experiences to teach others an important skill.

Entering Eyes

When AOT starts we see a massive Titan attacking one of the town's 50-meter-high walls. These walls have protected the townspeople for one hundred years. People have come to trust them. Now that trust is shattered. One moment the townspeople are peacefully going about their business. The next moment a massive Titan hand is grasping the top of a giant wall ready to tear it down. The townspeople at first stare at the Titan in shock and then flee.

This scene unfolds in a series of shots that are accompanied by eerie and foreboding music. The first three shots in the scene as are shown below in (1-3).

Viewers eventually realize that what the townspeople in (3) are staring at is the huge red Titan hand in (4). These shots below are stills we have clipped from AOT. In the show, of course, they are moving images.

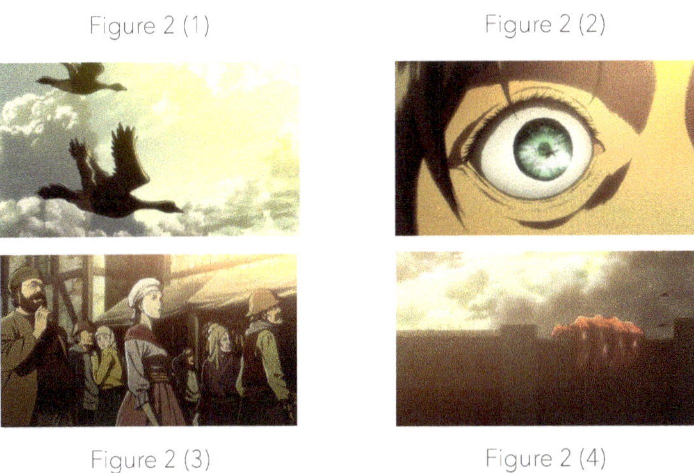

Figure 2. Eren and the townspeople spot a Titan's hand (WIT Studio)

In (1) we see birds flying across the sky. Then in (2) we see Eren's eye with the image of the birds flying across it. While it is hard to see them in a still picture, they are quite clear in the video as they move across Eren's eye.

Then, in (3)—and in some following shots not shown here—we see people staring up in shock at the massive Titan hand in (4). When viewers see Eren's eye in shot 2, they realize he is looking at the birds flying in the air, the birds they have just seen in (1). Eventually, the birds fly across the top of the wall and over the Titan's hand. While the townspeople's attention is immediately drawn to the massive hand, Eren's gaze is fixated on the birds and their flight.

When we see the shot of Eren's eye—with an image of the birds flying across his retina—we, as viewers, are positioned as if we were staring, up close and personal, directly into Eren's eye. This is not at all a "natural" image. In fact, it would be an odd thing to do to a person and would rarely occur in everyday life (unless you were an eye doctor). This is an artificial image, an image designed to affect us in a certain way. It is an image made to get us to act in a certain way as viewers.

This image of Eren's eye is not a realistic image like a photograph or realistic painting. On the other hand, it is not a line drawing. It is replete with details like a realistic image, unlike a line drawing, but not with the realism of a photograph or film. It is an anime image.

By anime we do not just mean cartoon like images or animation. We mean a hand-drawn or computer-generated animation of the sort typical of Japanese anime. Japanese anime (which may be imitated in other countries) designs images in a distinctive way. By "image" here we mean both a single static image or an animation containing a changing image. In the case of the image in (2), it is not static in AOT, but moves; viewers see the birds in flight across Eren's eye.

We want to know what a designed image like (2) does. We believe it is relevant to how deep human engagement and learning work. Humans only learn, or, at least, learn well, when they are engaged. The designed image in (2), in its context, certainly creates engagement. And, of course, the image communicates something to the viewer and communication is a form of learning.

In this shot we learn that Eren is looking at the birds. There are different ways this could have been communicated. We could have learned much the same thing in words ("Eren stared intently at the flying birds"). Or we could have learned it in line drawings. In fact, like many anime series, AOT is based on a manga and the manga is made of black and white line drawings. They, too, could communicate much the same thing. Different ways to communicate have different effects. We will later be concerned with the differences between communication in words and communication in designed images, including anime designed images.

However, communication is not the key goal of the image in (2). The key goal is to make the viewer jump into Eren's head (to enter into his head through his eye). The designers want the viewer to sense, feel, and think from Eren's embodied perspective in the virtual world, not from their own perspective as someone looking at images on a screen. They want the viewer to look through Eren's eyes, in two senses: go through them into his mind and look out at the world through them.

Why do the designers of the AOT anime want viewers to do this? They want viewers, over the entirety of AOT, to build up in their own minds a view of who Eren is, what motivates him, and how to assess his actions. They want viewers to construct Eren as a character for themselves. To do this, they want the viewer to move continuously between two different perspectives. One perspective is an outside perspective composed of what viewers see and hear about Eren from their perspective as a viewer living outside the virtual world of AOT. The other perspective—a process which starts in AOT with the image in (2)—is an inside perspective composed of what viewers have sensed, felt, and thought from inside Eren, from his own embodied perspective in his world (AOT's virtual world).

Seeing the birds fly across Eren's eye starts a process of trying to mirror in our own mind and body what Eren is seeing, feeling, and thinking. Mirroring is not just a capacity of human beings' mirror neurons, which allow humans to imitate others in the privacy of their own mind (Hickok 2014; Ramachandran 2000). It is a yet more general capacity based on our evolution as social animals.

The designers of AOT do not want to tell us directly and didactically who Eren is, what motivates him, and whether his actions are good or bad, impulsive or planned, truthful or not. They want us to discover this for ourselves and to discover it by living within Eren, as well as by observing him from the outside. Across all the episodes of AOT—from childhood to adulthood—Eren is a massively complex character. But then, every human, in their own way—when and if we ever get to know them as intensely as we come to know Eren—is massively complex and never knowable just from an outside perspective.

The designers of AOT want us to answer questions about Eren—Who is Eren? What motivates him? Is he good or bad?—for ourselves by using not just outside evidence, as we might in school or a court of law, but also an inside evidence based on having "walked in Eren's shoes." We viewers have to continuously juxtapose our own sensing, feeling, and thinking with Eren's sensing, feeling, and thinking as we have vicariously experienced it, not just inferred it from outside, detached evidence.

When we enter Eren's eyes and mind, we come to feel his overwhelming urge to fly free like the birds, rather than be trapped like a bird in a cage or cattle in a pen behind walls that have inevitably failed. The other townspeople see the walls as safety and their fear now leads them to flee inwards towards the safety of the inner walls that have not yet failed. Eren's insight ("inner sight") beckons him outward toward freedom. Is this, though, just a child-like fantasy in the face of terror or is Eren holding on to hope and getting the glint of an idea that might grow into a plan?

Eren, it seems, retreats into a fantasy of flight. Yet this simple fantasy, acted out in his head, will issue into his own idea of—and his obsession with—freedom (defined in his own terms). A great deal of AOT will be about what freedom means or can mean to humans and how it relates to walls, rights, war, choices, history, and who does or does not count as a human. These larger issues both start with Eren's eye and are embodied in Eren throughout the course of AOT, an Eren we both observe and observe through.

AOT continually uses designed sensation—for example, images of eyes, birds, and other specific sensations created by words, movements, actions, sounds, and music—to embody and concretize "abstract" ideas about freedom, choice, responsibility, character, and the nature of humanity. Such ideas—the stuff of philosophy—only really exist as they are acted out in, and shape, lived history. They are not just philosophy, they are the stuff of life, society, and history. Philosophy can most certainly illuminate them but must stem from and return to the ground of lived experience.

Eren, while he is sensing the birds in flight, is moving in his mind from sensation (birds) to sense making (about constraint and freedom). And, we viewers, too, start down that path when we enter Eren's eye and mind and mirror his feelings, thinking, and being. This is just the beginning of the path; it is but a tentative first step. We will spend a long time in AOT looking at and looking through Eren, not just looking, but sensing and feeling beyond sight as well. We will inhabit Eren's body and mind even though Eren is a virtual character and not real person—a magic trick indeed.

When we talk about sensing, feeling, and thinking from Eren's embodied perspective within the specific context he is in, we are talking about one meaning of the term "empathy," a strong form of empathy. Humans evolved the ability to engage in this sort of empathy—and to have it even for fictional characters—because they are social animals. To social animals, it is crucial to be able to figure out what other animals of your kind are feeling, thinking, and planning to do. Being able to think about what others are thinking has been called a "theory of mind" (Goldman 2006; Gopnik 1993). We humans early in life learn that others have minds like ours.

But a theory of mind is not empathy in the deep sense. A theory of mind means I can try to guess what you are feeling and thinking by asking myself how I would feel and think in your position. Empathy is a yet more powerful theory of mind. It is about trying to feel and think from your perspective realizing that you are not me, you are a being with a different background and different experiences than mine. And, for a moment, I inhabit your being and leave mine behind. It is a sort of out of body experience.

All humans can make pretty good predictions about what others who share their own background, culture, and experiences will feel or think in given circumstances. It is much harder to predict what people different from us will feel and think in given circumstances. This ability would not have been important when we were hunters and gatherers living among a small group that shared nearly everything. It is crucial, though, in the "modern" world where most of us live amongst diversity. Indeed, the only way modern people, people living in diverse communities in a global world, can achieve understanding and peace is through empathy in the sense we are using the term.

The state of conflict and "us" versus "them" hatreds in the United States and across the world today tell us this is not something that is easy for humans. It has to be learned and good art and media can be a key force for teaching empathy.

Empathy requires practice. It requires living with care and attention among others, even others, like Eren, in virtual worlds (where we can do less harm and risk less damage). It requires, as well, that we have a theory of other humans that is not based just on ourselves, but on the nature of humans as types of creatures who enact common humanity in quite diverse ways. It requires that feeling for and with others (an inside view) reciprocally interacts with intellectual analysis (an outside view), but intellectual analysis grounded in situated cases and concrete sensations. One without the other, as we will see, can be dangerous. AOT is at one and the same time training for empathy and an analysis/theory of the human condition.

Deep Canvasing

Humans can view other humans in two different ways. We can view another human as an abstract decontextualized category (gay, African-American, immigrant, and so forth) or as a specific contextualized individual (Susie, my half-Asian, half-Irish immigrant neighbor who has such cute kids and who helped me last week when I tripped and fell in my yard and hurt my head and who I once drove to her doctor's appointment when her car suddenly would not start...). Situational Susie is not eclipsed by her categories, though abstract Susie can be when she becomes a symbol of one's views on immigration.

When you are trying to change someone's mind on an issue (for example, immigration or gay marriage) that they strongly associate with their social identity (for example, being a part of a group that believes "white" people are being replaced by minorities and immigrants)—you will not accomplish this by arguing over categories directly. You have to start at an experiential level

(McRaney 2022). You can do so by finding some experience they have had in the past where they have related in a personal way to someone like Susie. This allows them to complexify the issue, for example, the issue of immigration, that they have come to treat purely categorially and too simplistically in their mind. It triggers feelings and emotions that make them more willing to elaborate, reflect on, and reconsider their abstract beliefs about immigrants in terms of real people like Susie.

What you are doing is finding a past experience that can make the person simulate in his or her mind situational realities and the concomitant feelings and emotions they trigger. This grounds them in lived experience and not abstract categories and bloodless logic. They can begin convincing themselves to change their own minds, maybe not in a total way, but, at least, in a way that makes them see issues as more complex and nuanced than they did before. Of course, if they have no past experiences with people like Susie that you can get them to re-experience, you can give them new experiences. Good media can do this. So can real world experiences, though sometimes these are harder to set up. What you cannot do successfully is give them evidence and logic with no experience, feelings, or social bonding (McRaney 2022; Pinker 2015).

It has long been known that humans have a much harder time hurting or killing someone they see face to face than someone they can harm from a distance without seeing them. Many people who can drop a bomb out of plane cannot shoot someone in the face. It is hard to rail against immigrants when Susie pops into your mind and heart.

A method of engaging people in political conversations called "deep canvasing" seeks to get people to recall and reflect on issues they have strong political opinions about using the guidance of an interviewer who seeks reflection on actual experiences and not an argument (McRaney 2022):

> Once that real, lived memory was out in the open, you could (if done correctly) steer the conversation away from the world of conclusions with their facts googled for support, away from ideological abstractions and into the world of concrete details from that individual's personal experiences. (p. 30)

Deep canvasing, even when the interviewer strongly disagrees with the interviewee's stance, involves listening and respecting, not arguing over evidence or conclusions. It seeks to help people uncover motivations and to trigger emotional responses to issues based on experiences. It seeks to create in emotional responses and dawning realizations that bypass dichotomies, abstractions, and taken-for-granted categories. In the act, people can change their own minds.

In everyday life, people mostly argue not to reach truth but to defend their "team," which is integral in defending themselves when they feel their team is threatened (Asch 1951; Geil & Moshman 1198; Sunstein 1999). People are social animals and they defend their herd. People very often know little about what they claim to know and their information often comes from a narrow range of sources that offer them more a sense of worth and belonging than deep knowledge. Change happens when people have the opportunity to change teams for the better—and if you want to change them, you better be offering a good team that will accept them and allow them to matter. So, we must worry not just about the bad things about other people's teams, but about the limitations of our own, as well. Most people will not leave their team to be alone or a second-class player on another team.

Deep canvasing recruits the beginnings of deep empathy. It seeks to trigger empathy, that is, feeling and thinking in and through the situated placement of someone else in the world and our own personal (not categorial) relationship to this placement.

We have used examples of people trying to garner support for issues like immigration and gay marriage. And, indeed, this where deep canvasing started and has mostly been used, for liberal causes. But the situation would be the same if a person who supports wide gun ownership wanted to change the mind, even partially, of someone opposed to guns. Here, too, abstract analytical rational arguments will not work. Conversation must start with people's lived experiences, experiences that are concrete and replete with nuances and complexities categories miss.

When we engage others to feel and think in terms of experiences and not categories, they may very well not be entirely converted. But people will move closer to each other. They will see that issues and humans are complex and do not fit all that well into categories. We will not always convert others, but empathy and compassion can be much more powerful forces in society than conversion, because conversion is rare and long term and empathy and compassion can create bonds across diversity good enough that we can live with other and not harm each other. That is the start, at least, of flourishing beyond group solidarity at the expense of others.

Deep Empathy

Empathy is what connects humans. For humans, a sense of belonging—that is mattering to others—is a deep biological need. We are social animals (Atzil, Gao, Fradkin, & Barrett 2018; Brooks 2011). This leads, of course, to forming and maintaining connections, but it can also lead to "us" versus "them" distinctions as a way of forming and maintaining our connections by contrasting "us" to "them."

As we indicated above, there are two different kinds of empathy. Perspective taking is the ability to take someone else's perspective in a cognitive way. By observing and reflecting on a person, we seek to infer what the other person is feeling, thinking, and intending. This sort of empathy does not imply that we wish the other well. I may want to understand your perspective so that I can manipulate you. Indeed, good salesmen are good at inferring other people's feelings and thoughts and using them to position their sales pitch.

A second type of empathy we can call "deep empathy," though we just used the word "empathy" above for deep empathy. This sort of empathy is not just cognitive, it is emotional as well. We do not in deep empathy try to infer what the other feels and thinks, we want to feel and think it ourselves as if we were them.

It's the ability to actually enter the "mind space" of another person so that you can sense their feelings and emotions. In a sense, your identity merges with theirs. The separateness between you and them fades away. Your "self-boundary" melts away, so that in a sense – or to an extent – you become them:

> If you experience "deep empathy" then it becomes impossible to inflict pain or suffering on other people, at least intentionally. In deep empathy, you recoil from other people's pain in the same way that you recoil from your own pain. You are reluctant to harm them in the same way that you are reluctant to harm yourself. (Taylor 2015)

Deep empathy raises a profound dilemma for humans. We can really only be sure about our judgments of others and their deeds if we have empathized with them in a deep sense. Indeed, we often feel this way about ourselves. We feel others cannot really understand us or judge us unless they really know how we felt and sense the world and others in it. Yet, someone may be so evil in our eyes that we would be repulsed to empathize with them, to enter their minds.

The same issue arises with texts. You cannot really understand and deeply critique a text unless you have first read it as a "compliant reader" trying to understand and believe what it says—to see why anyone would be drawn to it—and only afterwards read it as a resistant reader ready now to critique it and even fight against it with real understanding. Yet a text may be so evil in your view that you refuse to engage with it in a deep way as a form of understanding even for critique.

Whether to engage with a person or a text emphatically is a moral decision. Different people will make this decision in different ways. In the end, when we decide not to engage empathically, we simply dismiss or condemn a person or a text as beyond the pale. Thus is the path of war and it is sometimes necessary for survival, though it is a path that can lead to mutual destruction.

AOT designs repeated ways for us to enter Eren and empathize with him. We meet him as a headstrong but sweet little boy. He ends up, in the view of some, a genocidal maniac and, in the view of others, a hero. AOT tests and builds our empathy skills in a tough case indeed. It is one that resonates with our fractured, dangerous, conflict-filled, violent times. Anyone alive to our times—who feels the "Titans" are at our gates ready to end humanity—will, when they judge Eren, judge humanity, too. They will think of themselves, as well, and how they would have faced his challenges, which are not unlike our own today. When we look Into Eren's eyes, we, ironically, also look into our own.

CHAPTER 3

INTUITION

In the last chapter we talked about empathy. Empathy is essential if we are to live together in a diverse world. It is a force that allows us imaginatively to enter other humans, come to understand them better, and to see them as fellow human beings even amid differences and disagreements. Without empathy, humans are fated to be trapped within the borders—behind the walls—of their social groups, the groups that give them a sense of belonging, mattering, and social worth, but sometimes deny such worth to others. AOT, like other good media, allows us to engage in—even practice—empathy for characters quite different from ourselves, caught up in strange worlds that yet resonate with our own. Despite these differences, with empathy we come to see and feel deep similarities—or, at least, important contact points—between Eren and ourself and between his world and ours.

In this chapter we are going to talk about a close relative of empathy, namely intuition. Intuition is a crucial source of discovery and creativity. Without it, more analytic and rational forms of thinking and problem solving can become stunted. Yet, intuition plays even less of a role in formal schooling than does empathy. Schools, at least, sometimes give lip service to empathy as a character trait, but rarely broach the topic of intuition. Given the importance of intuition in human learning, problem solving, and creativity this is, indeed, a paradox.

Understanding Intuition

Intuition is the ability to understand something immediately, without the need for conscious reasoning. One example is the often-told story of Wagner Dodge, a smokejumper who survived the Mann Gulch Fire in August 1949 (Mc-Gilchrist 2021, p. 1157). Dodge and his fellow firefighters were in danger of being entrapped by the fire they were fighting since it was moving much faster than they had anticipated and was now less than 100 yards away. As they were trying desperately to escape, Dodge got a sudden idea that was something he had never thought of before. He stopped to set a small fire in the area directly in front of himself, thereby creating a burned-over area that the fire would bypass because there was nothing left there to burn. He laid down in the burned over area and survived the fire as it passed by either side of him. Almost all the other fire-fighters died because, in all the confusion, they failed to follow Dodge's lead. Dodge did not come to the solution by conscious reasoning—there was no time for that—it just came to him when he desperately needed it.

Another example, one that we will deal with in more depth below, is the common phenomenon where a scientist, mathematician, or artist has worked a great deal on a problem with conscious effort and only later, when they have stopped thinking about the problem—perhaps they are out walking or daydreaming—does the solution to the problem just seem to come to them.

In both these cases, a solution seems to come to a person "out of the blue". Yet this solution is the result of mental processing, but mental processing that takes place in the brain outside of a person's conscious awareness. This mental processing delivers the solution to the conscious part of the brain. Of course, only when Dodge tried it or when a scientist, mathematician, or artist tests it in practice do they find out whether it is correct. Intuition is not always correct, but it often is.

In both cases, even though the mental processing that led to a solution was unconscious, this unconscious mental processing was fueled by—was using—past conscious work the person had done. In Dodge's case, that work was all the past experiences he had had fighting fires and the knowledge it led to in his long career as a fire fighter. In the case of the mathematician, scientist, or artist, it was not just their long-term experiences in math, science, or art, but, in particular, the conscious effort they had devoted to a specific problem they could not yet solve. Intuition seems to come free, but it is a reward for previous hard work.

People sometimes use the words "intuition" and "insight" in the same or overlapping ways. Sometimes they use them differently, often "intuition" for a "gut feeling" and "insight" for a "bolt out of the blue." We will use "intuition" for both cases.

One good way, as we have already hinted above, to understand intuition, a potentially potent force in anyone's life, is to look at mathematicians. Indeed, we can begin to get a good understanding of how the human mind-brain works by looking at mathematicians. How mathematicians think and solve problems can teach us—even if we hate or fear math—a good deal about how we all think and solve problems.

We usually think of mathematicians as solving problems step by step, manipulating symbols and following the "rules" of mathematics in a process of explicit and overt conscious reasoning. And, indeed, that is a good part of what they do. But very often they say that is not how they find a solution to a problem they are interested in.

When the mathematician Anna Sfard (1994) interviewed some of her fellow mathematicians, every one of them told her they could not think about mathematics without making pictures (mentally or physically). When they were seeking a solution to a problem they could not yet prove, they did not think by manipulating mathematical symbols, but, rather, by manipulating images. She concluded:

> When the abstract construct is supported by an image schema, the perception of its salient characteristics may become much more like our perception of the properties of physical bodies: it is immediate, it is holistic, and it is not mediated by a long chain of inferences. It is this ability to grasp ideas in a direct quasi-synthetic way, which, according to the mathematicians I talked to, gives them the feeling of 'true' understanding. (p. 18)

So, many mathematicians start not with words or symbols, which are abstract, but with images (and, as we will see later, metaphors), which are not abstract. A picture or a diagram often allows us to focus on a whole and not its parts in isolation. It allows us to focus on a whole where the parts "hang together" in a way that is more than the sum of the parts. This is what has been called a "gestalt." Sfard points out that this is often how we see the bodies of humans and animals. We recognize them as wholes, not a sum of discrete parts.

Sfard also points out the mathematicians she spoke to talked about using metaphors to guide their thinking. One mathematician, for example, said to her:

> To understand a new concept I must create an appropriate metaphor. A personification. Or a spatial metaphor. A metaphor of structure. Only then can I answer questions, solve problems ... without the metaphor I just can't do it. And once we find an answer, we remember what we perceived by insight better than anything we arrived at by more everyday means. (pp. 12-13)

Metaphors are a type of image expressed in words. Metaphors guide us when we are on uncharted ground exploring a new area where we have no old signposts. Like many others, Andrew Reynolds (2021) has stressed metaphor's role in science:

> Metaphor and analogy allow us to recognize similarities in the dissimilar. …the philosopher Mary Hesse showed how important the use of metaphor and analogy is in the expansion of scientific explanation by means of model making. The solar system model of the atom, the billiard ball model of gases, and the wave theory of light are all examples of how metaphors are used to create useful scientific models and theories.

The solar system model of the atom, like other fruitful metaphors in science, was an intuition, an inspiration. It was an image that led to more focused analytical study that, eventually, showed it to be inadequate. But that progress only occurred because the metaphor opened the path. Further progress requires new metaphors, such as the "electron cloud model" which is currently the most sophisticated and widely accepted model of the atom.

Many mathematicians say that a solution to a problem they have been thinking about for a long time has come to them as an immediate insight or realization, but not in the form of a fully worked out proof. The solution comes to them as an image, metaphor, or spatial pattern of relationships that they just feel is right, though they cannot yet formally prove it. Their insight then sets them on a path to use their more analytical skills to find a formal proof. Mathematics as a discipline demands proof even though mathematicians often discover solutions as inspirations that just "come to them." The proof comes later.

The famous mathematician and philosopher Henri Poincare (1914, pp. 129-130) claimed that it is by overt logical reasoning that we prove things, but it is by intuition that we discover them:

> Logic teaches us that on such and such a road we are sure of not meeting an obstacle; it does not tell us which is the road that leads to the desired end. For this it is necessary to see the end from afar, and the faculty which teaches us to see is intuition. Without it, the geometrician would be like a writer well up in grammar but destitute of ideas.

In doing mathematics, science, playing chess, creating a painting, or composing music—and in many other activities in life—there are a great many possibilities to consider when trying to solve a problem or create a new work. There are too many to go through each one methodically. Somehow one must make an insightful guess as to where to start, a process the American philosopher C.S. Peirce called "abduction" in his studies of science

(Douven 2021). The neuroscientist Iain McGilchrist (2021, pp. 376) puts the point this way:

> …if mathematicians, or scientists, or chess players, or poets, or artists, or composers had to consider methodically all the possibilities, there would not be enough time in the history of the universe. In reality only a very limited number of self-selecting forms present themselves, vaguely at first, and more clearly as the business of creation continues, more like a picture gradually coming into focus than the following of steps towards a goal.

The human mind can, outside of our conscious awareness, mull over a great many possibilities and come to see patterns and regularities that are suggestive places to focus our more conscious attention and efforts on. The mind does not stop working on what we have been devoting conscious effort to when we cease our efforts. It continues to work outside our conscious awareness or focus.

We might make a discovery about our work or an art project while working in the garden or commuting to work, when we are sleeping, when we are daydreaming, or when we are just "playing around" in our mind with images, metaphors, and ideas without any immediate goal. The brain never shuts off and it is churning away in various directions even when we are preoccupied with other things or just not focusing on much of anything. This is sometimes called the brain's "default mode" (Barnett 2020). One of the mathematicians who Sfard interviewed said: "'Having a result' without knowing how it was obtained is perhaps the most striking phenomenon in the work of a mathematician."

Intuition comes, though, only to a prepared mind. While the human brain can, outside of conscious focus, mull over things—seek to find patterns and relationships—it needs material to work with. The mathematician who discovers a result by intuition has worked long and hard doing mathematics more consciously and effortfully, working away on analysis and proofs. This is the fodder the mind works with to find connections and relationships we have not been able yet to discover consciously in our analytic efforts. Often this happens after a mathematician has been working on a specific problem for a while, but it can happen when mathematicians face a brand-new problem and gain an insight based on their wealth of experience in mathematics as a whole.

Intuition is the capacity of the unconscious part of the brain to use past experience or previous conscious work on a specific problem to come up with a solution to it. It works because the unconscious brain is constantly seeking for patterns, associations, regularities in the myriad details it has stored in it. It is constantly seeking for "gestalts," that is, for wholes that make sense of their parts in ways that go beyond just a sum of these parts.

Learning intuition requires that people work on problems that they cannot just solve in a rote manner based on simple trial and error or based on past experience alone. It requires problems that they can work on in an open-ended, exploratory way, even playful way, considering a space of possibilities and multiple ways to fit pieces together into a meaningful whole. It also requires a wealth of different sorts of problem-solving experiences in an area (whether it be art, science, a profession, or a passion-driven activity like cooking, gaming, or gardening) that gives a person a sense of the "lay of the land" (the way different aspects of the area fit together and compare and contrast with each other as in a landscape).

Intuition drives discovery and creativity. It is a must for people who want to flourish in their work or life and sometimes even just to survive.

Thinking Visually

Humans can think visually or verbally (in terms of words). Later we will argue that these are both forms of mental simulation where we manipulate images or words (or other sorts of symbols) in our minds. There are two different types of visual thinking (Grandin 2022; Kozhevnikov & Shepherd 2005). There are people who visualize in terms of pictures (realistic images) of objects and scenes. There are other people who think in terms of manipulating spatial structures and patterns in their minds (much like manipulating 3D puzzles). The former people are often artists of some sort and the latter scientists or mathematicians of some sort.

People can also think verbally in terms of words (Gee 2004). Here, too, there are two different types of such thinking. When we are using language in mostly literal terms, verbal thinking is sequential, concatenating one element after another linearly in terms of grammatical properties. However, there is also a form of verbal thinking in terms of metaphors and other forms of figurative language and in terms of the different situations contextually associated with words in use. This type of verbal thinking is a verbal kin of visual thinking, using words to generate images or patterns.

Many humans can think in all four of the ways we have discussed and most can learn to engage in one type or another better with teaching and practice.

Some people, however, are strongly oriented to one type or another and there is a "disability" (aphantasia) in which a person cannot think in terms of realistic images at all (Grandin 2022).

School heavily favors sequential verbal thinking, as do some professions such as the law. Each form of thinking is good at solving different sorts of problems. Therefore, it is important that people learn to think and solve problems in different ways and that workplaces (and schools) use teams of people adept at different forms of thinking and integrating them for problem solving and creativity.

The Brain: An Association Engine

The human brain is a massive association engine. The brain represents elements from past experience in terms of connections among ensembles of neurons (Churchland 2013; Eagleman 2020; Seligman, Railton, Baumesiter, & Sripada 2016; Swaab 2014). These connections represent all of the associations (patterns and regularities) a person has discovered in past experience at a given time in life. These associations are used to recall, remember, imagine, predict, plan, and carry out actions, as well as to make sense of new experiences.

Experience—which is composed of sensations from the real world or from media—furnishes our brain and is the basis of everything we learn, believe, and know. We saw above—and will see more later—that language (words and syntax) is a quite different form of experience than are images and the sensations we get from the world. Obviously, creatures without human language furnish their brains with no need for language of the form humans have. Language certainly gives humans powers other animals do not have—as well as some problems they don't have—but we can only understand these powers when we see how language connects to (non-verbal) sensation and the neural connections/mental associations such sensation gives rise to in our brains, a topic we deal with later.

Imagine you have taken a trip to Paris. The associations among food, wine, restaurants, and lifestyle you formed on your trip to Paris—the patterns you discovered in how these things relate to each other—play a role in your memories about Paris, how you think and reason about Paris, what sorts of predications you might make about Paris and Parisians, and, perhaps, in fantasies you imagine in your head. They are all represented in connections among neurons in your brain that activate when you are remembering, thinking, predicting, or fanaticizing about Paris (all forms of mental simulation). But these associations can also activate unconsciously (automatically) as when you order a French wine without even thinking about the matter because "deep down" you associate French wines with good times in Paris.

The brain can activate associations on automatic pilot without conscious awareness in order to engage in fluid behavior that is fast and efficient. When you first learn to dance, you have to think consciously about every step, both in terms of how the steps connect to each other and how they connect to your muscles and body. After enough practice, you can activate all the associations you have formed about the dance steps to, say, do the tango without any need for conscious attention and reflection. These associations now activate automatically and fluidly. Indeed, if you begin to think about them consciously, you may lose your rhythm and stumble. The same thing happens with good athletes and musicians. It happens with language learning, as well. When you are learning a new language, you must pay conscious attention to much that later, when you are more proficient, will go on automatically.

However, if you eventually want to learn something new or take your now routine performances to a higher level, you must bring back to conscious awareness what you have previously automatized so that you can work out new ideas and behaviors. Then, with practice, you can re-automatize what you have learned and turn it back into fluid automatic performance. This has been called the "cycle of expertise" (Bereiter & Scardamalia 1993), a process of conscious learning that eventually becomes automatic mastery and then is later brought back to conscious awareness for new learning and later re-entry into a state of automatic mastery at a new level. It is the heart and soul of life-long learning.

The massive web of associations in our brain—associations we discovered in experiences in the world or via media—is the foundation not just of habits (where we act on automatic pilot), but of our powers of intuition. This web is the data base the brain uses for intuition, for discovering insights, good questions to ask, and possible solutions that we have not been able to reach through focused conscious analysis. Once we have the results of intuition, we can engage in focused analysis to test and validate these results. But without intuition we can be lost in the details of the trees and never understand the big picture that is the forest.

The quality of our intuition powers depends on the nature and breath of our experiences in the world and from media, because experience is what connects ("wires") the brain. Therefore, the most important question a teacher or mentor can ask is: What sorts of experiences do I need to give learners to furnish their brains and empower their powers of intuition and insight? Teachers and mentors need to know how specific experiences can fit with others to create a fruitful base both of details, facts, and categories useful for solving problems (analysis) and of materials that the brain can mine for patterns and relationships that can fuel new insights and discoveries (intuition).

Many a person has worked long and hard on the details of a problem only later to see, in a flash of intuition, a deeper pattern in the details that leads to a solution. Seeing the forest (the big picture, a pattern, a gestalt) has led to seeing the trees (the details, the parts of the whole) in a new and better way. The phenomenon of intuition has been called "the eureka effect" or "the Aha! Moment." While the Eureka Moment is named after the ancient Greek scientist Archimedes, who supposedly ran through the streets naked shouting "Eureka" ("I have found it") after a trip to public bath had led him to an intuitive insight into how to solve a problem a local king has tasked him with, it is both a common everyday experience and an integral part of science.

Here is a simple example from language understanding. It is hard to make sense of the sentence "The haystack was important because the cloth ripped" (Bransford & Johnson 1972). You can work a good deal on trying to make sense of it with little effect. If I now show you the phrase "a parachutist," your mind immediately makes sense of the sentence. What has happened here is that "a parachutist" has immediately linked the details of the sentence—its string of words which make little sense—to your web of associations in your brain that connect these details to a "big picture" (a context, a pattern). You sense an immediate moment of insight into what the sentence could mean and, indeed, cannot any longer see the sentence as senseless. It is a little "Aha! Moment."

When teachers and mentors focus students on a specific problem—for example, a specific equation in mathematics—they should treat this equation like a puzzle piece that can—and is meant to—lock onto other pieces to create a bigger picture. When people do a puzzle, they clearly see and know each piece is incomplete and needs other pieces to make a larger meaningful whole. They know, as well, that each piece will fit into neighbors before the neighborhoods make a yet bigger whole.

Teachers should not treat the equation as an isolated string of details like the sentence "The haystack was important because the cloth ripped." This sentence is grammatical, of course, and makes a sort of literal grammatical sense, but it is not meaningful in a way that gives it useful meaning. The equation can be grammatical in the same way, but not meaningful in any contextualized sense. Students need some sort of a key (like the edges of a puzzle piece or like the word "parachutist" for the sentence) that lets their mind fit the equation together with other parts of the puzzle so they can eventually see the big picture that give math its deep meaning.

Teachers and mentors must always look both ways: towards the trees (facts, details, specific problems) and the forest (the larger pattern that gives the facts, details, and specific problems deeper meaning). The interaction of these two is the heart of the matter: intuition gives us ideas to pursue more analytically and analysis gives our brain more material to connect into its web of associations that underwrite intuition. Intuition offers patterns and context that make details make deep sense and more details, presented the right way, give the mind-brain more fodder for intuition.

Empathy and Intuition

Empathy and intuition are closely related. Empathy is deep insight into another living being. Intuition is deep insight into a situation. Both are the products of much unconscious processing of the brain—activating associations and searching for relationships, connections, and patterns. Both issue in an insight coupled with feeling. In the case of empathy, we feel the feelings of another person and tune into ("feel") their thinking. We do this without making inferences from external evidence, but from a form of intuition based on our experience of ourselves and other living beings as fellow experiencers of our shared world. In the case of intuition, we feel that something is right or not (we have a "gut feeling"). Again, this is not based on inferences from external evidence, but from how our brain has sorted through the connections (the web of associations) in it that represent the record of our experiences in the world and in media.

Both empathy and intuition are only as good as the range and depth of experiences we have had in life. Both empathy and intuition are stunted when our experiences in life have been stunted. People who are weak in empathy or intuition must rely almost entirely on their conscious reasoning and analytic and logical abilities and these can be quite limited—even misleading or dangerous—without empathy and intuition.

Empathy and intuition take a back seat—or no seat at all—in school and in some work settings. Yet they have a front seat in human lives that are creative, flexible, pro-social, humane, and flourishing.

CHAPTER 4

BALANCE

Empathy and intuition are important aspects of flourishing humans. It is hard for people to have empathy for others when they themselves are not flourishing, especially if they live with fear and anxiety. It is hard to have empathy or develop deep powers of intuition if a person's social relations and experiences in life are limited, especially if a person's social belonging relies heavily on a division between "us" (the people to whom I matter and who matter to me) and "them" (not us).

In the U.S. today—and across a good deal of the rest of the world—inequality is at very high levels. Research has shown that high levels of inequality make people in society—not just the poor, but many others, as well—feel that what they do in society does not really matter, that they are not able to participate in the wider society in any truly meaningful way (Pickett & Wilkinson 2009; Wilkinson & Pickett 2019). They feel that the "game is rigged." In turn, these feelings often lead to a lack of both physical and mental health.

To flourish, humans first have to flourish as living beings in the same way all living beings do. At the heart of flourishing as a living being is the necessity of achieving balance between self and world. This state is called "homeostasis" by biologists (Barnett 2020). To discuss such balance, let's start with AOT.

Out of Balance

When we first meet Eren in Episode 1 in AOT, we quickly come to realize that he is out of balance—out of step—with his world. The people who live within the walls have been told by their government and their religion (a religion devoted to the idea that God made the walls) that their minds and hearts should be focused on life inside the walls. They should not think about or even discuss what is outside the walls. And the people are content. There has not been an attack on the walls for a hundred years. Life within the walls is ordained by God, it is the ways things are meant to me. Eren, however, sees the walls as a prison and longs to go free outside them, a dream that appears unrealistic since there are human-eating Titans outside the walls.

Eren is small and not very strong, yet he runs head long to fight bullies who are harassing other kids. He never wins and gets beat up unless his adopted sister Mikasa is with him. Mikasa is a great fighter and feared by all the bullies in town. Though only a child, Eren castigates the Garrison Regiment police officers for drinking on duty because there is, they believe, no serious threat to the walls they are supposed to defend. They think he is "a strange kid."

Eren tells Mikasa he wants to join the Survey Corps, the small regiment that ventures outside the walls to investigate and fight the Titans. For the most part, the Survey Corps is a suicide mission. Furthermore, the townspeople look down on the Corps as a waste of taxpayer money. They have no significant effect on the Titans, and, after all, life is meant to be spent inside the walls. Mikasa and Eren's mother are horrified he wants to join the Survey Corps; they cannot fathom his decision, and fully intend to stop him.

Things only get worse for Eren. Not long after we meet Eren, Titans attack the outer wall of Paradis Island, rip a hole in it, enter and attack the people inside. The people try to flee to safety behind the inner walls, but, in the act, a great many are destroyed by the Titan horde. Eren and Mikasa are in the courtyard below the outer wall when the attack happens and they, too, flee. As Eren and Mikasa flee, they see that Eren's mother is trapped under the wreckage of their house, destroyed by a Titan. They try frantically to save her, but they cannot free her. Eventually, Hannes, a member of the Garrison Regiment, runs up to them, gathers them up, and, against Eren's wishes, takes them to safety just as a Titan approaches. As they flee, Eren looks back only to see his mother picked up and eaten by the Titan. Eren, only a child, is not just out of balance with his world; he is now a victim of a massive trauma, the sort that changes people for a lifetime.

Humans are living beings. Living beings differ from non-living ones in one key respect: they do not just passively receive the effects of the environment on them (Capra & Luisi 2014; Davies 2019; Kauffman 2019; Zimmer 2021). They actively respond to these effects. They engage in reciprocal interactions with their environment. The environment acts on them and they act back on the environment. All living things decide how to respond to the actions of the environment on them or even initiate actions to change how the environment will interact with them. This is true even of single-cell slime molds who have no brains.

Life is about two actors interacting, the living being and its environment. Living things survive—and, better, if they can, flourish—if they are in balance with their environment. Balance means that the environment does not overwhelm the creature and the creature does not deplete or destroy its environment or cease to be able to transact with it. When a living being cannot act back on its environment, it is on the verge of death.

Some animals are social animals, humans among them. For social animals, balance with the environment does not mean just a balance with the physical world. For humans, as social animals, their need to belong—to matter to others—is as strong a biological urge as their need for food or propagation (Safina 2020; Sapolsky 2017; Tomasello 2019). Just as a lack of balance with the physical world (e.g., too little food, too much danger) can cause dangerous stress and cause damage to the creature's organs, so, too, in the case of social animals, can a lack of balance with the social world (e.g., rejection, loss of face, failure to be nurtured as a child, unfairness).

Balance is the key property for survival and flourishing for living beings and social balance is an additional key property for social animals. If we care about nurturing, educating, or otherwise helping humans our priority would be to know about, care about, and do something about their state of balance with the world, physical and social.

Eren is unbalanced with his environment physically and socially. He is weak and "strange." And, yet, if we wanted to help him, we would face a dilemma. The balance that his fellow townspeople have achieved is, in a sense, a false balance. It is based on assumptions formed based on what the government and religion say is the truth and what daily habits seem to indicate are the right things to believe and do, all of which turn out to be false. Viewers and the people of Paradis will eventually discover that the government is corrupt and lying and their religion is based on untruths propagated by the founding king of the state.

On the other hand, just celebrating Eren's opposition to the *status quo* will not work since the Barbarians are quite literally, in AOT, at the gates. What to do, then? What will become of Eren and his balance with a world now thrown into ever greater chaos by the Titan attack? Indeed, what will happen to the citizens, government, religion, and the state's institutions in this new world? What happens when an old balance is destroyed and a new one is not yet at hand, has yet to be discovered? This is in large part what AOT is about: How do humans survive and flourish—and can they—in the face of massive change, chaos, and lack of knowledge? It's a good topic, because it is one every human faces today in our world, a world filled with crises, changes, complexity, and dangers.

The whole course of Eren's life—and the lives of his friends—in AOT is an attempt to decide how to react back to the physical and social world when both keep changing in chaotic and complex ways. And they seek more than mere survival, though often this is difficult enough in AOT's world. They seek flourishing which they see as freedom, though freedom means different things to each of them.

Sensation and Allostasis

All living things must interact with the world across their porous boundaries. They must let good things in (food, resources, energy) and keep bad things out. They must keep in balance with the world—to be in it and part of it, but not overwhelmed by it—a state called "homeostasis." Sensation and feeling in living beings exist, first and foremost, to help them to achieve and maintain homeostasis in response to environmental stresses (challenges) (Solms 2021; Zimmer 2021). Flourishing creatures dance with their environment; they do not destroy it or get destroyed by it.

Homeostasis requires an organism to act to maintain some stability through change, to achieve a dynamically changing balance between itself and its world. The organism must use internal resources (energy) to face challenges from its environment (e.g., to find food, seek or build shelter, and avoid predators), but retain enough for emergencies (e.g., to face an attack or a significant change in its environment). It always must retain enough resources to be able to seek new resources when they are running low. This process of working to achieve and maintain or restore homeostasis (balance) is called allostasis. Allostasis is a form of resource management (Barnett 2020; Sapolsky 1994). It is the very work of being and staying alive. "Allostasis" means working (to survive) and when the burden from this work gets overwhelming creatures go into "allostatic overload".

For social animals, homeostasis and allostasis act at the social level as well. Humans must achieve balance ("harmony") with their social world, with other humans and their social groups, as well as with the physical world. For humans, social interactions can be challenges and potential stressors just as can interactions with the physical world. They must manage their physical, mental, economic, and social resources (e.g., status and social connections) to deal with social challenges and strife and not be overwhelmed by them.

When living creatures suffer too much exposure to stress—physical or social, if they are social animals—their internal organs suffer significant damage due to the release of chemicals ("stress hormones") that in the short run can be helpful for emergencies, but in the long run are highly toxic. These chemicals prime a creature's body to face emergencies but are damaging to its organs when they are in its body too long or too often. This damage undermines a creature's ability to engage in allostasis and, thus, its ability to gain and manage new resources. Creatures in this state—human or otherwise—are said to have allostatic overload (McEwen 2006).

Since allostatic overload can be measured by the amount of stress chemicals in a body across time, this gives us a concrete way to assess any creature's state of wellbeing and flourishing. More generally, we can say that any teaching or technological practice that enhances allostasis is enhancing wellbeing and any that leads to allostatic overload is toxic. Work on trauma has shown that beings with allostatic overload cannot learn well, so teaching or assessing them without remedying their allostatic overload is profound malpractice (Burke Harris 2018; Perry & Szalavitz 2006).

Allostatic Overload

Humans cannot flourish unless they first flourish as living beings. They cannot flourish as living beings if they have allostatic overload or, for other reasons, cannot properly manage their internal resources. Only when their basic needs as a living being are met can they also flourish as a distinctive type of living being, a human animal.

It is a sad fact that in today's world a great many humans live with allostatic overload (Wilkinson & Pickett 2019). This is not just caused by specific traumatic events (like war or extreme climate change), but it is also caused by extreme inequality in a society. Extreme inequality—which is prevalent today in the United States and many other places in the world—affects both poor and more well-off people badly. It stresses people because it destroys people's deep desire for fairness (a pan-human trait found even in some other animals) and their need to feel that what they do in society matters (another pan-human trait).

When designers design for good human learning and human flourishing—the core form of teaching—they need to be aware of the allostatic state of the people they are seeking to teach. They may need to alleviate allostatic overload or teach people new ways to cope with stresses and challenges before that can move into new forms of teaching and learning.

For example, it is well known that humans will learn poorly if we trigger negative stereotypes about them (Steele & Aronson 1995, 1998). If a group of people is stereotyped as less good at math than others, they will do poorly in math if we trigger (remind them of) this stereotype in our teaching. They will do better if we do not. So, teachers need not only to be sure they do not trigger stereotypes, they need also, in the long run, to teach people to evade and defeat stereotypes and other internalized viewpoints that deskill them.

All good teaching requires care for different people's contexts, knowledge of their state of balance with the world, and work to undo harms done to them. Thanks to the state of society, schooling, and the world today, nearly all of us have suffered harm and harbor harmful ideas about ourselves or others. Good experience design for learning ("teaching') is often a form of therapy as well.

In AOT, Eren has allostatic overload. He is a case study in childhood trauma. And it is a case study—dramatic and metaphorical as it is—that resonates with the world we live in today. But, too, Eren's society—like ours—has allostatic overload. It cannot learn well and cannot budget its resources well to deal with the change and disruption it faces.

CHAPTER 5

ATMOSPHERE

Humans and many other animals can pay attention in two different ways. They can pay broad attention or narrow attention. In broad attention, they pay attention to the big picture, to a scene as an integrated whole. In narrow attention, they pay attention to a specific part or detail of the whole. Many species of birds use one eye (the right eye connected to the left brain) to pay attention to small details like finding pieces of grain in pebbles or sand (McGilchrist 2021, pp. 36-37). They use the other eye (the left one connected to the right brain) to pay attention to the whole scene they are in, to the wider environment, in order to keep "an eye out" for predators or other dangers.

Humans do not use separate eyes for each form of attention. They can switch between one and the other. They can size up a scene or situation in a wholistic way and then narrow in on the details. They can switch back to the big picture when their attention to details seems not to be working well. They can also, at one and the same time, pay narrow attention to details in a focused way while remaining aware of the broader scene or situation in a backgrounded way (McGilchrist 2009, 2019, 2021).

Indeed, this is how vision works in humans. The center of the eye sees a narrow part of the visual field in a highly sharp and focused way while our peripheral vision (stemming from the rest of our eye) is vague (blurry), but we can switch what is in the periphery to the center quickly (by moving our heads) if something important pops up in the periphery of our vision. Often, we are unaware of what is in our peripheral vision until something of importance pops up in it.

Broad attention has many functions in humans. One important aspect of broad attention is that it sometimes has a special feel to it, a feeling we will call a "sense of atmosphere." This feeling—which is related to our sense of how our body is positioned in space—is deeply important for humans. Atmosphere is also an important aspect of media, whether books, films, or video games.

Sense of Atmosphere

When a child enters a new classroom, she assesses the whole scene in terms of how it feels—for example, inviting or foreboding—to prepare for how she will act and interact. When she later pays attention to details—to the other students, her math problems, the teacher—she acts and reacts to these details in terms of her assessment of the overall atmosphere of the classroom and will track this atmosphere as it changes.

We saw in the last chapter that the basis of life, survival, and flourishing is balance. A living creature must create, maintain, repair, and enhance the balance between self (its bodily integrity and resources) and world (the world's impact on the creature) in its transactions with the world.

To ensure balance, a living being must be aware of where its boundaries are in the world at any given time and place and what the state of balance is between the being and the world at those boundaries. Let's call this awareness of where a self's boundaries are and what their state of balance is, at a given time and place, a sense of placement. Any self must be able to sense how well placed it is and must work to maintain, improve, or restore its balance on this basis.

A sense of placement in the world can be manifested as a whole-body multi-sensory set of feelings at the skin and within the body, a sensation that we will call a sense of atmosphere. "Atmosphere" is a word suggested by the Finnish architect Juhani Pallasmaa (2012, 2014).

When the weather dramatically changes, you immediately and automatically sense the implications of the change—a change in your placement in the world—for the integrity of your boundaries. When the sun is out, the sky is clear, birds are chirping, and the world is vibrant with colors, you feel one way about your placement in the world and when clouds roll in threatening rain and wind and things turn dark and colors fade to gray, you feel another way. These feelings are whole body feelings (often triggering other emotions as well). The reactions of all your senses are combined into one gestalt. They are a reaction to the world sensed as a gestalt, not yet sensed in terms of specific details, which come later.

The way selves respond to weather is much the way they respond to any placement in the world. So, we can use the word "atmosphere" here more broadly, as English already does. When you cross from a rich neighborhood into a poor one, your sense of atmosphere changes just like it does for weather. Perhaps, it is not surprising that English uses the words "climate" and "atmo-sphere" literally for weather conditions and figuratively for other sorts of environmental, social, and situational conditions. There is something similar about them even at the biological level.

Awareness of, the sensing of, atmosphere is a "big picture" sort of coupling with the world. It can lead to a desire to enter further into an experience in a way that will resolve the atmosphere into more details or a desire to flee from it. Or, it can cause a person to want to enter into detailed interaction with the environment but with caution.

Atmosphere is immersive in a wholistic way, a way we can call "atmospheric immersion." Atmosphere can tell us to flee or remain. We can revel in atmosphere without moving too quickly to details and tasks. On a hike through the woods, we can feel "in the midst" of things, a connected, integrated part of the whole. Or, our attention, can focus more narrowly as we resolve a sense of atmosphere into details, categories, and tasks we set ourselves beyond just being there. Atmosphere, as a gestalt, however, can linger in the background and sometimes return in full to the foreground. On a hike you can be enticed by a beautiful flower, stop, pay close attention to it, and wonder what type of flower it is and whether it would make a good addition to your garden at home, and then return, with the joy the flower has brought you, to a more total immersion in and appreciation of your forest hike.

While humans have an innate need to feel safe and secure, and often use their sense of atmosphere to judge whether things are safe, they are not always and everywhere satisfied with a sense of complete safety. In real life, humans are often energized by a sense of atmosphere that is inviting, but still evokes mystery or even a sense of some risk or challenge (see Chapter 9 below).

Video Games and Atmosphere

The term "atmosphere" is often used when designers or players talk about video games (and, of course, other media). As with other aspects of sensation, video games are a good place to study atmosphere. This is so because video games are a designed world wherein players can have experiences much like they do in the real world. The player, often via an avatar (a surrogate body), senses, feels, chooses, and acts in a virtual world. As in the real world, players can feel they are "immersed" in the game world. They feel a certain sense of atmosphere when they begin the game and, when the game moves to a new level, a different atmosphere may arise and players will quickly feel that too.

Players rely on this sense of atmosphere to guide them as they go on in the game. The atmosphere of the game can lead players to immerse themselves "in the midst" as integral parts of the game world or, if the atmosphere turns them off, quit the game. Of course, they regularly exit their full immersion in the atmosphere to solve specific problems with a focus on details and even abstract principles (e.g., don't forget to block and strafe when fighting this type of boss).

Here is what Matthew Bentley (2013) has to say about atmosphere in video games:

> ...atmosphere is the feeling that is touched upon by only that particular combination of imagery, sound, music (or lack thereof), story, gameplay and the sense of agency which games are so well-known for. It is a sense of immersion within the game world, but is not principally composed of immersion alone. ... It is the odd yet essential "X-factor" of games, the incongruous immersive edge that comes from the right combination of elements, in the right way. In the same way that the right key unlocks the right door, a good game can get access to our imagination via the right atmospheric engagement. Games seem to do this extremely well, because they involve the player as an active and integral part of the world - being an agent in the world has the power to immerse ourselves more in the feeling of it more fully than with a film, a TV program, or a novel, if done right.

Bentley's statement above can readily be applied to classrooms. Atmosphere in a game operates like it does in the real world. The atmosphere of the game world, like that in the real world, triggers our sense of safety, mystery, and danger, as well as the overall "feel" of the game world. Depending on the game and how good it is, the atmosphere of a game can draw us in or repel us in different ways.

Atmosphere is an invitation to situate yourself in the game world in a certain way at a given time and place. We swim in it and it guides us as to when, where, and how we should exit immersion and focus on a necessary task (much as the flower on the hike enticed us to stop and focus for a while). The way your sense of atmosphere situates you in the game world affects your choices and how you proceed. Should you move with caution or jump right in? Should you be a child at heart or a serious adult? Is something off or odd or is this pretty "normal"? What can you expect here? Do you want to be here?

And, of course, as in the real world, atmosphere can change in games and, when it does, players sense it immediately. We might say that atmosphere is the player's initial orientation to the game or a new part of a game in terms of how the player should go on to feel and respond, predict, expect, and act. As in the real world, we alternate between the big picture and the details and they nourish and enrich each other.

Atmosphere in a game can be so replete and filled out that little is left to the player's imagination. Sometimes it can feel imposed. Or, the atmosphere can be so confusing that the player really does not know where she is or what is expected of her or what might come at her. The sweet spot is in the middle where the atmosphere is rich enough to trigger feelings of placement, but not so rich that it does not invite the player to contribute to it with her own personal feelings, emotions, and imagination. Here is Matthew Bentley again:

> The single largest constructor of atmosphere is the player's imagination. But that imagination has to be fed, and nurtured, via the game - specifically, the game has to allow gaps or 'space' for the player's mind to fill in. If you say too much, you leave no room to breathe. You have to create enough space for the player to be partially-process-oriented in the way their brain processes the game, as opposed to 100% goal-oriented. ... Modern games tend to detract from atmosphere principally by leaving no cognitive gaps - there is too much infinitude of stimuli and too much given away - not necessarily plot-wise, but in terms of an unwillingness on the part of the designers not to constantly bludgeon the player's subconscious with detail.

Interestingly, there are corollaries to this gap between detail and emotional imagination in all fields of art- but again, more on that later.

Again, Bentley's remarks can be applied to lessons in classrooms. While games are a particularly good place to study atmosphere, all designed experiences have some sort of atmosphere. A classroom does, as do buildings, novels, paintings, dance, and movies. The classroom, in fact, shares with video games the power to make the student an agent in the world, though sadly many do not, certainly not at the level of participatory immersion video games create.

In education, we most often use the term "atmosphere," when talking about classroom atmosphere, just for the sorts of talk and social interactions going on in the classroom. This misses the fact that classrooms, like a forest or a video game, are a "world" filled with sensations of all different sorts interacting with feelings and emotions of different sorts. For some people, just the image of a traditional classroom, without any talk or texts or interactions, turns them off. If an atmosphere feels unsafe or uninviting, we are reluctant to spend time on more focused tasks within it. We would rather flee it.

CHAPTER 6

TENSION AND RELEASE

In the last chapter we discussed the dynamic balance between atmosphere (a sense of and feeling for the big picture) and details. There can be tension between atmosphere and details. A student could feel a tension between her sense of the atmosphere of her classroom—for example, a sense that coverage matters more than real understanding—and how much she enjoys the math problems she is given and how badly she wants to explore them further without the need to move on too fast to the next goal. Tension is often felt as a lack of balance and, in this example, the student may well feel just such a lack of balance. However, tension is not always a bad thing. It can also be good and important to human learning and engagement with the world.

Good Stress

Allostatic load is a measure of stress (Barrett 2020). Stress hormones are released when we need extra energy in challenging situations. These hormones become dangerous and toxic to our organs when they are too often activated or stay continuously in the body for long periods of time. However, humans need stress at the right level. Too little stress in life leaves them unable to cope with challenges when they come, as they always will (Jamieson, Black, Pelaia, Gravelding, Gordils & Reis 2022).

Humans flourish under conditions where stress is held within certain bonds and spaced out in time. The dynamic balance humans need to flourish requires a certain tension between feeling challenged (stressed) and yet, feeling that the challenge is doable and can lead to resolution. Challenge brings tension and resolution brings rest, release, and resolution. Life for any creature who survives, let alone flourishes, is composed of repeated cycles of challenge (tension)—resolution (release) engagements across time that make the creature more and more skilled and able to handle future challenges.

Music and Life

Cycles of tension and release are critical to any creature's survival and flourishing. Music is a good example because the build-up and release of tension lies at its center. A piece of music, for example, can create tension through changes of intensity and speed. As it gets ever louder and faster, this often creates excitement and anticipation. Flowing with the mighty current of heightened notes, you wonder how far it can go. Then, all of a sudden, the intensity lowers and the music calms down, releasing the tension. You feel both the tension and release in your body and your emotions.

The pianist Daniel Barenboim (2009) has argued that playing with less intensity by lowering the volume can also create tension too. And if it is done right, this can be even more effective than raising intensity. A lower volume calls for a greater need eventually to increase intensity and that is when tension arises. To that end, a unique strategy of his is to play softer when more intensity is expected in order to build up tension and then release it when he increases the intensity.

Music has a great many ways to create—and play with—tension and release. This is a large part of what gives us pleasure in music, the rhythm of anticipation and resolution which often continues as a cycle. The writing collective *Denver Taste* argues that the dynamic of tension and release is not just the basis of music but of life as well:

> From our biology to our psychology and even to our religious and philosophical worldviews, tension and release are everywhere. Music, then, isn't just some weird tension and release game we play for fun. Instead, it's the purest expression of the dynamic that is essential to all living things. Even to life itself.

> By turning back to music, we can actually learn a lot about life itself, since they both have the same fundamental dynamic. In fact, music is the expression of this dynamic in the abstract language of sound. It builds us up, only to drop us down. But hey, that's what life is all about. Not the building up, nor the easing down. But the playing with different tensions and different modes of release, and the experiencing of joy from moving from one to the other. (https://mytasteculture.com/featured-articles/tension-and-release-i-music)

CHAPTER 7

EMOTION

So far, we have talked about five deep aspects of humans central to their wellbeing: empathy, intuition, balance, atmosphere, and tension and release. These are all forms of feeling. Empathy is feeling with and through another. Intuition is a "gut feeling" or a flash of insight that comes from within. Balance, or a lack of it, is a physical property that we feel as health and wellbeing or as sickness and anxiety. Atmosphere is a feeling based on a sense of our placement in the world, a feeling that can be good and enticing or bad and uninviting. Tension and release is the feeling associated with the basic cycle of life.

Schools stress cognition and yet when we start to think about the fundamental nature of humans, we realize we must start with non-cognitive elements. This is not, of course, because cognition is unimportant. It is because cognition only functions well when it is guided by feelings and emotions. Of course, feelings and emotions can lead cognition astray—intuition, for example, is not always right—but nonetheless, as we will see, cognition in the absence of feelings and emotions does not function well and can even be dangerous. The important thing is to understand how feelings and emotions work, where they come from, and to have good ones and not be led by bad ones.

In this chapter we want to talk directly about feelings and emotions. The two words are used in confusing and overlapping ways in everyday language. They are also used in different ways in academic research where controversies abound. Sometimes they are together called "affect." For the time being we will just use the word "feeling" to mean both feelings (like hunger) or emotions (like anger). We will discuss the differences between feelings and emotions later.

A New Revolution

The view many people in Western culture hold about feeling goes far back in history at least to the Ancient Greeks (Konstan 2006; Solomon 1976). On this view, humans have two parts. One part is "higher" and rational and should be in control. The other side is "lower" and passionate and can easily go out of control. And, of course, most of us humans have experienced times when anger, fear, grief, or lust has seemed to go out of control and take over our bodies. This divide persisted into modern cognitive science which studied cognition as the source of learning, thinking, and intelligence and saw feeling mostly as a force that could override good reasoning.

To this day, much "rigorous" work in areas like science or math education deals only with thinking and problem solving not feelings, nor, we might add, with empathy, intuition, balance, atmosphere, or tension and release. Researchers are aware, of course, that anxiety about math or science—or even feeling hungry—can interfere with learning, but once such negative feelings are removed, they act as if feelings have little to do with learning math and science.

There has been, however, over the last few decades, a revolution in the study of feelings and cognition, a revolution largely stemming from neuroscience (Barnett 2017; Damasio & Carvalho 2013; Damasio 2018; McGilchirst 2021; Mlodinow 2022; Solms 2021). Humans, it turns out, cannot think or decide without feelings. Feelings motivate, guide, and assess thinking and deciding.

Anime—and AOT is no exception—displays characters' feelings and emotions quite dramatically. Indeed, Eren, when he discovers he has the power to turn into a Titan, becomes emblematic of the traditional view of feeling. When he goes into a rage he turns into a Titan and becomes a monster. Initially we see him as a hopeful monster because we believe he is fighting for a good cause. Later, when we know more, things become more complex. We come to think and feel differently about Eren, as person and as a Titan.

At the same time, AOT and much other anime, explores the intricate connections among feelings and emotions, intuition, and reasoning in social contexts. Emotions can go out of control, but there is no progress, no persistence, no overcoming, no recovery from failure, no creative solutions without feeling and emotion, sometimes strong ones. It is interesting that by the end of AOT, when Eren is on a mission to save "his people" by destroying most of the rest of the world, it is impossible to tell whether he is guided by blind passion or intense rationalization. The two seem to meld.

To discuss feelings and emotions we must first discuss sensation, since feelings and emotions are simply the ways we humans become consciously aware of our internal sensations.

Sensation

Humans have outer sense organs that sense the outer world: Vision, hearing, touch, smell, and taste. And, they have internal sense organs that sense the inner workings of their body. These inner sense organs sense our physical balance, body position (proprioception), and the changing states of our internal organs as the world and chemicals affect them. Our sense of pain—we have pain receptors all over and inside our body—is between outer and inner.

Imagine you are surfing out on the ocean. As you surf a wave, your outer sense organs are sensing (detecting) data from physical properties in the world (like light waves, sound waves, air and water molecules, and physical contacts on your skin). Your inner sense organs are sensing (detecting) the effects of the world on the insides of your body (e.g., a racing heart, higher blood pressure, tightening muscles, and "butterflies" in your stomach). You need not be consciously aware of this sensing. You may very well be paying avid attention to just staying on the surfboard.

Your sense organs detect data (e.g., how light is reflecting off surfaces or how your heart is racing) and they send this data to your brain. The brain processes and deals with this data in ways you are not necessarily conscious of, but ways that have effects on your body and behaviors nonetheless. This data is mined by your brain to assess its implications for your homeostasis (balance with the world) and to allow your brain to engage in work that leads to actions to repair, enhance, or maintain your homeostasis. For example, if you are surfing, and are any good at it, your sense organs are continually sensing your balance on the surf board and correcting it to keep you on the board, in balance with the wave.

There is much terminological disagreement in how to deal with sensation (Barrett 2017, 2020; LeDoux 2019; Solms 2021; Sapolsky 2017; Smith 2015). So, we will have to be clear here about how we are using the word and readers need to be aware that others use the word differently or use different words.

Our sense organs can detect data from the world—for example, light rays—and send this data to the brain without our having any conscious awareness of what is going on. We will call this "unconscious sensing." It is a form of detection. Our senses can detect things and send data to the brain without conscious awareness much as a thermostat can detect changes in temperature and act on them without any consciousness.

However, if we become aware of these unconscious sensations—something we will call "conscious sensation"—we feel or experience something. In the case of touch, if the surfer becomes consciously aware of the unconscious sensations on her skin causing her to shiver, she will feel cold. If she becomes consciously aware of the qualities of light impinging on her retinas, she will experience a specific hue and shade of color. If she becomes consciously aware of the effects the surfing is having on the sensors inside her body, making her heart race and her muscles tighten, she may well feel excitement.

Psychologists usually study sensation (unconscious and conscious) one sense at a time. But in the wild our senses operate together, interacting with each other, to create what we might call a "dynamic ensemble of sensation," a constellation, pattern, gestalt of sensory data that constantly changes across time. We can be aware of parts of this ensemble and change our focus of attention to be aware of other parts of it as need be.

Inner Feelings

When you are surfing you cannot pay conscious attention to everything impinging on your senses. Conscious attention is narrow and limited. It exists to select what is most important at the time and deal with it. When you do become aware of what your inner sense organs are sensing (detecting), this awareness, as we have just seen, is experienced as a feeling. For example, if you become aware of your heart racing, your muscles tightening, and "butterflies" in your stomach as you surf a big wave, you may feel excitement. Someone else may feel fear.

Inner feelings like excitement and fear are contextually sensitive. The same inner sensations (e.g., a racing heart, higher blood pressure, tightening muscles, and "butterflies" in your stomach) can in one context (say on a roller coaster) be felt as fear and in another context (say when winning a tight tennis match) be felt as excitement. Indeed, one and the same person might find a roller coaster exciting in one mood and fear inducing in another. Many a person has been unsure whether what their inner organs were trying to tell them was lust or love, anxiety or anticipation, jealousy or protectiveness and needed to (consciously) think more about the matter.

Emotions and Emotional Systems

As we said earlier, the words "feeling" and "emotion" are used in overlapping and complex ways in everyday language and defined differently by different academic authors. For some authors, there is no real difference between the terms "feeling" and "emotion." They argue that we tend to use emotion terms (e.g., "anger") when the inner sensations we are feeling were caused by entanglement with other people and feeling terms (e.g., "hunger") when they were caused by less social situations. Because humans are social animals and a sense of belonging is essential to their wellbeing, emotions (socially focused feelings) are in some ways more complex than the inner feelings for which we do not use emotion terms (Solms 2021).

We should note that there is also a body of work—often in or related to therapy—that treats emotions as non-conscious elements buried deeply in our unconscious minds, but able, through effort, to be brought into the light of consciousness. You may have lived for years unknowingly resenting your father and discover it and deal with it only later in therapy. We are not using the word this way. For us, in this work, emotions are not only feelings triggered by states of our inner body that we become aware of, but also feelings entangled with others and our nature as social animals.

Finally, and more importantly, there is an important body of work that argues humans have a set of basic emotions that they share with all mammals and some other animal species (Panksepp 1998 and Panksepp & Bevin 2012). These "raw" emotions are triggered in the mid-brain, an evolutionarily earlier brain than the cerebral cortex (which controls our so-called "higher thinking"). The parts of the mid-brain that trigger these raw emotions give rise to their own form of basic consciousness. This is not a rationalizing ("cognitive") form of consciousness, but a brute form of awareness. We are aware, but not in any inferential way, of how things, at this basic level, feel to us in terms of feelings like hunger and emotions like rage.

In humans, in the course of socialization, we learn to control these basic emotions by cognitive processes in the cortex (except when they go "out of control"). Furthermore, through their interactions with higher cognitive processes, these basic emotions and their combinations give rise to a myriad of more subtle feelings and emotions—things like regret, jealousy, and nostalgia. These more nuanced emotions are more culturally variable.

The view that the mid-brain controls and causes the expressions of these basic emotions is strongly supported by the fact that humans and animals missing their cortexes can still feel and express feelings and emotions and behave on their basis. For example, a rat missing her cortex can still nurture and care for her young (Panksepp & Bevin 2012).

Jaak Panksepp (Panksepp 1998 and Panksepp & Bevin 2012) is the major figure in this area. He uses the names below for seven basic panhuman emotions (or "emotional systems") discovered through deep brain stimulation studies. Panksepp capitalizes his terms for the basic emotions because he wants to distinguish them from colloquial use where different cultures use different words for these basic emotions.

1. LUST. Erotic feelings guide your sexual behaviors.
2. SEEKING. Expectancy, interest, curiosity, surprise guide searching behaviors.
3. RAGE. Frustration or anger guide avenging behaviors.
4. FEAR. Feelings of threat guide fight, flight, or freeze behaviors.
5. PANIC/GRIEF. Separation anxiety or other forms of loss guide behaviors that seek reunion or mourn the loss.
6. CARE. Feelings of attachment causes behaviors that care for and protect others.
7. PLAY. Feelings of fun arouse our basic human need to play.

Note that these basic emotions are paired with behaviors that they motivate and guide. The basic emotions—or emotional systems—are core to human life and are often dramatically displayed in anime and other media. As we have said, they are subject to learning in human socialization and to higher-order thinking processes that shape them into a myriad of cross-culturally diverse shades, nuances, and complexities for which we have a bevy of different names (Mesquita 2022). But the basic emotions are there in the mid-brain and form the base emotional colors from which a myriad of others come by admixture and addition of other elements. And, indeed, they can, in certain contexts, still come out in all their primordially basic nature, as many people who have been caught up in raw anger or lust well know.

Feelings as Guides to and Assessors of Action

When our outer and inner sense organs are reacting to the world without our conscious awareness, the brain is using sense data about the world's effects on our outer and inner sense organs to decide what this data implies for our state of homeostasis (our wellbeing or lack of it) and what should be done by the body to maintain, repair, or enhance homeostasis.

Our inner feelings and emotions—like hunger, excitement, and fear—exist to help guide and assess action consciously (Barnett 2017; Damasio 2018; Mc-Gilchirst 2021; Mlodinow 2022; Solms 2021). The feeling or emotion tells us that something is, here and now, going right or wrong with our body and that we should act to maintain, repair, or enhance the body's homeostasis, its balance with the world. The feeling or emotion also assesses the action. The action is considered good if it maintains or enhances good feelings or emotions or if it lessens or removes bad ones. So, for example, a feeling of hunger motivates us to think about how to get food and to go get it. The feeling assesses the success of our actions in the sense that what removes the feeling of hunger is good and what does not is not.

Feelings and emotions are produced by our awareness of our inner states and needs. They tell us to act, for example, our feeling of hunger tells us to seek food. However, our brain does not tell us why it reached this decision, for example to make us aware of hunger and motivate us to seek food. The same inner states that we come to feel as hunger can be caused not just by a lack of food *per se*, but by a lack of certain key nutrients in the food we are eating. This often happens when people eat too much industrial ("fast") food (Moss 2013; Warner 2013). This food is lacking in certain important minerals, though it is not lacking in calories. After eating it, people often still feel hungry and eat more of it because their body wants to get key nutrients it expects in food, but which are not in this food. The brain, of course, does not tell us that our hunger is caused by a nutrient problem and not a calories problem. This requires education about food, something many Americans do not have. More generally humans, as social animals, need education about the sources of feelings and emotions.

In many cases schooling deals poorly with feelings and emotions. Teachers and researchers are aware of them, but believe they must be controlled. In one classroom we were in, a little girl, during reading time, bounced in her chair and said "I'm so happy" and the teacher told her to calm down, sit still, and pay attention. In school, some teachers—and even some researchers—feel feelings (note the paradox) have little to do with the content of learning, for example, learning something like algebra. However, we will see later that feelings and emotions are integral to learning and no learning takes place without them.

Just in terms of the basic emotions, no deep learning takes place without SEEKING and CARE. PLAY, which we often see as the opposite of working at our studies, can also be an essential part of learning. If you are not seeking for something, you do not pursue it. If you do not care, you do not pay attention. When you play, in the right way and contexts, your powers of intuition can grow, especially when play is exploratory.

CHAPTER 8

PERSONHOOD

It is paradoxical that, for humans, the world is full of things (stable objects), when science has taught us there are no such things as things, only particles, waves, processes, and lots of empty space (Hoffman 2019). And, too, philosophers have taught us we have no access to things anyway, only to how they appear to our senses (Garfield 2022). Now, while the issue of things is interesting and we will discuss it here, for us humans, there is one thing that is most important to us and that is other people. As we do with inanimate things, we assume that ourself and other humans are stable unitary entities. However, to a large extent, we create this unity in our heads.

We saw in the last chapter, that if you become aware of your inner sensations—the ways your organs are reacting to the world—this awareness is expressed in humans and some other animals as feelings or emotions. Something similar happens when you become aware of what your outer sense organs are sensing (detecting) from the outer world. This awareness also has a very specific quality to humans (and other animals, we presume). This quality in the case of touch is called "feeling," just as in the case of inner sensations. If you become aware while you are surfing of how the ocean water is making contact with your skin (touch), you may "feel cold". Excitement and being cold are feelings (personal subjective experiences) that result from your awareness of how the world is affecting your inner or outer sense organs. If you do not become consciously aware of these effects, your body still detects them—and reacts to them—but you do not feel anything, do not have a subjective personal experience of these effects.

However, we do not use the word "feeling" for any other of our outer senses except touch. If you become aware of the greenish-blue color of the ocean water around you when you are surfing, you do not say anything like "the water feels greenish-blue" (in comparison to "the water feels cold" in the case of touch). You say "the water looks greenish-blue." We call our awareness of what the world is doing to our skin a feeling ("feels cold"), but not our awareness of what the world is doing to our eyes, here we say "looks greenish-blue." In the case of our ears, nose, and taste sensors we also talk about how things sound (e.g., loud), smell (e.g., musty), or taste (e.g., sour), not how they feel.

Qualia

Philosophers have long sought a term for what exactly red (color), loud (sound), musty (smell), sour (taste), and cold (touch) are as conscious sensations. One term they have commonly used is "qualia" (Chalmers 1996). "Qualia" is a name for the subjective experience we have when we become aware of outer sensations, that is, the effects the world is having on our outer sense organs. Now, we do sometimes use the word "feeling" here in a slightly different way from how we use it for inner feelings. We do say things like "this shade of red has a different feel than that" or "People born blind don't know what it feels like to see." So, though it might be good to call both inner feelings like excitement and outer sensations like blue or loud "feelings"—they are "kin"—we usually don't in general, and philosophers sometimes settle for the word "qualia".

It is not clear what "qualia" as a "subjective experience" or even "feeling" in the case of inner feelings like excitement really are scientifically. There are disagreements here. Yet, we humans know well what it feels like to feel excitement or fear and how a different hue and shade of red looks ("feels") different from another one. We also know these experiences are specific, concrete, and personal, and hard to put into words. We know they are something others have, but in ways we can never be sure are the same as ours, since they are private and personal.

Philosophers have long pointed out that we humans have access only to feelings and qualia. We are, in a sense, trapped in a feeling and qualia prison. We never directly confront the "stuff" that causes them in the world. That stuff, according to physicists, is composed of particles and waves and lots of empty space. These are things we never sense directly and we have no sense whatsoever of experiencing them. Our favorite chair seems solid, not a bunch of particles and waves surrounded by air molecules all operating in empty space.

We never directly confront what is "out there" save in terms of its effects on our sense organs. Furthermore, different sorts of animals have different sense organs or the same ones (like eyes) that work differently in different species and, so, each kind of creature, including humans, only senses (unconsciously or consciously) their own version of the world, not what is "really" out there. Each creature's version of the world has been called its "*umwelt*" (von Uexküll 1934/2010), their own species-specific world. It is arrogant of humans to think their *umwelt* (the way the world appears to them) is "the world."

Qualia as Trackers of "Reality"

Our outer sensations of which we are aware—the subjective personal way we experience color, taste, sound, smell, and touch ("qualia")—exist to help us keep track of the things in the world. However, this is no simple task. All we experience are qualia, the way our senses take in the physical properties of the world. We never directly confront a "thing" behind and apart from the qualia presented to our senses. We construct things as continuously existing entities that count as the same thing across time and change in our mind-brains.

Certain things—like our favorite chair in the living room—seem to us obviously one thing. They do not change much and we have had lots of encounters with them. But, for many things in the world, we would be hard pressed to say whether they are the same. It is hard to know whether the humming bird you saw last week and the one you now see in a similar location are or are not the same bird.

Tracking things can get quite hard in some cases. How much can a car or building be modified before it is not the same car or building? When mining companies take the top off a mountain is it the same mountain? When a restaurant changes owners but does not much modify the menu is it the same restaurant? AOT was made by a different anime studio in its last season and a half than in its first three. Most people saw it as the same show despite differences in graphics and the "feel" of the show. In other cases, people have come to see a series they are watching as "not the same show anymore" when change has gone too far. Is America today the same America as when it was founded, as it was after World War II, or the one you grew up in? Americans are fighting over this today even though, in some ways, it is not even clear what it could really mean.

After the ecumenical council Vatican 2 (1962-1965) some Catholics no longer saw the Catholic Church as the same religion. Key changes that made them feel this way had much more to do with sensation than theology, changes like saying Mass in English (or another vernacular language) and not Latin; having thc pricst facc thc congregation rather than stand at the alter with his back to the congregation; and replacing Gregorian chant with more modern music. In a great many cases, judgements of sameness are made in how a thing affects our outer and inner senses (feelings).

The case of other people is the most complicated one for humans. As social animals, it is crucial for us to know who we are dealing with. Yet we are sometimes unsure whether someone we have encountered is someone we have met before or not. Even more importantly we are sometimes unsure someone we know is the "same person" in the sense that they may have changed so much that they have become foreign or strange to us. It is almost as if we feel someone different is now inhabiting a body we once knew.

Tracking sameness is crucial because it constructs whatever stability our world has for us. We use such judgments to determine how we will behave and how we will value people and things. Many older Americans ("Baby Boomers") think of America today as a quite different country from the one they grew up in. Is it? There is no "right" answer, since all things always change. But how people feel about this question of sameness deeply affects their behaviors, beliefs, and values.

It has become not uncommon in the U.S that people who were liberals earlier in life have become ardent right-wing conservatives, sometimes with racist and conspiracy-theory riven beliefs (Corn 2022). In some cases, their families have disowned them—even publicly in the case of some politicians—and can no longer recognize them as who they once were.

In the U.S., different people who call themselves "Christians" debate, sometimes furiously, over who are the "real Christians". Indeed, some branches of Christianity argue that when you have become "born again"—have accepted Christ as your personal savior—you have become a different person and should limit your dealings with others, even in your own family, who are not "born again."

Similar things, in different areas, are happening all over the world, and always have. However, today, driven by the great pace of change and the crises we face across the globe, they appear to be even more common and dislocating. Modern media—and most certainly some good anime—get us to reflect on stability and change and on the nature of personhood and institutions in ways that can make us more reflective about our ourselves, others, and society.

Characters in Media

Authors of books, films, video games, and anime face the same problem we all do in life. In life we construct whatever unity another person has for us across all the changes that happen to that person and our relationship. Indeed, we do the same for ourself. This is the very stuff of social life. Authors must create characters, that is, fictional persons (or other sorts of living or fantasy beings) and give us enough material to create/construct enough unity for them so we view them as a single character. Of course, media often plays with this unity. Think of Dr. Jekyll and Mr. Hyde; Dorian Gray; Superman; Jack Torrance (played by Jack Nicholson in the movie) in the *Shining*; and Norman Bates in *Psycho*.

Humans even have to construct their own sense of a unitary self. Many people feel they are not "the same person" when they take (illegal or legal) drugs and medicine. When they are old, they sometimes feel they are quite different than they were when they were young and some people have changed their political and other views and values significantly over their life time. Mental illness or strokes can utterly transform a person in mind, body, and behavior. Trans people transition into "who they really are" as, in a sense, do Christian people who become "born again."

People spend time and money in therapy trying to accept themselves; forgive themselves; find themselves; find their "real self," and radically change themselves. We tell young people they should be all they can be; discover who they are; be their best self; accept who they are; get in contact with their inner self; and live their dream. We say things to other people like: you are better than that; you are not who I thought you were; you can't help yourself; you have no idea who you are; you are two different people; you are living a lie; I am not sure who you are; I know you better than you know yourself; don't sell yourself short; you think too highly of yourself; you are too selfless; there is nothing to you; you are more important than you think; you've lost yourself; if only you were the person I thought you were; your old self was better, and on and on.

People have many different social identities. A person could be, at one and the same time, a wife, committed feminist, parent, musician, Mexican-American, professor, ardent runner, committed political liberal, devout Catholic, activist for the disabled, and a person who owns and values their status as a person with ADHD. Such a person will speak, act, and behave differently when acting out of each of these identities. And these identities can change over time and new ones can arise.

What, though, constitutes a person's "core identity," their "personhood" that underlies all their changing social identities? Social theorists have been better at identifying and celebrating multiple identities than they have at theorizing core identities, other than pointing out that such core identities are, at least partly, constructed by how a person "stories" their life in terms of a coherent story with a clear plot, even if their life does not seem so coherent to others or to themselves when storying gets hard, as it often does (Bourdieu 1991; Brockmeier & Carbaugh 2001; Gee 2015, 2020; McAdams & McLean 2013).

Character as in "Good Character"

The word "character" also has the meaning of a person with traits like integrity and courage. When we say someone has "character" in this sense—a form of high praise—it is often not exactly clear what we mean. Virtues like honesty, loyalty, courage, self-sacrifice, self-control, fairness, patience, perseverance, generosity, as well as being caring, responsible, humble, hard-working, trustworthy, sensitive, empathic, ethical, self-disciplined, kind, and non-aggressive have been associated with character. And this is only a partial list. There is a field of education called "character education" meant to teach teachers how to teach character, though some people think character is an inherent trait. Character education has, at times, been politicized and identified with support for capitalism and a conservative stance on society (Smagorinsky & Taxel 2005).

The phrase "a person with good character" often seems to overlap or mean little more than "a good person." What can people really mean or be doing with the word "character?" In many ways, the word represents a person's—in some way, most people's—ideal for what a human ought to be. In this ideal sense, many people believe a person can have good character regardless of their religion or political stance, that character transcends religious and political debates.

Few of us live up to any ideal, even our own, on a daily basis. We differ over how the virtues associated with character might be enacted in different contexts. Yet most of us want to have a good character, want others to, and believe society would be much better off if we all did. Humans are drawn to ideals. It is essential that we discuss ideals, give models of them, debate them, contextualize them, but leave them with some sense of transcendence. Discussing, debating, and reflecting on character—and the uses and misuses people can make of ideals in service of their own religious and political views—is central to any pluralistic society.

Character is, in many ways, the label under which we can discuss morality, ethics, and goodness when they are detached, as much as they can be, from specific religions, political positions, and cultures. There is, of course, a need to engage fully with religious, political, and cultural diversity. But there is also a deep need to spend some time trying to transcend them in a search for more widely shared ideals, ideals core to the nature of humans as living beings and as humans.

Earlier we discussed empathy, intuition, balance, atmosphere, tension and release, and feelings and emotions. These are all constituents of our inner life and of our embodiment in the world. Personhood—and the several senses of "character"—as well as the nature of things and institutions in the world is the ontology (stuff) of the human *umwelt*. Things, institutions, and persons are open to us only via sensation (qualia and inner feeling and emotions) and we create their solidity and unity, such as it is, out of all the ways we have sensed them in the past. They are what we call, in the next section, "sensuous constructions." The "nature" of things, institutions, and people is the heart and soul of media and should be at the heart of an education. In the next section we will look at how AOT constructs Eren as a character and how this process raises important issues for reflection and discussion.

What is a human? What are human institutions and why are they so vexed? What is the difference between an inanimate thing and a living thing? What makes a country or a culture a country or a culture? How much can they change and still be the same? What is the human *umwelt* and how does it compare to the *umwelts* of other living beings? How do we help humans, institutions, and life on earth survive and flourish, especially today in a world facing so much change, complexity, and crisis? These are profoundly important and utterly basic questions. They should be the core curriculum of any human seeking after understanding. Of course, we will have to later take up the question of whether and why a human should seek understanding, that is, an education that transcends the pragmatics of daily life.

Eren: Things and Individuals as Sensuous Constructions

People and things, as we experience them, are one and many. They are one, specific, individual (a given person, thing, or institution), and utterly unique but that oneness is made from a composite of sensations over time. A person we know is both a quite specific entity and yet also a composite of many different sensations that were part of many different experiences across time. A person is both one and many. So, too, are things and institutions.

The name "Eren" names a character in AOT, but Eren, as a character that we experience across a series of encounters, is what we might call a "sensuous construction" (a construction made from different sensual experiences across time). Every time we encounter him, he is replete with sensual features, some the same and other different across time. Each time we encounter him he carries the cloud of all the earlier sensual features we have experienced in regard to him. Each appearance of Eren will change the cloud. If the cloud loses its gestalt/wholistic character, we will cease to see Eren as the same person or will feel he changed beyond recognition.

To see how individual people are sensuous constructions, let's take as our example, then, Eren in AOT. He is made by us viewers based on the experiences the designers of AOT give us of him. We meet Eren as a young boy and watch him grow up. We see him act, react to, and express feelings differently with friends, family, enemies, fellow soldiers, and people he doesn't know. We perceive differences in how he acts, feels, and appears in many different social situations and in many different environments. As we all do, he behaves and expresses feelings and emotions in different ways at different times and in different contexts.

Eren is affected differently by different people and so he seems a different sort of person with different sorts of people, yet we see him, nonetheless, as the same person. He gets sick, becomes badly injured, seems at times to be mentally ill and behaves in odd ways. And, of course, we eventually see him not just in his human form, but in his Titan one. Yet, many of us even see Eren the human and Eren the Titan as the "same person." Indeed, media often shows us how expansive our acceptance of a person as the "same person" can be.

Each time we experience Eren, our experience is made up of the ways he looks, sounds, moves, emotes, and how these ways have made us feel. This is all coupled with any connections our brain has made to other information we have gained from the scripts in AOT or reading and discussion outside the anime series. Each such experience constitutes a changing web of associations that makes up Eren as a person/character in our mind-brain (the sensuous construction that is Eren).

If we want to continue to feel that Eren is the "same person", we have to perceive the set of associations that compose him as related to each other in a wholistic (gestalt like) way. However, the ways Eren appears and acts at different times and in different contexts in AOT can stretch and even come close to breaking his "unity" as the "same person." Mikasa, Eren's closest friend from childhood on—and a woman who loves him and is totally devoted to him—says at one point late in AOT:

> *Everyone says Eren has changed.*
> *I've thought, too.*
>
> *But...maybe all of us are wrong.*
>
> *Maybe Eren was this way from the start. And if this is the real him...*
>
> *...I...I...wonder what I saw in him..*
>
> (E87 The Dawn of Humanity)

Figure 3. Eren Jaeger
(WIT Studio & MAPPA Studio)

What constitutes a person's "real self" ("the real him") is a fundamental problem for us humans as social animals. Here are four images of Eren across time in AOT. Each is part of an ensemble of sensation and feeling connected to others that all together constitute for us "Eren" as a unitary "thing," a person, if they do. We see how qualia and feelings can allow human beings to track a "thing" (here, Eren) in the world despite massive and constant change. It is a necessary trick for survival and one that can be used by media designers to great effect. AOT challenges the limits of what constitutes "one person"—a person we know—for viewers.

A good deal of Japanese anime is concerned with the themes "what makes a thing a living thing" and "what makes a creature a human being." Anime often has characters that look very different from each, such as doll like creatures (that may or may not be alive), robotic beings, shape shifters, seemingly inanimate things that talk, talking animals, spirits, and humans who look and behave in odd ways, alongside good-looking youthful characters with big eyes that are a staple of anime. Who is human or not, good or not, friend or foe, to be trusted or not, is problematized and often not readily predictable. Good creatures do bad things and bad ones do good things and they are often not consistent or predicable. We as viewers must—as we do in life—construct as much consistency and coherence as we can, realizing that there are limits to consistency and coherence in real life, as well as media.

AOT stretches Eren as a character almost beyond the breaking point. We see him early on as a sweet but headstrong child and, through many changes, we see him, in the end, as a monster engaged in genocide, a genocide that, nonetheless, he thinks is the only moral way forward. We viewers have no trouble recognizing him as the same character (person), but we are made to wonder why we do so. We are made to ask whether he has changed radically or we were mistaken about who he "really" is/was. Is he acting freely or out of compulsion or trauma? Is he mentally ill or endowed with profound insight? What really are his motives? Can we trust what he says are his motives? Does he even really understand his motives?

Late in AOT, Eren says he has never liked Mikasa, his closest life-long friend and a woman who loves him. Is this how he really has always felt, feels now, or is he lying to protect her from himself? We have seen so much about him in AOT and know so much about him and yet, in the end, he remains an enigma (generating lots of discussion on line).

Eren is, in many respects, a character for our times. As people in the United States, and in many other places, take up more and more combative identities against others and sometimes become people their friends cannot recognize—often encouraged by social media that has convinced them of conspiracies and or alternate ("red pill") realities—Eren comes to seem a concrete example of a more general trend in our world. His world looks strange at first and then oddly familiar. This is one of the fortes of anime: to make the "normal" strange and the strange revealing. Indeed, it has been said that such "making strange" is one of the main functions of art (Shklovsky 1965).

CHAPTER 9

LANDSCAPES AND FLOW

In Chapter 5 we looked at atmosphere, a form of feeling about how we are placed in an environment. Here we will look at placement in the environment in a different way. We will take up how humans, stemming from their evolutionary history, respond to nature in the sense of landscapes.

In this chapter we will look at four "higher order" feelings that strongly affect how compelling an experience is to a human. Higher-order feelings are feelings or emotions that are melded with higher-order cognitive states (Panksepp 1998 and Panksepp & Bevin 2012). Raw emotions like rage or lust involve no reasoning process or inferencing. They are triggered and we act. Since humans are socialized early in life, engage in social learning, and have higher-order reasoning capacities, they (sometimes) learn to control their emotions and meld them with reasoning, inferencing, or reflection. This process gives rise to a myriad of different emotions and emotion terms like remorse, regret, guilt, shame, distress, anguish, (as well as terms like rue and compunction which are literary terms), and others, all mixtures of the basic emotion of PANIC/GRIEF (see Chapter 7) with social and cultural learning and inferences about context.

Four Higher-order Feelings

Humans only store experiences in the web of associations in their brains if these experiences have caused them to care about them. The four higher-order feelings about landscapes that we will discuss here make humans care about and continually engage with an experience.

These higher-order feelings were first studied in terms of how humans respond to landscapes. However, they apply more widely to other sorts of experiences. Nonetheless, landscapes are primordial to humans. Humans' evolutionary history has taught them to respond in different ways to different sorts of landscapes for survival, flourishing, and learning. More widely, human physical and mental health requires that humans are "grounded" in the material world of dirt, air, water, and life outdoors. Unfortunately, as humans got more modern, they became less and less grounded. This has reached an extreme today we humans stare endlessly at screens.

In Chapter 6, we discussed tension and release as an essential sensory part of achieving dynamic balance. Just as we breath in and out, are active and then sleep, live in light and darkness, work and relax, socialize and spend time alone time, seek excitement and then peace, and engage with many other such cycles, tension and release are poles around a center that constitutes balance amidst change.

While the sensory relationship between humans and nature is primordial for humans in terms of dynamic balance, it is a relationship that is often greatly disrupted in modern life. The core concept of homeostasis (biological balance) is defined around the give and take between living things and their environments. For all living creatures their environment is first and foremost the material world. As is the case for all living beings, human health requires a balance between self and world. Too many too strong challenges (stresses) from the world are bad for humans, but so are too few, because failing to learn how to deal productively with challenges is a sure way to die in nature.

Research on landscape aesthetics has shown that natural settings and landscapes can produce emotional states of wellbeing in humans (Stuart-Smith 2020). They attract us to stay and linger or entice us to set out and explore. This research has shown that images of urban scenes generally result in negative feelings whereas the opposite is true after viewing images from nature (Hartig 2008). People shown scenes of cities with trees and other vegetation show less fear and more delight than they do when they are shown scenes of treeless city scenes (Roe et al. 2013).

Considerable recent work on health argues that humans need much more contact with the earth than they normally get:

> Research has shown that taking group nature walks, for example, is linked with lower depression, less stress and better mental health and well-being. Other research has shown that spending long stretches of time in the woods – a so-called «forest bath» – can boost the number of white blood cells that fight viruses and tumors. (Miller 2017)

Like all animals, humans evolved to interact with nature—they need, for their survival, to get from nature not only resources that nourish the body, but resources that nurture learning and imagination. Work in environmental psychology by Rachel and Stephen Kaplan (1989) has argued that humans have certain needs in regard to nature and these needs influence how they interact with nature at the level of sensation, imagination, and behavior.

According to Kaplan and Kaplan (1989), when early humans entered nature, before we had tamed and destroyed so much of it, they wanted their surroundings to be coherent and not confusing (to make sense in terms of parts and wholes); they wanted it to engage them, to be a realm of activity and stimulation, to have a certain complexity; they wanted a map, in their head and later on paper, so they knew how to move around and get in and out of an area; and they wanted mystery, a sense that there were things to discover. The Kaplans called these four needs a need for "coherence" (a sense of parts and wholes, how things "hang together"); "complexity" (engagement and stimulation); "legibility" (a map); and "mystery" or "anticipation."

These needs—coherence, complexity, legibility, and mystery—give rise to four core human higher-order feelings. As emotions we can label them as a) a feeling of coherence (a feeling that things hang or fit together in a coherent and meaningful way); b) a feeling of engagement (a feeling that things are complex enough and in the right way to entice us and draw us in); c) a feeling of legibility (a feeling that we are not lost); and d) a feeling of mystery (a sense of wonder and anticipation).

Each of these feelings involves also a cognitive state. It takes reasoning to understand that something is or is not coherent, complex in the right way, legible, or mysterious, so these are cognitive states as well as effective ones. Because they are so important to humans and because humans are "turned on" by them, they are also feelings. They make us feel in ways that entice, attract, and draw us in in different ways. So, these four things are needs, feelings, and cognitive states all at once.

It is clear that these four feelings are adaptive in that they would have helped our ancestors to survive and even flourish. They are adaptive for modern humans—who are now more than ever isolated from nature—in that they lower human beings' anxieties and bring them excitement, imagination, and feelings of competence and of belonging to and in the world.

Mystery is interesting here. In the research, it is the most consistent and impactful variable. Humans feel very positive about mystery and eager to engage with it when it is safe, but also a bit risky. They like to be a little bit on the edge. Of course, when mystery is associated with serious threat and danger, it no longer causes positive feelings in most humans (but there are those who get even more energized).

Mystery is clearly another release and tension feeling, a dance where we do not want to resolve the mystery too soon, since a large part of the excitement and fun of it is in the process of solving it and not just, or sometimes even at all, in having solved it. And, with mystery, there is also the balance between safety and risk that at the right level is exhilarating.

Yet it is also clear that the other three needs are release and tension feelings as well. Here, too, we want resolution/release to come but too soon or too simply: We want things to be coherent, to make sense, for parts to form unified wholes, but, perhaps, not too fast and not all at once, since by delaying we might discover new unities. We want things to engage and stimulate us, but do not want our sense of engagement and stimulation to end too soon, to be too simple, too predictable, to be merely titillating and not inspiring and life enhancing. We want a map, but we want to discover it and still have some unchartered realms on it. For those who want to linger in nature and not just get in and out quickly, mapping can be more engaging than the map it issues in.

These four needs apply beyond nature. We humans have these needs in our encounters with cities and in our social encounters with people. We have them, as well, in our encounters with art, media, and teaching and learning situations.

We want things to make sense, but not so simple that they foreclose deeper appreciation and understanding; we want them to be engaging and stimulating, but not to end too soon or be too trivial; we want to have a map or know the rules, but have a hand in making or unmaking them; and we want mystery, but a good one, with twists and turns. And we want, or should want if we are to flourish, the resolution of all these needs as stopping off points for reflection and refueling before we head off to other uncharted or less well charted territories.

Immersion and the Self

Now we want to discuss the nature of a mental state where humans engage in intense mental effort but are completely absorbed in what they are doing in a way that they "lose themselves." They pay little attention to themselves as a self separate from their task. This is a form of immersion that the psychologist

Mihaly Csikszentmihalyi (2009) called "flow". In a state of flow, Csikszent-mihalyi argued, actions and awareness are merged and a person loses the sort ruminations about self we humans so often engage in.

Flow involves people engaging in an activity on automatic pilot (without much conscious reflection and reasoning), but is more than that. It also involves complete concentration, clarity of goals, a feeling that time has either sped up or slowed down, a feeling of effortless mastery, a balance between challenge and skill, a feeling of control over the task we are engaged in, and often a feeling of deep satisfaction.

The topic of consciousness has been written about for thousands of years with much controversy and little agreement. Without broaching this massive literature, we can distinguish between two types of consciousness: conscious awareness and self-consciousness. Humans can sense (detect) things in the world and in their bodies without being consciously aware they are doing so. When you rush out the door, caught up with thoughts about what you need to do, you detect that the door is open wide enough to get through or open it wider, if need be, but you need not be consciously aware of these properties of the door. Asked later, you would have no idea. But sometimes you are aware of what you sense and this awareness comes with "feeling," for example, the "feel" (subjective qualities) of a specific shade of blue or the feel (say, anger) of specific internal states of your body and its inner organs.

Such conscious awareness is something we share with many animals. It is not well understood yet either biologically or philosophically. However, it is much less mysterious and controversial than self-consciousness. Self-consciousness is when we think overtly about ourselves, when we reflect on ourselves. Self-consciousness seems to involve a self ("I") thinking about a self ("me") and so gives us the feeling we have in us two selves, an observer and an observed.

Humans, being able to think about themselves, have long believed the thinker here ("I") is a self that someone transcends and commands their body. It is the "real" us and many have believed it can live on past death. This sense of self has been the subject of much philosophy that has argued that it an illusion created by our brains and, some have argued, especially in some Eastern philosophy, that it is an illusion we are too attached to and should get over. It has also been the subject of much therapy and self-help where people search for their "true selves" (and somehow miraculously never seem to find one they regret having found).

When humans are not engaged in a specific task or goal their mind often ruminates about different things. This is called the "default mode" of the brain

(Buckner, Andrews-Hanna, & Schacter 2008). Our brains never turn off. When we are not using our brain for a specific task, the brain does not shut down but engages in things like daydreaming, ruminating, associating, and dreaming. Very often our ruminations are about ourselves, for some people obsessively so due to anxiety or trauma.

We humans, however, can, and often do, engage with the world without thinking about ourselves. When an expert dancer, musician, or surgeon is performing, they often experience their actions as spontaneous, not as the product of their self planning, reasoning, or calculating. They are not reflecting on themselves ("me the surgeon", "me the dancer"); they are at one with, attuned to, connected to, embedded in their activity and its environment.

This feeling of selfless immersion can happen in big picture mode or in details mode. We can lose our focus on ourself when we are immersed in a forest walk; a surgeon can lose her focus on herself when she is operating on automatic pilot during surgery in a wholistic way. But we can lose our self when we stop in our hike and pay intense attention to a stunning flower; the surgeon can face a specific problem that has arisen in surgery and concentrate with total engagement on detailed problem with no reflection herself. In both cases, we are intensely absorbed in and by an activity in which we have lost our sense of a separate spectating reflective self.

The real issue here is not whether we are caught up in the big picture (a whole that is more than its parts) or dealing with specific details is when we should engage in self-consciousness and when we should not. Self-consciousness breaks selfish immersion (flow) because it detaches us from our task and creates a certain duality between the self and its activity and the objects or other people involved in it.

There are certainly times you do not want self-consciousness to break selfless immersion. For example, thinking reflectively about what you are doing while dancing can make you less fluid or even cause you to trip over your own feet. You need to be caught up in, part of, the dance. Athletes worrying that they will fail—or are failures—usually do fail.

Selfless immersion is often associated with expertise because it makes for fluid and successful performance, whether driving a car, playing a musical instrument, giving a lecture, or doing surgery. It is often associated as well with enjoyment in losing ourselves in the midst of our activities in the world or our engagement with media. It is striking how much humans enjoy losing themselves, shutting down our internal monologue about our self.

However, when we are trying to learn something new or when we are teaching newcomers, it is often necessary to engage in a reflective, self-conscious stance on our activity as a learner or teacher. Teachers must do this because after they become experts, they may have long forgotten what it felt like to be a beginner without embodied knowledge. And, too, when we are engaged with the world or media, it is sometimes necessary to take a reflective self-conscious stance when things have gone wrong, for example, if we have come to realize that our taken-for-granted mastery needs changing or if we come to feel that the media we are losing ourselves in is not, perhaps, all that good for us.

A reflective, self-conscious stance enables us to monitor our behavior, plan our next moves, and try out different things. But in many cases gaining expertise will eventually mean casting off this monitoring, planning, and training and leaving our self-consciousness behind in the service of immersion.

For novices, self-conscious attention improves performance and learning. But this is not true for experts. Once a skill is mastered, things change dramatically:

> When experts "choke" under pressure, it is often excessive attention to themselves—in the guise either of their own performance or their own affective and cognitive states—that is the culprit. (Garfield 2022, p. 109)

Experience designers (teachers) want learners to grow from self-consciousness into immersive mastery. They want learners to lose themselves in experience so that they can by-pass their self-centered fears and worries. And they want sometimes to have their learners break immersion to engage in reflective exploration and questioning about their relationship to what they learning.

Finding and losing the self—self-consciousness alternating with selfless immersion—is another balancing act. We do not have a name for it, but it is an ever-present phenomenon in experience. There is a balance point around which we alternate between a focus on the self and immersion in the world but orient toward a center where self and world are integrated and reciprocal. Since there is no word for this higher-order feeling (it is a form of being both a separate self and yet still in and "at one" with the world), so, let's call it: "self-balance". In self-balance we alternate around a center where self and world never become too far apart. We are not alienated from the world (physical or social) and we are not dominated by it. We can add it to coherence, mystery, complexity, and legibility.

While coherence, mystery, complexity, and legibility are founded in our relationship with nature, they—and self-balance (a good dance between immersion and self-consciousness)—are also crucial parts of any good designed experience for learning, development, and flourishing. For too many young people, school—and more and more the world we all live in—lacks coherence, good mystery, good complexity, and legibility. School and the world do not entice them, draw them in, make them feel grounded. School and the world make them spend too much time in worrying about the self and too little in immersion where they stop thinking about themselves as the dancer and start being the dance.

CHAPTER 10

IMAGES

So far, in the previous chapters, we have discussed phenomena—empathy, intuition, balance, atmosphere, tension and release, emotion, personhood/character, landscape aesthetics, and higher-order feelings like mystery, coherence, legibility, complexity, and self-balance—that stand somewhat apart from the sort of analytical, logical, and fact-retention skills that constitute, by and large, the focus of formal schooling. We have not yet dealt directly with the sort of "intelligence" school is most focused on. We will soon get to this sort of intelligence, but first we need to discuss the human capacity for mental simulation, the ability to create images and moving images in one's head.

From Simulation to Images

Simulation is the place where phenomena like intuition and empathy meet more rational and logical analysis. In the course of evolution humans evolved a capacity to engage in mental simulation far beyond what other animals can do. This capacity, much later human development, led to the capacity to draw and paint realistic images on surfaces, a capacity no other animal has.

We saw, when we discussed mathematicians in Chapter 3, that images (either realistic ones or patterns that can be manipulated) are crucial to their ability to discover new solutions. Einstein achieved his major breakthroughs in physics by performing visual experiments in his head rather than in a laboratory. He simulated phenomena—like imagining a person on a rocket chasing a beam of light—as a way to trigger intuition and think through the implications of the simulated experience. Einstein's visual experiments were called "Gedankenexperiment" ("thought experiments"). Einstein put the matter this way (Einstein 1995, p. 36):

> …Words or the language, as they are written or spoken, do not seem to play any role in my mechanism of thought. The psychical entities which seem to serve as elements in thought are certain signs and more or less clear images which can be "voluntarily" reproduced and combined…but taken from a psychological viewpoint, this combinatory play seems to be the essential feature in productive thought — before there is any connection with logical construction in words or other kinds of signs which can be communicated to others.

Our early ancestors, even those before we *Homo sapiens* evolved, knew how to form images in their heads. Lots of animals can do this. It requires that you have a brain with neurons that can respond to stimuli from the world, store them as a form of memory, and then use them to form (activate) an image in your mind-brain. "Image" is not really the right word here, because we can form mental versions of sensations that come not just to our eyes but to our other senses as well (such as imagining smells, sounds, textures, and so forth).

However, *Homo sapiens* (us)—one species of the genus *Homo*, all the rest of which are now extinct—developed the ability to form not just images, but full-blown simulations in their minds. In these simulations we can walk around as ourselves, role play someone or something else, make choices, see the consequences of these choices, re-run the simulation and see what happens if we make a different choice, travel to fantasy realms and even die and come back to life. It is a *Homo sapiens* superpower.

In this chapter we are going to look at how images and the ability to simulate came about and what some of the consequences were. We will argue that this process gave rise to four major new human feelings, ones that drive humans to this day. These new feelings arose when humans gained new sensations and became aware of them, sensations that came from new activities.

Aesthetic Objects

Our discussion here of the factual details of the evolution of realistic image making is based on Lorblanchet & Bahn 2017 with additional background from Clottes 2016; Curtis 2006; David 2017; and Desdemaines-Hugon 2010. Much of the interpretation of the important of these factual details is our own. Long before *Homo sapiens* evolved, *Homo erectus*, a close relative of *Homo sapiens* that evolved in Africa about 1.9 million years ago (Higham 2021), collected objects they found "beautiful," such as distinctive pebbles and shells they found on the beach, and took them home. They had learned to value an object for how it affected them, not because, or just because, of its usefulness. We do the same thing today. To see a pebble as beautiful means that we imagine it—value it in our minds—in a certain way, a way that gives the pebble a sensual property that we did not sense directly (like color) but added to it, namely, beauty.

Later, *Homo erectus*, who had been making tools for a long time, started to craft beautiful round spheres (called "bolas") out of chunks of rock, objects with no known use. They also started to make hand axes that were not just useful, but that looked good (e.g., highly symmetrical) as well. In some cases, they worked on the original rock from which they carved the axe so as to leave in place a fossil shell that just happened to be embedded in the center of the hand axe they were making. The shell had no function; it just made the axe all the more aesthetic. Often, they kept these beautiful hand axes and did not use them.

Homo erectus had discovered what we call "aesthetics." What "beauty" means has long been contested by philosophers. All we can say is that *Homo erectus* found well-made bolas and symmetrical hand axes distinctive, compelling, attractive (attracting) and valued them not just for their use, but in their own right.

Homo erectus had learned to transfer, in their imaginations, objects from the mundane world to another realm, a realm of personal meaning and value that transcended pragmatic action. They created a realm filled with objects whose value transcended the everyday mess of working to survive in the material (and dangerous) world. They had created the realm of the ideal, an alternative world humans would never stop looking for. Many of us, even in selecting pretty pebbles on the beach today, keep searching for ever better ones, ever more special ones, an ideal one (which we never seem to find). The ideal becomes a realm that competes with the real world.

One telling example of the search for the ideal that has filled human history is love. For Plato, love had to have an "ideal object" (Madigan 2011). Lovers seek an embodiment of an ideal in each other that is essentially eternal and transcendent. Real people fall short, always embodying the contingency and messiness of the material world. An ideal becomes an essence, not an actual object. Actual objects can only gesture towards the ideal.

While some animals find particular colors attractive in a mate, humans are not just attracted to aesthetic objects, they are aware they are so attracted and value the objects apart from any use they have (e.g., attracting a mate). When *Homo erectus* gained the capacity, the power, to perceive beauty, how did this make them feel? *Homo erectus* probably did not have language like ours, but feelings aren't words anyway. They surely felt, as we do, some form of delight or attraction. But they also felt a feeling of transcending or exceeding the mundane world, bettering it or perfecting it—or just discovering it on the beach—bringing out or finding its hidden meaning. This feeling is a powerful one, since, in it, people realize their capacity to give and create value beyond the material world and the pragmatic use of things. And then, alas, they must ever search for it.

Tools

Homo habilis, an earlier relative of *Homo sapiens* than *Homo erectus*—the name means "skillful man"—made tools more than 2 million years ago. They did so by striking one rock against another one to create fractures with sharp edges that could be used for cutting and scarping. Eventually *Homo erectus* made more complicated tools called "hand axes." With two curved, flaked surfaces forming the cutting edge (a technique known as bifacial working), these tools proved sharper and more effective.

A few animal species can make or use tools, crows and chimpanzees, for example. But none of them make tools in anything like the numbers that *Homo habilis* and *Homo erectus* did. None of them keep stores of tools at a home base. And none of them make anything as elaborate as a *Homo erectus* hand axe, let alone the many tools that would follow. Tools from the start were a *Homo* specialty.

When *Homo habilis* and *Homo erectus* gained the power to make tools—and perfect them ever more and more—and were aware of their tools as tools and tool making as a process, how did this make them feel? Whatever feelings or constellations of feelings crafting and using well-made tools gave our early ancestors, they surely encompassed a feeling of having an extended body. Much as a blind person's cane extends his or her body further out into the world or a rifle allows one to kill at a distance, tools augmented the powers of the body. The person using a good tool feels extended and expanded.

This effect of this sort of bodily extension reaches an interesting point in video games. The human mind and body are made in such a way that when a person controls an avatar in a game they feel as if their body extends into the virtual world. That is why young children often jump in their chair as they make their character jump in the virtual world. A game controller is a unique sort of tool. It is like a blind person's cane that allows the gamer to "tap" the virtual world and bring it into close contact with their body.

Person + tool constituted a new expanded self that had more power in and on the world than the unexpanded body. This surely was the beginning of the ability of humans to dominate animals. In the course of history, humans sought and still seek ever greater extensions of their bodies, their mind's powers, and their life spans through technology.

We have the term "cyborg" for a being with both organic and biomechanical body parts, but person + tool was the beginning here. We humans have ever since searched to empower our bodies further and further, to make up for our weaknesses and imperfections. This, too, is a form of the search for the ideal.

Social Distinction

A bola was an aesthetic object to *Homo erectus*. A hand axe could be just a tool, but if it was made distinctively, it could also be an aesthetic object. But objects were also social to early humans and still are to us today. The maker of an aesthetic object, or the owner of one, could gain social status, just as today someone who paints well or someone who owns a great painting can gain status, though status of different sorts.

Different groups of early humans made tools in different ways and these ways of making gave each group an identity as tool makers and users of tools of that sort. Indeed, then and now, social groups and cultures are identifiable in terms of the things they make, use, own, and display.

Objects, then, can be used to signal status within a group and membership in and solidarity with the group. Within a Hells Angels biker group, your bike, your leather jacket, your boots, and other objects such as jewelry, can display your identity as a biker of the Hells Angels sort (solidarity) and gain you individual status within the group if they are distinctive in the right way. Of course, these objects are always accompanied by distinctive ways of behaving, interacting with others, and how you use language.

Imagine an upscale restaurant and a biker bar. Everything in them will look quite different—the objects, décor, and the people—in a great many ways. Humans use just such appearances to predict what will happen, how people will behave, how they themselves might be treated, in each place. They may find one place full of "people like me," even though they know none of them, and not the other. A person may well choose not to go into the one or the other place. Humans as social animals use appearances, how things look and feel, to predict who is safe to interact with and who not.

Humans are social animals. Social animals have a biological need to belong to and contribute to social groups within their species. Many social animals—including our relatives the chimpanzees—are hostile to members of their species with whom they do not share a group (Safina 2020). Within a social group, very often different members have different degrees of status, that is, higher or lower standing in the group in terms of how others treat them. Group members have to be able both to recognize other members and to recognize the different statuses of each member in the group.

Some social species have groups in which status conflicts are low—while others have groups in which they are intense—but few species have groups in which status plays no role. Humans, like baboons, are a species in which status conflicts and worries can be intense and this has long been a trait in humans, though it can be mitigated in certain contexts (Sapolsky 1994, 2021).

Recognizing other members of one's group or the status of group members is easy, of course, if the group is small and everyone sees everyone regularly. Save for social insects, most social animals only see themselves as members of relatively small social groups such as families, troops, or clans that rarely get much bigger than 100 members and are often much smaller (Safina 2020). Humans, however, can feel they are a member of very big groups, groups that contain a great many people they have never seen and never will see, such as groups based on cultures, religions, and nations.

Chimpanzees would never eat in any restaurant (if they had restaurants) filled with other chimpanzees they do not know. They are very aggressive with other chimps they do not know. However, humans can go to a city they do not live in and eat in a restaurant filled with strangers. In the animal world (save for ants and termites and some other insects) this is unique. They can do this just so long as most of the people in the restaurant look and behave in ways that seem expectable and safe enough to constitute people "like us" (Jackson 2019; Storr 2021). In the United States this judgement is often class based and, of course, for some people can involve race (and other invidious divides) as well.

Humans can feel a social affiliation with a larger group of others than any other (non-insect) creature, with groups that far surpass the number of people they could ever meet or know. They can pull off this feat because they can predict from appearances whether the people in a new space are sufficiently "like them" to enter that space and feel comfortable. Appearances become social signals of identity.

There may have been a time when many Americans recognized almost all other Americans as fellow Americans. However that might be, America today is rife with different contesting groups that go to no pains to mask their disdain for other groups. They wear their identity "on their sleeve," so to speak. Video of the January 6th insurrection in Washington shows hordes of people who readily recognize each other—and are easily recognized by their enemies—by their clothes, speech, and symbols (a red MAGA hat, Q on signs and clothing, a "Don't Tread on Me" flag, and guns, for example) as people who have found a shared identity, one now well known to Americans. It is exactly all these visible markers that allow them to feel solidarity with each other when they have never met and before they have yet talked to people in the crowd. And it allows them to feel disdain for others.

These objects are not inherently meaningful. Make America Great Again (MAGA) was a saying originally associated with Ronald Reagan. Another color or another saying would have worked as well on the red MAGA hat as long as it served as a predicable signal of being "one of us" for the people in this very expanded social group.

Humans are tropic to status (Storr 2021). They pay a good deal of attention to it and worry about it a good deal. Certain objects and practices become markers of a person's status within a group or of a group's status in comparison to other groups. In this latter role they become markers of solidarity with a group: "people like us" wear certain things, cook certain dishes, listen to certain sorts of music, and so forth.

Within the group of people who attended the January 6th insurrection, a person could gain individual status by having the most distinctive or extreme markers of their pro-Trump identity. And they all signaled solidarity by showing up with similar "regalia" (a word that means decorations or insignia indicative of an office or membership, formerly royalty, but now used more broadly and often referring to special styles of dress). And, of course, we can note that our use of the term "insurrection" contributes here not just a literal meaning, but serves also as a marker of social identity. You knew the minute we used the word "insurrection" we do not own red MAGA hats.

While humans had previously transferred an object from the mundane world to the realm of the ideal, now they transferred objects from the mundane world to the realm of a world of social status and solidarity. Just as a beautiful object has value in a realm (the ideal) beyond its use value, an object like a Harley motorcycle or a red Trump hat has value beyond its use as well. It marks a social identity. The ideal realm and the realm of status and solidarity are imaginative constructions, and they are strongly tied to images.

Using objects, clothing, food, and such things—and how we interact with them—as signs of status and solidarity allowed humans to organize into much larger groups than any other animals can (other than ants and some other social insects). The object becomes a sign (e.g., the red MAGA hat) and its meaning ("we are Trump people") can travel far and wide with it, allowing people to recognize "people like us" widely across space. It allows them to accept as fellow group members even people they have never seen before. This gave rise to an imaginary identity, an identity that does not reside in kinship or close interactions (the source of trust for most animals and our early human ancestors), but in wider affiliation among people who do not know and may never know each other, but share "membership" in a very big social group. Chimpanzees could never have done it.

Imaginary identity here does not mean a "false identity" or that people with the identity are deluded (though they can be deluded by how good the identity is for them or others). It means that the identity is replete with images that anyone in the group, and often those outside it, associate with the identity.

Imaginary identities are only maintained and can easily be manipulated by images (realistic ones or more abstract signs and symbols). Such extended groups based on imaginary identities give rise to new feelings. Humans have long felt kinship, friendship, and local community ties in strong ways. But now they have learned to feel ties to others they do not see regularly or know at all. This feeling has no common name, it is the attachment we feel to groups larger than our local communities. Such groups transcend the here and now and constitute a new and different realm or world of value conjured from imagination. This feeling portends the long history of nationalism, xenophobia, inequality, racism, and war. We could call it, for want of a better word, a feeling of an extended social body. Tools gave rise to the feeling of having an extended physical body. Social signs gave rise to the feeling of having an extended social identity beyond kith, kin, and local community. If "extended social identity" sounds too academic to you, we could use the term Benedict Anderson (1983) did, "imagined communities," and talk about a feeling of affiliation with an imagined community. People in such groups—and we are all in some, whether it be a religion, ethnic group, culture, or affiliation with people with whom we share deep interests or passions—can often recognize each other before they talk.

Just as the extended body has led humanity on a very long dance with technology to enhance our powers, expanded social attachment has led humanity on a very long search for empowering their "imagined communities" over others.

Images on Surfaces

Making tools, aesthetic objects, and social signs of status or solidarity require the ability to form images in one's head—not just static images but sequences of images like the steps to make an elaborate tool—a form of brain-based simulation. It is interesting that the ability to make realistic images on a surface came much later in history than the ability to simulate images in our head. There were bolas, hand axes, and even rocks with patterns of lines made on them long before anyone bothered to—or, perhaps, could—draw or paint a realistic image of an animal or a human on a surface (for example, on a rock or cave wall).

Something happened to *Homo sapiens*—to us—about 60, 000 years ago (Lorblanchet & Bahn 2017). Across the world *Homo sapiens* began to draw realistic looking images. This was the time in which some members of *Homo sapiens* had first left Africa. They arrived in Australia about 60, 000 years ago and in Western Europe a bit later, about 45,000 years ago. Others spread elsewhere and, as we know, eventually filled the earth. And, of course, some stayed in Africa. When *Homo sapiens* arrived in Europe, their cousins, another species of humans, the Neanderthals, were already there.

The first drawings in human evolution were painted patterns of lines on rocks, some dating back 70, 000 years. Drawing and painting realistic images came later. The earliest example of such pictorial art so far found was discovered in a cave on the Indonesian island of Sulawesi (Vergano 2014). This art has been dated to be at least 43,900 years old. In these images, Pleistocene humans (*Homo sapiens*) depicted several figures that seem to be human, though some of them have snouts or a tail or a bird's beak. These are human-animal hybrids and, of course, while we moderns believe such things only exist in the imagination, the people that drew them may well have thought otherwise.

Another interesting fact, other than the lateness of realistic image making in evolutionary history, is that the early makers of realistic images drew many different types of animals, but nearly never drew plants or trees or environmental scenes. They often drew and painted animals quite realistically and dramatically, but drew humans as stick figures. They were not drawing and painting to document their world, but for some other reason.

There is an image of a bird-headed man in France's Lascaux Cave (Clottes 2016). Lascaux Cave is a Paleolithic cave system in southwestern France. It contains some of the most famous examples of prehistoric cave paintings, mostly of animals. The paintings in Lascaux date to about 20,000 years ago, so are younger than those from Sulawesi. The bird-headed man is the only figure of a human being on the walls of the cave complex in Lascaux. The painting shows this bird-headed human lying on the ground, apparently dead, in front of a bison—drawn and painted with majestic realism—whose entrails are hanging out. He is drawn as a stick figure. A broken spear lays on the ground near him and to its left is what looks like a stick with a bird on the top (perhaps a stick or wand used by the bird-headed man in the way shamans across the world do to this day), an image which resonates with the fact that the man appears to have a bird-shaped head.

We modern *Homo sapiens* understand animals very differently than did our early relatives painting in those caves. We cannot understand what these animals meant as images, unless we first understand what they meant in the mundane lives of these early humans. Early humans lived in a world replete with mighty animals. There were, in their world, a great many more and more powerful animals than we moderns have ever seen. Humans were, indeed, a small force in the face of this might, mere stick figures. They had no horns, or claws, or fur and their numbers were vastly smaller than other animal species they saw. Humans then were not the dominate animals—not even near it—on earth.

Ancient humans lived within the same web of life as these animals, needed some of them for food, and saw them not as inferior to humans but as dominant. And, long having had a sense of aesthetics, they admired them for their majesty and power. When they learned to draw and paint, they placed images of these animals on rocks and cave walls.

We cannot know for sure what these images of animals on cave walls meant to the people who made them and saw them. Some are in deep dark parts of the caves where no one lived and where, it has often been assumed, people were engaging in rituals, not unlike those humans engaged in churches and cathedrals much later in history. While we cannot know for sure what the European cave paintings meant, we can gain some insight here from a culture that painted such images a bit earlier, but a culture that still exists, the Aboriginals in Australia.

Caves in Australia

Homo sapiens reached Australia some 60,000 (or more) years ago and eventually started drawing and painting on rocks and walls. And they still do today (Chaloupka 1993; Lawlor 1991; Lorblanchet & Bahn 2017). For Australian Aboriginals, images on rocks and cave walls are not just art, they are an integral part of mythologies and cosmogonies. They tell Aboriginals who they are, how to act, and give meaning to every feature and animal in the landscapes in which they live. For them, the Earth—often called "Country" by Aboriginals—was created and exists today as part of what is sometimes called "Dreamtime," but is better called "Dreaming." When Aboriginal people use the English word "Country," it does not mean just land or a nation. It comprises an integration of culture, language, nature, and land as these are intertwined in a group's life now and in the past.

The images of animals Aboriginals made on rocks and cave walls are more than pictures of animals as we moderns conceive them. They are creator-beings who emerged from the Earth (Country) in the Dreaming. The creator beings have not left, they are still there as features of the environment like hills, rivers, and ravines, and in the animals, and, too, in the paintings on rocks and cave walls. Aboriginals do not consider "Dreamtime" as a time, but as an ever-present state:

> Hence, if we try to use an English word, we should avoid the term 'Dreamtime' and use the word 'Dreaming' instead. It expresses better the timeless concept of moving from 'dream' to reality which in itself is an act of creation and the basis of many Aboriginal creation myths (Lawlor 1991, p. 37).

These creator beings provided the laws that govern the universe and that govern the relations among humans and between humans and all other life. In some cases, these creator beings themselves drew on the walls of rock shelters and often incorporated themselves into the images produced. In other cases, they allowed themselves to be set in an image on stone and were present there. Past, present, and future are inextricably linked and are essentially one. As their images on rocks and walls fade, people repaint them within the context of Dreaming.

For Aboriginals, rock and cave art are aesthetic expressions and explanations of how things came to be, how social order, including land ownership and custodial responsibilities, should work, and how people and all living beings are connected to each other and should relate to each other. They are integrated parts of rituals, daily practices, mythic beliefs, and the fabric of culture, language, and nature (Country).

Back to the European Caves

Many scholars have speculated that the paintings in the European caves were part of rituals where a priest like figure, an early shaman, intervened with the spirits of animals, ancestors, or gods to seek help for their community (Sidky 2017). There are shamans across the world still today in many different cultures. Here, too, it is likely that we are seeing aesthetic images that are integrated into a seamless web of culture, language, environment, and social membership.

The shaman became a force that could mediate between humans and spirts. Originally, it appears, the shaman traveled to the world where the spirits of animals lived to beg them to keep their bodies in the mundane world available for hunting and the survival of humans. Humans have long been able to see animals, and not just themselves, as having two selves, a spiritual one and a corporeal one. Shamans still exist all over the world and play the same role (Dubois 2009; Taussig 1987). Their spirit can leave their body and travel to other worlds to placate spirits, gods, and demons in the service of their human community.

Shamans, as we know them today and in history, are healers. They heal physical, mental, and spiritual disorders for individuals or for the community as a whole. This healing is often effective, thanks to the fact that the human body responds to emotions by producing chemicals that can have good or bad effects on our health. Shamanic healing only works, though, when the shaman's rituals are performed for and before community members. It is the belief that flows through the group, coupled with the shaman's performance, that gives rise to healing.

Outer and Inner Images

What did our relatives in Australia and in the European caves and elsewhere feel when they painted on the rocks and engaged in rituals? After all, they had discovered an immense new power, the power to create, outside their heads, images of what they could imagine in their heads. It seems, given the cave paintings, they felt the presence of spirits. They felt, in one sense of the word, spirituality. They felt that another world—or other worlds—had opened up to them, the domains of beings that were more powerful, whether they were good or evil, than humans. This domain came also to include a part of themselves, a part which transcended their "mere" humanity, transcended their body which could suffer and die. This part—the human spirit or soul—cannot die and it is the part of the shaman that travels across space and time.

Humans sense the world and form associations in their brain. The brain, thanks to the human capacity for simulation, can replay these sensations in the private video game in our mind. We say "video game in our mind," rather than the more traditional "theater in our mind," because humans, in their mental simulations, can role play as themselves or others, make choices, and "start over" when they are unhappy with the results.

Drawing and painting images on surfaces and then incorporating them into rituals is the invention of an exterior simulation that can mimic our inner simulations. Just as tool making fueled an endless development of technology, this capacity to externalize one's imagination (simulation capacities)—first in paintings incorporated into rituals—has fueled an endless development of media.

The first drawers and painters of realistic pictures undoubtedly also felt a form of authorship, but authorship as what we might call an "imaginator" for the community (a role different from, but akin to the shaman). The products of these imaginators—the cave paintings, for example—both powered and were powered by myth, the creation of the group's story. However, this was myth not just as words—though myths are also stories in words—but as images—here, animals—that were thought to be more than mere representations (depictions), but images of things (like the dying bison) with import, with a message for us, with, perhaps, powers beyond what we see, but which we can feel. These are sensuous symbols, not the drier stuff of words.

Imaginators: Media Designers as Designers of Experiences

Designers for learning need to design for humans as they are. We are still what *Homo sapiens* was 50,000 years ago, though now in a modern high-tech world where humans are destroying life on earth. *Homo sapiens* 60,000 years ago were modern cognitively and biologically (Higham 2021), but still lived in a world where they were not a dominant part of the web of nature (or Country for the Australians). Humans today still seek the ideal, extended bodies, extended social bodies, and spirits or spirituality. That search, as it became ever more modern, took on both life-enhancing forms and toxic forms. It is the job of good experience designers to mitigate the toxic forms and support or create life-enhancing forms, forms for flourishing for humans, but not at the cost of other life on earth.

In this chapter we have seen that humans, starting with the things they could sense in the world, like a pebble on the beach, created in their minds four different worlds or realms that have profoundly affected human history and powered immense developments across that history: the realm of the ideal (aesthetics); the realm of the extended body (technology); the realm of imagined communities, the extended social body (nationalism); and the realm of spirts (spirituality and religion). Humans live in and across the real world (their human *umwelt*) and these four worlds, worlds that are the products of the human capacity to simulate (imagine). And they release the products of simulation (art, tools, imagined communities, and spirts) into the world they live in.

CHAPTER 11

AOT: FOUR FEELINGS

We have discussed four feelings that go back to the dawn of our species and still drive us today. These feelings fulfill survival and flourishing needs in humans. The four feelings are a) transcendence through contact with the ideal; b) the feeling of bodily extension; c) the feeling of being a part of an extended social group (imagined community); and d) the presence of spirits and spirituality. These are all feelings of gaining more power than the mundane world usually allows us to feel in the press for survival. These four feelings and the search for them are also themes that have run through human history, literature, and other media.

A good deal of dramatic media uses these four feelings using to develop their story. When this is done well, these themes get viewers (or players in video games) to think about and reflect on important issues in history and society, issues that should be an integral part of an intellectually and socially relevant education. AOT is no exception here. We will take a brief look now at how these feelings/themes work in AOT.

The below four themes/feelings are crucial to AOT. We can represent them diagrammatically as:

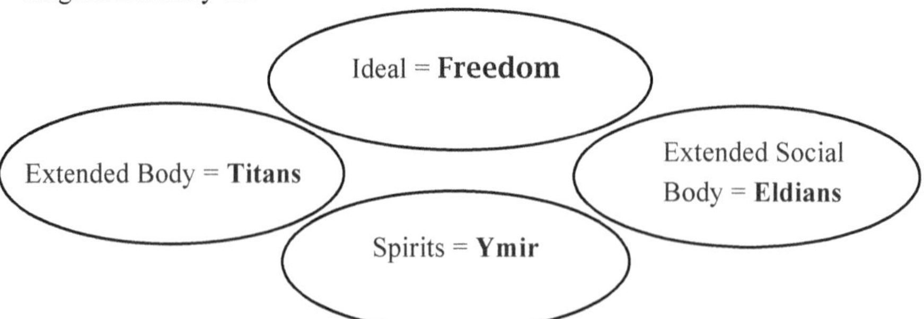

Let's consider each of these in turn. They are all related closely to each other and work together to create a good deal of the story and drama in AOT. They also create a good deal of reflection on—and discussion on social media sites about—the intellectual, social, and moral issues they raise.

Spirits

We will start with spirits. Long ago, a young girl named Ymir was a slave of a leader—a man named Fritz—of a small tribe, a group of people called Eldians. One day, after Ymir had committed a minor transgression, king Fritz sought to punish her. He had her chased by his soldiers. As she was being pursued, she ran to hide in a hole in a giant tree and fell into a hidden underground pond beneath the tree. In the pond, as she is drowning, a giant creature of branching light touched her and turned her from a mere human into a Titan and the origin of all other Titans. Titans are beings who can switch from human form into gigantic creatures with super strength and powers—extended bodies indeed.

Despite how Fritz had treated her, Ymir remained loyal to him. She used her Titan powers, together with his army, to help him conquer neighboring groups and made Eldia into an empire. When Ymir died, her powers were split into what eventually became Nine Titans, all her progeny, each with distinctive powers. These Titans continued to fight for Eldia and ensure its continued dominance. Ymir—now an embodied spirit—was transported to the "Coordinate" (a space outside time and space) where she gives aid to the royal family when they need it.

This may all seem strange, indeed, to modern people. But it is not strange either to watchers of anime or to the diverse mythologies that have existed across history and the world. It should not seem strange to anyone who has read the Old Testament where God helps his chosen people to conquer other tribes and become a powerful force in the world, supported by powerful warrior leaders (called Judges in the Old Testament). Indeed, it has been common in history that a group of people believe their god—to them, the real god—supports them and wants them to conquer others. And, too, the world of the Old Testament is filled with creatures as impressive as the Titans, creatures like the Behemoth, Leviathan, Cherubim, and Nephilim.

The Extended Body

Like all empires in history, Eldia eventually met its match. A country called Marley—a country which previously Eldia had conquered—manages to co-opt and control several of Eldia's Titans. They use them to conquer Eldia, as Eldia had done to them in the past. When Eldia is defeated, its current king, a man also named Fritz, flees with some of his people to a remote island named

Paradis Island. He renounces the use of Titans for warfare since it has brought too much suffering to the world and made Eldians a hated group. He uses the powers of Ymir to wipe his people's memories clean so they will not remember their past. He then builds massive walls around Paradis Island to keep his people isolated from, and ignorant of, the rest of the world.

Marley has captured many Eldians who did not make it to Paradis. They live as an oppressed and hated minority in ghetto like conditions in Marley. Marley wants to attack Paradis, take its natural resources, and kill the Eldians within its walls. Before they do so, in order to ensure the Eldians do not leave Paradis, Marley places a new form of unintelligent Titan in large numbers outside the walls of Paradis to kill any Paradisian Eldians that venture outside the walls.

The intelligent Titans (the nine) are a perfect example of the dream of an extended body come true. They are creatures massive in size and in power. Each intelligent Titan—the ones from Ymir—can switch between being a human and being a Titan. In Titan form, each has its own superpower. Further, their human bodies can heal from even grievous injuries. There is a price, however, to be paid for being a Titan. A Titan only lives for 13 years and then their Titan powers must be passed on to someone else. Furthermore, they spend their lives fighting wars and killing others, but have the intelligence to have doubts about this and even feel guilt.

The protagonist of AOT is an Eldian boy named Eren Jaeger who lives on Paradis Island. Unlike most of his fellow citizens, he hates living behind the walls of Paradis. He desires freedom and thinks it exists somewhere outside the walls. He does not, at the beginning, know there are other humans on earth, but he knows there are (unintelligent) Titans outside the walls that could and would kill him. His road to freedom seems to be blocked until he discovers that he himself has the power to turn into a Titan, eventually even to become the Founding Titan, the most powerful Titan of all.

With such great power, Eren now faces a great dilemma, a dilemma which plays out across the whole course of AOT. His dilemma is whether and how to use his powers, powers that have few limits. Should he help bring peace to the world, even though so many other nations despise Eldians for their violent imperial past? Or, should he engage in genocide to wipe out all others, save for the Eldians on Paradis so they can live in peace? Eren represents a common human fantasy: What would you do if you had ultimate power? His dilemma and how it works out in AOT dramatizes deep moral issues, ones that have played out in different ways across human history.

The Extended Social Body

The issue of the extended social body—the larger imagined community of Eldians—is at the heart of AOT as well. When Eldia was a small tribal kingdom, people belonged to a well-defined, not very large tribe, the largest sort of grouping in early human history before there were nations. Thanks to the Titans, however, this tribe becomes a nation and an empire. What it means now to be an Eldian becomes a quite different matter.

After Eldia is conquered, being an Eldian means something different again. What is the relationship of the Eldians in Marley to the Eldians on Paradis Island? The ones in Marley are taught that the Eldians on Paradis are devils who brought ruin and destruction to the earth. They need to support Marley to atone for the sins of their people. Yet some Marleyan Eldians see all Eldians as "the children of Ymir." When Eren sets out to save the people of Paradis Island, he faces the dilemma of what to make of the Marley Eldians who live in—and in many cases support—Marley.

When AOT starts, the people of Paradis Island—Eldians in exile—do not know there are other humans on earth. They just know they are there and that Titans are outside their walls. When they use the word "humanity" they mean themselves. Thanks to the fact that the king that brought them to Paradis wiped their memories clean, they do not know their past and so now are members of a quite different extended group.

Paradis is a large island and the Paradisan Eldians live within three massive circular concentric walls. The poor live in the outer rung separated by one wall from the Titans on the outside. The rich live in the center separated by three walls from the Titans. Those in between live in the middle. As in all human societies, since humans ceased to live in small hunter-gatherer bands, the citizens of Paradis see themselves as a member of one large group most of whose members they do not know and will probably never see. They use the normal signs and symbols of government and civil society to mark out their national identity. At the same time, this common identity is divided by the signs and symbols of class divisions.

The less well-off Eldians believe their membership in the extended social body (the imagined community) of Paradis Eldians is essential to their safety. If and when they are attacked by Titans, the poorer people close to the outer wall expect help from their government and from their better off fellow citizens. After all, they are all Eldians. When the walls are finally attacked by

Marleyan Titans, these people find out they are sorely mistaken. Those richer people living behind the inner walls view those who flee the attack as poor and unworthy "migrants" who will compete for jobs and food. The poorer citizens find themselves either recruited to go out and die fighting the Titans to save their "betters" or left to live as second-class citizens (not unlike the Eldians in Marley) in their own country.

At a larger level, the whole structure of the Eldian social body is a fake. The current king is not the real king, he is not the real successor of the King Fritz who brought his people to the island. The real king is in hiding. The man on the throne is a powerless dupe of the rich behind the third wall who use him and the government to increase their own wealth, power, and safety. When the larger society eventually finds out the government is a fake, they are at a loss of what to do. Perhaps any government is better than none, especially in the face of Titan attacks. If they overthrow the current government, how do they know they will not face chaos and civil war? This question—whether it is better to follow a bad government than to take the risk of the chaos of revolution or no government—has fueled a good deal of political discussion in the West since the ancient Greeks and St. Augustine (Herbert 1963; Raeder 2003).

The Ideal

The protagonist of AOT—Eren—is a young boy when we first meet him. He lives near the outer wall that eventually is brought down by a massive Titan. Eren is impetuous, passionate, and fiercely loyal to his friends. On the day he sees a massive Titan rise up to breach the wall, he stares at a flock of birds flying across the top of the wall, above the Titan's hand, and out into the wild. At that moment, Eren is deeply aware that his people are trapped like a bird in a cage or cattle in a pen behind their walls. They are in a prison of their own making. He realizes that the only way to gain freedom is not to retreat behind the other walls, as all the townspeople are running to do, but to move forward, out past the walls, to fight the Titans and live beyond the walls. He vows that, when he is old enough, he will join the Scouts, the only regiment of the army that ventures outside the walls, often suicidally, to face the Titans.

Eren's ideal—an ideal that drives him and, too, his friends—is to "go free." And, indeed, this has been an ideal for a great many humans across history who felt trapped in their circumstances, who were treated as second-class citizens, or who were oppressed by government. This ideal is associated, for Eren, with birds as symbols of freedom. The insignia of the Survey Corps—the troops that go outside the walls—is a stylized image of bird wings. Birds in AOT are a distinctive symbol of an ideal realm that transcends the mess and danger of the mundane world. It becomes Eren's mission to find this ideal world and, as so often happens in our world, his search for an ideal realm takes many turns and leads to many problems. Is there a realm of true freedom? Can humans live harmoniously in freedom without constraints or will it become a realm of the strong against the weak, what Hobbes called "the state of nature" (Zagorin 2009).

When the Titan attacks the walls, Eren becomes obsessed with escape and freedom, but he has already been well prepared for this by an earlier encounter with his friend Armin. Armin has found a secret—and illegal—book his grandfather has hidden. It is a book about the outside world, a world that the Eldians in Paradis know nothing about. Their knowledge of their past and the wider world has been wiped clean. Armin rushes to show the book to Eren and tells him:

> *My grandpa was hiding this...*
> *A book about the outside world!*
> *It says the majority of the world is covered*
> *by a huge body of water called the "sea."*
> *And it's all saltwater!*
> *...*
> *And there's more...*
> *Flaming water! Frozen earth!*
> *Plains of sand, white as snow!*
> *I'm sure the outside world*
> *is many times bigger than the world inside the walls!*
> *...*
> *Wouldn't it be great if, one day, we could go explore the outside world, too?*
> (E5 First Battle)

Much later, when Eren has discovered his Titan powers and he is fighting against Marleyan Titans to save Paradis, he remembers this moment with Armin. We are told his thoughts as he tries, in his Titan form, to move a massive rock to seal the hole in the wall made by the Titan he long ago saw attack the wall:

> *From the time we are born,*
> *we are free...*
> *It does not matter how strong*
> *those who deny us that freedom are...*

Flaming water... Frozen earth... I don't care what it is!
The one who sees them
will be the freest person in the world!
Fight...
I'd willingly give my life for that!
It doesn't matter how terrifying the world is.
It doesn't matter how cruel the world is!
Fight...
Fight!
Fight!
Fight!
(E13 Primal Desires)

Eren sees fighting against the Marleyan Titans as the price to be paid for freedom. Freedom is so precious to him that it is worth any cost to attain, including suffering and death. When he says he is willing to give his life for such freedom, he means he is willing to die so his friends can attain it. For Eren, such freedom is the birthright of any and all humans. When asked why he seeks freedom, he replies: "Because I was born into this world". However, at this point, Eren believes that the only humans on earth are the Eldians on Paradis Island. When he finds out there are other humans, his views will change. He will face the problem so many in human history have faced: Who are the real humans, the ones worthy of respect?

Eren's original view of freedom is what has been called "negative liberty" which means freedom from constraints (Hiruta 2021). Eren wants to be free of the walled cage he lives in and its government and institutions that he believes dupe the people into a false sense of trust and safety. He believes the world beyond the walls is open and free, a state of nature in which he and his friends can live free of institutional constraints. However, by the time in AOT when Eren and his friends actually see the ocean, they have become aware that there are other humans out there across the sea, humans who despise the Eldians on Paradis Island and want to kill them. These other humans believe Eldians are evil because of their history of using Titans in war to colonize others. Eren says:

On the other side of the sea... is freedom.
That's what I always believed.
But I was wrong.
On the other side of the sea...
are enemies.
...
Hey...

> *If we kill all our enemies... over there... (pointing)*
> *...will we finally... be free?*
> (E59 The Other Side of the Wall)

Eren no longer sees the outside as a world of limitless possibilities. It is filled with enemies and he takes a view of it now that is much like Hobbes' "state of nature." The "state of nature" Hobbes argued was a war of every man against every man because in the state of nature there is no government. In the state of nature there are no rules, only the freedom to fight (Lloyd & S Sreedhar 2022, Sections 3-6). Eren realizes this as he says to his brother:

> *If someone is willing to take my freedom... I won't hesitate to take theirs.*
> (E79 Memories of the Future)

Here Eren realizes that in the state of nature everyone has the freedom to take what they want and so only the strongest survive. In AOT, Eren moves from an ideal of freedom that means being free of society and its constraints to a proponent of genocide: the way to freedom for him and his people, especially is, he believes, to destroy all the other humans on earth, thereby creating the open and free world he dreamed of for his people.

A colorful character in AOT, Kenny Ackerman, who among other things is an infamous serial killer known "Kenny the Ripper," says as he is dying: "Every last person I've seen was the same way. Whether it was booze, women or even God. Family, the king, dreams, children, power... They couldn't keep going unless they were drunk on something. They were all slaves to something." By the end of AOT, as Eren seeks to use the full power of the Founding Titan to kill everyone on earth except the Eldians of Paradis, he has become drunk on his ideal and is willing to create hell on earth to bring it into existence. Such has been the case for many utopians in human history.

In AOT, contact with a spirit gave (originally, Eldian) humans a powerful extended body (Titans) that ultimately leads to war and hatred as extended social bodies fight for power, held together more by symbols than by the real merit of their governments or beliefs. In AOT, an idealistic young man (Eren) searches for an ideal world of freedom from governments, constraints, and war and finds the path to that world paved with genocide. It is a powerful tale of desires that have driven humans through history since they went into dark caves and sought to transcend themselves through the intervention of spirits whose powers, then and now, they could rarely tame.

CHAPTER 12

ACTING

Humans do not solve problems the way computers do. Computers operate by manipulating strings of symbols. Humans can solve problems this way, but they are much better at solving problems by imagining themselves doing and manipulating things in their minds via simulation. This is so because, like all animals, humans evolved to act in the service of their survival and, if possible, flourishing. Thinking, feeling, and emoting all evolved in humans to subserve action in the sense that they tell us when we need to act to maintain, repair, or enhance our state of homeostasis (balance with the world). And they work best when they act together in the service of action. It has been shown that humans think better when they are moving, walking, gesturing, or outdoors (Paul 2021). Computers do not have bodies. Humans not only have them, they use them along with the brains to think and solve problems.

Schooling without Caring

The psychologist Arthur Glenberg (2011) has shown, in his "Moved by Reading" interventions with children, that when children are encouraged to simulate (with concrete, physical action in their heads or with manipulables) the texts they are reading, they achieve large gains in learning. Glenberg found that when children act out the words on the page their reading comprehension can double. Words are best understood not in terms of definitions but in terms of how they relate to actions and scenarios in the world.

School often asks students to think and solve problems outside of the context of action, with no movement or bodily engagement, without triggering simulation, outside of physical environments that are motivating, and by focusing on manipulating strings of symbols or words. This is a perfect recipe for making people look and act less smart than they are. Of course, some students do well in this scenario although the evidence is that what they learn is not retained all that long past their schooling, if even that long.

Humans decide and reason best when they have an action to take whose outcome affectively matters to them, that they care about it (Barsalou 2008; Glenberg 1997, Glenberg & Gallese 2012; Immordino-Yang & Damasio 2007). "Matters" here means that something is "at stake" for the human in how the action turns out. Research has shown that humans think more logically and rationally if they are given a problem that triggers their caring (Cosmides 1989; Wason 1966, 1968). For example, if you give humans a problem where they must follow a rule and use abstract symbols (e.g., numbers) to apply the rule, they often do poorly. If you give them the same problem, but in terms of following a rule about how to catch cheaters who are violating the rule, they do much better, even though the problem is logically the same. Humans are built by evolution to care about cheating and fairness, since as social animals cheating and a lack of fairness can endanger their social wellbeing.

This raises a deep problem with a good deal of formal schooling. Humans act to solve problems well only when they care about the outcome. Some things—like unfairness—create deep caring in humans. Other things—like passing a test of memory retention—are much less motivating to many humans (though, of course, some care a great deal). School often offers problems in an abstract form, not in terms of concrete realities that create caring. And, in many cases, students do not know why they are supposed to care, at any deep level, about the work they are given in school. No one tells them and sometimes there is no good reason to care.

Why should anyone care about solving algebra problems, one after the other, on a sheet of paper? There are perfectly good and deep reasons to engage with algebra, but solving problems outside of a context that gives the activity motivating (life-enhancing) meaning is not going to allow students to discover those reasons. Nor is telling them that learning algebra is good for getting a job or for getting into a good college when they do not know what those jobs are, cannot afford a good college, or have no idea what college really amounts to and what makes one better than another.

When we act to achieve a goal, we cannot pay conscious attention to everything around us. Conscious attention is limited and takes effort. We pay conscious attention to—focus on—only what is most relevant to us (most relevant in terms of our goals) at the time. What guides our conscious judgments about relevance is a feeling, the feeling of caring, the feeling that something matters to us, that something is at stake for us in the outcome of an action. Caring tells us what to pay attention to as relevant in a given situation.

Caring is the motivator of attention. Any aspect of an experience that triggers caring—for whatever reason—designates that aspect as relevant to what we want to accomplish in taking an action. Caring is our conscious awareness of a need, a need that may stem from the unconscious workings of our mind and inner states of our body or from a conscious plan, a need to solve a problem relevant to maintaining, repairing, or improving our physical and social balance with the world.

One famous experiment (Chabris & Simons 2018) showed clearly how humans pay conscious attention only to what they care about. Subjects in this experiment were asked to watch a short video in which six people (three in white shirts and three in black shirts) pass basketballs to each other. They were asked to keep a count of the number of passes made by the people in white shirts. So, what they were asked to care about was the number of passes. During the video, a person in a gorilla suit strolls into the video, faces the camera and thumps their chest, and then leaves, spending nine seconds on screen. Half of the subjects missed the gorilla and were shocked when it is pointed out to them on a replay of the video. Basketball passes were relevant, the gorilla was not.

The Basic Circuit of Human Action

Human actions have a basic structure. We can call this structure "the basic circuit of human action." When the conditions of the basic circuit of human action are not met, humans think, decide, and act much less effectively than they otherwise can. So, one good way to make humans look stupid is to ask them to act when the basic circuit of human action is "short-circuited" in some way. The basic circuit of human action is seen below:

Table 1. The basic circuit of human action

Step 1	An inner sensation gives rise to a feeling (e.g., hunger)
Step 2	The feeling creates a need to act (here act to lessen the feeling of hunger).
Step 3	The need creates caring (here, caring about food). Caring guides our actions by indicating to us what we should pay attention to as relevant to our goal (here how to lessen the feeling of hunger). We pay attention to what we care about.
Step 4	The feeling, need, and caring activate both background knowledge and reasoning (planning) that together lead to a decision about how to act.
Step 5	Act.
Step 6	The original feeling (e.g., of hunger) assesses the outcome of the action we take to accomplish our goal (what makes good feelings remain or heighten or what lessens or removes bad ones is "good").
Step 7	We redo the action—start the whole circuit again—if the assessment of its outcome is poor.

Above we used hunger as an example of a feeling that motivates action. Of course, in a great many cases, the feelings that motivate action are more complex. When a student is asked to solve a series of algebra problems on a test and she works hard at it, she may have been motivated by a fear of some sort (not passing the test, not getting into a good college, disappointing her parents or friends, losing face in her peer group, and so forth). Or, she may have been motivated by a feeling for the beauty of algebra, a feeling of pleasure in doing algebra, or even a feeling of excitement at facing a challenge. Or, she may feel boredom, anger, or confusion and be motivated to avoid the algebra (another action).

We cannot know what feeling motivated a person—and they may well not be able to put it into words themselves—but if the person has no feeling, then the person does not know what to care about, how to pay attention, and what actions to take or how to assess them. In this case, the person may refuse to act or act oppositionally.

We can write the basic circuit for human action in short form as:

Feeling → need to act → caring → background knowledge + reasoning → decision → action → assessment → revision

Humans in most cases must learn the elements of the circuit of action. Certain sorts of inner sensations are felt as hunger by all humans. In other cases, humans will feel certain inner states differently because of past experience, social learning, or the context they are in. In certain contexts, or given different backgrounds, some people feel hunger as sinful or a sign of weakness, not as a basic desire for food. Some people, thrill seekers, have learned to feel inner sensations that others feel strongly as fear as intense excitement. Some people have learned to feel what others feel as pain as "gain" or, in some religions, "atonement" and this leads not to avoidance but to seeking more. Basic feelings, at a deep level, are similar for all humans, but once they get caught up with learning, the conscious mind, social groups and culture, they become much more nuanced, diverse, and lead to different actions and assessments.

People learn what to care about and how to care about it. Some people care passionately about "good food," either in the sense of highly nutritious food or gourmet food, others do not care about the one or the other or either. Some people care deeply about "losing face," looking bad to others, while other people care more about getting in other people's faces than losing face. Some people care deeply about animals and some do not. We humans have a strong tendency to see those who care little about what we care about as "not one of us," not a person like us. What people have learned to care about is formative for who they are.

Caring guides what we pay attention to, but people need to learn how to manage their attention, since it is a limited resource (Kahneman 2011). The need to learn when and where to focus and refocus their attention and how to make good judgements about degrees of relevance in an experience. For example, some people will pay attention to more things, refocus their attention more often, and more often test whether seemingly less relevant things are more relevant than they thought.

People's experiences in the world and within social groups determine their background knowledge—the web of associations on which they can draw to think, remember, plan, and imagine. And people's abilities to engage in conscious reasoning, analysis, and planning vary based not only on their backgrounds but on what forms of language, symbol systems, and imagery they have available to them. You cannot reason well about algebra if you do not know algebraic symbols in a fluid way. There are lots of spatial tasks you cannot do if you have not learned to manipulate 3D images well in your mind. You cannot construct an argument in biology if you have no control over the academic language of biology. You cannot do graffiti if you have not learned the symbols of a given group.

Action is essential for survival and flourishing and we humans learn how to act—the components of the basic circuit of human action—largely from our families and other social groups. We all face a deep problem—a common one in the modern world—where the actions we need to take for survival or flourishing are ones that none of our social groups have prepared us for or have prepared us for poorly. That is why we all need, throughout life, new teachers, new designers of experiences, and new groups that will teach us new ways to act and, in the process, make us new people or new and improved versions of ourself.

Social Animals

Now we need to return to the very basic point that humans act because inner sensations (states of their body)—and the feelings and emotions to which they give rise—motivate them to act. Like some other animal species, including sperm whales, parrots, and baboons, humans are social animals (Graziano 2013; Safina 2020; Tomasello 2014, 2019). They have what we might call social feelings. Such feelings are as physical as the feeling of hunger or the sorts of bodily agitations we sometimes interpret as anger, but they are caused by our need, as social animals, for belonging (Young 2008; Lieberman 2013). For a social animal nothing is worse than total social isolation.

We have seen that living creatures engage in allostasis (resource management) to maintain homeostasis (balance) in the face of environmental stressors (challenges). Social animals experience social interactions with members of their own species—in terms of acceptance, belonging, support—as potential stressors (Umberson & Montez 2010). Being a member of a group is a crucial survival and flourishing strategy for social animals, but it can be stressful as well.

In some social species, animals are most social not at the level of the species as a whole, but at the level of social groups (clans, tribes, bands, troops, ethnic groups, cultures, societies), groups whose members affiliate with each other (Safina 2015). No animal creates and maintains more social groups than do humans. Indeed, they create new ones all the time.

Social groups shape a member's basic circuit of human action, the basis of allostasis. In a great many cases, social groups teach their members how to carry out the basic circuit of human action. Aside from some innate associations, humans learn all the aspects of the basic circuit of human action from experience. This experience can just be out in the wild in the world, but it is often mediated or designed by social groups, initially families and then by larger groups like local communities, churches, institutions, and social groups of all different kinds. The learning that goes on in these designed learning experiences is often heavily emotionally charged by the human need to belong, which causes deep learning and acceptance. And, it is usually not much reflected on at a meta-level in terms of what it means for the self as an individual and other groups in society, which means it is often internalized in entirely uncritical ways.

Humans can, of course, belong to more than one social group; their brains are shaped by different social groups and they can face the world (or media) using different social group identities or several of them at once. A person can be undecided or even conflicted by what social group identity should be used at which time and place and this can create social stressors for humans. What humans cannot do is experience the world outside any and all social identities. Even the most basic biological processes—such as hunger and mating—are experienced and expressed in terms of social group identities. If someone does not express these things in socially recognizable ways (at least to some group), they are seen by other humans as wild, mad, or dangerous (unpredictable, untrustworthy).

Individual beings can be victims of their need to survive, but can, in the right circumstances, gain the freedom to seek flourishing and not just survival. So, too, social groups can be victims of their need to survive, and their members can be victims of their need to belong, but can, in the right circumstances, gain the freedom to seek flourishing for many, hopefully for all, and not just survival of the group itself alone. These circumstances crucially involve what we will call in the next section, "*A*-educators."

Allostatic Education

The perspective we have developed above suggests a different view of education. We associate education with schools and knowledge. The above perspective associates education with experiences in and out of school that enhance allostasis, that is, the work of surviving and hopefully flourishing. In this perspective, knowledge plays a role, of course, but in terms of our ability to feel and think (simulate, imagine) in the service of actions and choices that support our flourishing as individuals and as social animals.

This view of education is meant to be about individual and social group flourishing, but not to the detriment of other social groups and other forms of life. Let's call this more expansive and experiential sense of education, "allostatic education," "*A*-education" for short, education for human flourishing as social groups who are embedded in one species and one world.

Humans learn from experience. Beyond biological imperatives, as social animals, humans require teaching to know what to care about, how to care about it and why to care about it, what to do, how to feel, how to assess the results of their actions, and how best to recruit thinking in the service of action.

So, teaching in *A*-education is the job of people who design experiences with these goals in mind. Experience designers need to know how to recruit or create sensations and feelings that give rise to the sort of caring, actions, thinking, and emotions that support human flourishing.

Humans already have teachers/mentors in the social groups they have been socialized within. Social groups give humans a sense of belonging they long for, but often at a price to themselves and society. At any one time, any human's mind and body is limited by the experiences they have had and the social groups that have mentored those experiences. Such limitations can sometimes stultify an individual's growth as a human and be detrimental to other people who fall into a "them" versus "us" divide. And they can sometimes be detrimental to a pluralistic society in a highly changing world, since societies are always in danger of being torn apart by their competing clans.

So, teachers (experience designers) for *A*-education should design with one or more of the following three goals:

1. Design experiences to repair the weaknesses in the social groups to which learners already belong, making learners agents of social change in their own groups. By "weaknesses" here we mean aspects of a group that diminish or limit human flourishing.

2. Design experiences to give learners new social group memberships that enhance human flourishing.

3. Design experiences to enhance learners' meta-level understanding of social groups in society, including groups to which they do not belong, but which influence them and society nonetheless.

By "human flourishing" here we mean flourishing for individuals and groups but not at the expense of others and life on earth. Of course, there are tradeoffs here. Pain and death are part of life on earth. But the basic moral principle here is: "If something will hurt someone else or some other living thing, that is a reason not to do it and I need good and moral reasons to do otherwise." People who do not accept this principle are dangerous.

The moral of this chapter is that humans become seemingly stupid when they are asked to think outside of actions and caring in the service of their own flourishing as individuals and members of different social groups where they find belonging. Asking someone in school to fill in blanks with answers is an action. But it can be an action where, for some students, nothing seems to be at stake for them or where only failure looms. Asking students to listen quietly to a lecture is an action. Doing algebra problems is an action. Everything we do in school is a form of action, including coming in the classroom door in the morning. The issue of importance, however, is what feelings, forms of caring, and attentional processes these actions create in different students and how they intersect with their social identities. When these things differ across students, as they almost always do, the action being requested is not the same for everyone.

A test, a question, a pedagogy in school is not the same for everyone. It is not equitable unless, like a good experience designer, the teacher has taught all the students in class how to feel a need to act to learn what is to be learned, how to care about it, how to pay attention to what is relevant, how to recruit background knowledge and reasoning, and how to assess the results of their action. In doing this the teacher supplements the student's current social identities and makes of his or her class a new social group devoted to new actions. Now all the students are on the same page.

CHAPTER 13

LANGUAGE

In this chapter we take up the topic of communication and language. From the start we face two problems here. First, communication is so natural to us humans that we take its features for granted and we are rarely aware of how communication actually works. Second, when we talk about language, people often confound grammar and communication and have little conscious insight into how grammar does and does not relate to communication.

The notion of "context" plays a large role in all discussions of communication, but, alas, the concept is not all that well understood (Duranti & Goodwin 1992). We all know that words can take on different meanings in different contexts. Context is usually taken to be the whole setting in which a communication takes place, including the physical setting and the experiences, knowledge, and practices interlocutors share. When thought of this way the notion of context seems rather static.

Context is not a static thing, however. Imagine I want to offer someone criticism and want to be sure my words are understood and reacted to in the way I want them to be, say, as sympathetic, but firm; helpful, but not sugar coated. To do this I will select—based partly on my relations to and knowledge of the person—a setting (context) that I hope will facilitate my goals, one, for example, which is not threatening and not public. If the setting is not quite right, I might re-arrange it, redesign it a bit.

If no setting seems right, I might make a new one, engage in a larger design project, as some people do for wedding proposals or funerals. In all cases, I will not just hope the person reacts to and within the context the way I want, I will use words, tone of voice, and gestures to get them to construe (think about, interpret) aspects of the context in the way I want them to. Context supports the meanings of my words and the meanings of my words help my listener to construe or interpret aspects of the context in the right way. Words and context go together and interact dynamically and reciprocally, so much so that they become one system, not two isolated bits.

So, contexts are chosen, redesigned, or more wholly designed, and their significance to my words are shaped by my words and behaviors and, in turn, shape the meanings of and responses to my words. When we talk about meaning in language (save for an enterprise called "formal semantics") we must always think of words + context (as chosen, designed, or redesigned) in dynamic reciprocal interaction until they become one system.

Of course, sometimes we are forced to communicate in contexts that we have not chosen and have little opportunity to re-arrange. Nonetheless, often we still could have chosen just not to communicate and, even if we are forced to communicate, we still can use our words and behaviors to shape how the context is construed or interpreted.

To better understand communication, we will turn now to our ancient ancestors for whom communication was not yet a matter so taken for granted. 60,000 years ago, *Homo sapiens* had not had the human form of language all that long yet and they were just learning to draw or paint realistic looking pictures (Higham 2021).

Communication: Pictures

All living creatures are built to form and store associations. Some (like slime molds, single cell creatures that can solve mazes, Zimmer 2021) do this with chemicals and some with neurons. For animals with brains, associations that have been discovered in past experiences are stored as connections among neurons in the brain and are the basis of memory and planning (Eagleman 2020). From past experience an animal may learn to associate a certain plant with feeling sick or a banded snake with danger. When they experience these things again in the future their associations with sickness or danger will be activated and lead them to avoid the plant or the snake. Associations are used to guide our behavior, but they can be wrong. Certain banded snakes are quite dangerous, others are mimics, harmless snakes mimicking the pattern of dangerous ones to avoid predators.

Creatures tend to be quick to form associations. Associations that do not always work are still useful if we occasionally need to avoid a dangerous snake, even though we miss the company of non-dangerous ones. However, associations can easily get out of hand, especially for us humans who are associators *par excellence* and can find patterns in anything and everything, including the stars and tea leaves (Sapolsky 2017). When we associate one person of a given type with a certain trait and generalize that association to everyone of that type, we can end up damaging ourselves and others.

Association is also the basis of communication. Communication involves one creature trying to trigger associations in another creature's brain. For humans, this means trying to activate certain associations in another human's brain in order to get the other human to think (simulate) something or act in a certain way. Thinking involves activating associations in the "theater of our mind" (simulation) (Seligman, Railton, Baumeister, & Sripada 2016). Acting involves activating associations in our brain to guide action in a certain way. Communication is, thus, a sort of "mind manipulation" of other people, trying to get them to activate associations in their heads in ways we want them to so that they will think and act in ways we want.

If you want to communicate and have no language, you face grave limitations. You can gesture to things. For example, you could gesture to a predator and hope others realize, based on their past experience, they should associate what you are pointing to with danger and run away. Some animals can also use sounds that have become associated with specific sorts of things, like a particular type of predator. For example, vervet monkeys have different sounds to signal the presence of leopards (ground predators), eagles (sky predators), and snakes (tree predators). These forms of communication are very specific (Safina 2020). They allow for a very limited range of messages.

Drawing realistic pictures would be an improvement. This is something only humans can do and did for the first time about 60,000 years ago (Lorblanchet & Bahn 2017). Pictures can picture things not present and even combine aspects of things that do not in reality go together, for example, a horse with a long horn coming out of its forehead. Pictures can also be put into sequences or composed as scenarios.

But there is a problem with pictures. Since realistic images are so replete with details, they can trigger a wide array of associations and, thus, it is hard to be sure that the picture triggers the right associations (the ones you want) in the person you are communicating with. The person may trigger the wrong associations because they have had, unlike you, no past experiences with which to form the ones you want. Or, perhaps, they have them, but the picture activates other associations than the ones you want, because, for whatever reason, in this context, other associations are more strongly triggered in the person by the picture than the ones you intended.

So, pictures only communicate what you intend if you have prepared the ground, so to speak. You must place the picture in a context—or create a context—that will help guide the person to the associations you want the picture to trigger. In fact, someone else can draw the picture and you can still use it to communicate as long as you place it in the right sort of context, if such a context exists, or create such a context if it does not. We will see later that the same thing is true of words.

Long ago—for example, starting about 10,000 years ago and continuing thereafter in India, the American Southwest, Tanzania, and many other places across the world—there are pictures painted on rocks, rock walls, or in caves that look to modern people like (our conception of) aliens (Gulliford 2018; Westerby 2021). We have no idea what associations these pictures were intended to activate in the people at the time. We have not had many of the experiences they had, nor do we know exactly what the context was in which people used the pictures. We are prone to see aliens we have experienced in science fiction movies in their pictures and some people go far as to say the ancients had seen such aliens. This is the trouble with pictures: something must accompany them to tell viewers how to interpret them, where "interpret" here means activating the associations the drawer or painter (the communicator) intended to be activated.

Now, in some cases, as we saw in the Chapter 10, at least in respect to pictures of animals, we do know something about how early humans created a context within which the pictures would activate the intended associations. When ancient *Homo sapiens* painted pictures of animals on cave walls, they wanted the pictures to help them to communicate beliefs about spirits that were part of the identity of the social group.

They could not trust the pictures alone to do this. So, they incorporated the pictures into rituals involving music, dance, acting, dressing up as different sorts of beings, and, of course, words. Each person in the group participated in an embodied way in the performance. The performance was an experience and that experience was meant to ensure that everyone formed similar sorts of associations that allowed the group to communicate, believe, and act together. In this case, the associations they wanted to form and reinforce were about the relationship between the mundane world where humans hunted and killed animals and a spiritual world where the animals' spirits lived and could be beseeched (Sidky 2017). Once the community had had these experiences, the pictures could stand more on their own. The performance was a designed context, a new experience for newcomers to the rituals and an old one for others.

This was among the first examples of designed experience for learning that humans created outside of socializing children early in life as part of a family, where adults have always designed safe experiences for their children where they can learn without harm being done to them. The family forms individuals into kin and teaching and learning are crucial to this process. However, experiences like those designed in the caves formed the social body, the group as a whole. This was mostly extended kin early in human history, but a much larger and wider group later, what we earlier called "imagined communities" in Chapter 10.

Communication: Words

Words, of course, are a form of communication that, in some respects, are more powerful than pictures. Words do not require either what we are talking about or pictures of it to be present. While they certainly have powers pictures do not, they also have problems pictures do not.

Words, as we know them, are part of human language, a form of communication some have argued is unique to *Homo sapiens*. Others believe other human species had language of our sort, Neanderthals, for example. There is serious debate about the matter (Berwick & Chomsky 2015; Chomsky 2016). In this case, language would be unique to some members of the genus *Homo*.

Human language is composed of sequences of sounds (e.g., /b-ai-s-o-n/ for "bison") that have nothing to do with what they mean (here a type of animal). They aren't pictures. Words can be sequenced by the "rules" of grammar. So, if you know the language, you will agree with everyone else who knows the language as to how the words are put together to form a larger whole.

Words are like pictures, though, in that they are meant to trigger associations in people's brains. They are just much more general, so they can trigger many more associations. And this can be a problem, since, as we already saw with pictures, we need to narrow in on the "right" associations. A picture of a bison has to show its size, but the word "bison" does not indicate size without additional words. So, when the word "bison" is said you can imagine any size you want or not think about size at all. Words allow us to stay silent about things pictures must show.

So, just as for pictures, something must come with words (as rituals came with the cave paintings) to ensure that, when we use them, people activate the right associations. As with pictures, if people have not had experiences that would allow them to form the associations we want, we have to give such experiences to them—or somehow ensure they get them—before the words can work their magic. If they do have the requisite experiences, we still must ensure that other associations do not get in the way.

How do we do this for words? As with caves, we pick a context or design one which will guide the person we are communicating with to form the "right" associations (the ones we intend). This is design work, even the choice of the right context, let alone having to design one. As with the case of pictures, we may have to give people who have not had the requisite past experiences new experiences before the words will work. This new experience could be just a description in words, after all things like stories are vicarious experiences for humans. However, words are not always very good for this—remember the old saying: "a picture is worth a thousand words." So, often, the new experience is going to be actions in the world or via media that involve images and other sensations akin to the real world.

We can see what our ancestors were doing in those caves as using ritual (a type of context) not only to situate—pin down more concretely—the associations the pictures were meant to activate, but also to situate the associations the words in the ritual were meant to activate. Indeed, in those rituals, images, words, sounds, movements, dress, and the physical surroundings all worked together to ground associations that people could share then and there together.

Communication: Sensuous Constructions

A picture can be too specific. A photo of a specific bird captures all the specific features of that one bird, but each individual bird is different. That's why, when people are "birding" or "bird watching," they often do not use birding guidebooks with photos, beautiful as such photos are (eBird 2009). Birding books often use paintings, rather than photos. The paintings have been designed to highlight features a species of birds share, not features individual birds have. They are not as realistic as photos.

On the other hand, a purely verbal description of a species is less helpful since it is hard to visualize it. Vision and all other sensation are much more nuanced and concrete than words. Eastern Bluebirds, Western Scrub-Jays, and Indigo Buntings are all blue, but blue in different ways. They have different shades and patterns of blue that words capture poorly.

What we are very often offer in communication is something in the middle, not as specific as an individual bird and not as general as either a name or a verbal description of a species. The painting in the bird guide that abstracts from individual idiosyncrasies of individual birds but retains the birds' sensuous qualities is a good example of such a middle ground. It retains sensual features but goes beyond individual cases. Let's call such things sensuous constructions (see Chapter 14 below). Sensuous constructions intermix sensation and sense making. The painting in the bird book mixes a picture that has a sensual relation to birds with something more abstract than a photo but still much less abstract that a verbal description. On the other hand, a photo of a bird shows one specific bird and a word like "bird" names a general category.

The majestic pictures of a bison in an ancient cave, incorporated into rituals, was a sensuous construction. It was meant to capture not an individual bison and not just the idea of "bison species," but the majesty, power, and spiritual meaning of bison as (at the time) dominant beings. It made, through its sensuous details, a certain sense of the bison. That is why we moderns view the painting as "great art," though it was also great communication. The bison on the cave wall is sensuously replete but still a sign of something, namely the majesty and power of bison. It is midway between a photo and a word. Line drawings could do something similar but would be closer to words, but still not as abstract (general, categorial) as words.

When teachers, artists, and media designers design experiences for human learning and flourishing, they are in the business of creating useful, powerful, and life-enhancing sensuous constructions. They are in the same media business our ancient ancestors in Africa, Australia, Europe, and all over the world were in when they drew and painted on rocks and cave walls. They create sensuous constructions and place them in the contexts that dynamically and reciprocally let them do the work the designers want them to do.

We will discuss sensuous constructions further in the next chapter. In formal contexts of learning like schools they are rarely recognized for and used with the powers they are capable of. Sensuous constructions create a degree of abstraction but always leave that abstraction tied to sensation.

CHAPTER 14

SENSUOUS CONSTRUCTIONS

As we mentioned in the last chapter, birding—or, as some say, "bird watching"—has a good deal to teach us about how people learn and engage with problem solving more generally. Most birders carry a small bird guide into the field with them so they can look up birds they have spotted. Though many expert birders know the birds in their area with no need for a bird guide, for the rest the guide book is an important tool. Within some related groups of birds—like flycatchers and sparrows—different species can be so similar that looking them up in a bird guide is crucial if you want to identify them.

Some bird guides contain beautiful full color photos of birds. Of course, a photo captures just one bird (and individual birds vary even in the same species) in one position (e.g., facing forward or sitting sideways). The photos are a delight to look at, but they are not always that good for identifying birds. They are too specific and they do not draw one's attention to the features a birder can most readily use to identify the species in the wild (where the birder may get but a fleeting view of the bird).

All bird guides have verbal descriptions of each bird species under the species name. Verbal descriptions are too general and they cannot really capture the nuances and variations that we sense in the world. Several species of birds have blue on them and many more have brown or gray. Capturing the different shades of these colors in words is difficult. Describing the shapes of beaks, wings, and tails and the more subtle patterns and markings on birds is hard as well.

Another type of bird book uses paintings of birds, rather than the photos. The painting is designed to show a typical member of the species rather than a given individual. It places the bird in a way that clearly displays its most distinguishing features and some books have arrows pointing to the features that most clearly demarcate this species from others. No individual bird looks exactly like the picture, but most members of the species look enough like it to be identifiable. This depiction of a bird is less specific and concrete than the photo but more specific and concrete than a verbal description. It retains sensual features (we sense them, not read them), but still manages to be general enough to be about what a certain species has in common.

In the last chapter, we called depictions like these bird paintings in the bird guide "sensuous constructions." They are composed of sensory information (not verbal information) but still function in a more general way than sensing things in the world. They are half-way between words (or "concepts") and sensations. Sensuous constructions are important in learning and problem solving. They are how birders learn to identify birds and solve the problem of identifying a bird new to them. Sensuous constructions play this sort of sort of role in many other situations. We will also see that designers for learning often design sensuous constructions to teach, guide understanding, and entrench learning.

The Mediators

The human brain has two hemispheres that work differently but together (McGilchrist 2009, 2019, 2021). The right hemisphere sees things as connected and integrated, wholistically. It sees the big picture. The left hemisphere sees things in terms of details, parts, units, and general categories. The left hemisphere gives humans the power of detailed abstract categorical knowledge. The right gives them the power of seeing the big picture, the lay of the land, the connected nature of things more as processes than individual things. The sensuous construction mediates between these two. It keeps the embeddedness of the right hemisphere and moves towards, but not all the way to, the general categories of the left.

The painted picture in the bird book keeps some of the sensuous properties of specific birds, but stresses properties a species shares in order to render them a category without effacing their sensuousness. A picture is too specific, a species name too general. A description in words does add some details, but not in the nuanced terms typical of sensation.

Words as Sensuous Constructions

The great author Borges (2000) said it best:

> Words are symbols for shared memories. If I use a word, then you should have some experience of what the word stands for. If not, the word means nothing to you. (p. 117)

Words as parts of grammar are categorial and general (Gee 2017; Levinson 1983, 1995). If I tell you that "Durian is a fruit that smells bad," you need never have seen a durian or smelled it to know something general about it: it is in the category of fruit like apples and pears and it smells bad in some way (you know not what way). We will call this type of word meaning "structural meaning" (other terms for the same thing: general meaning, literal meaning, lexical meaning, type meaning).

Borges is talking about a different type of word meaning. Obviously if you know the categorial meaning of "durian," you don't know "nothing," you know it is a fruit. But you cannot "cash out" its general categorial meaning in terms of sensation and other experiences you have had with the fruit.

If you have had lots of experiences with durian—eating it, smelling it, touching it (it has a thorn-covered rind), cooking with it, buying it at H-Mart, perhaps experiencing it in Thailand, or even seen the trees it grows on—then you have a bevy of memories of it composed of former sensual experiences of the fruit and the contexts in which it resides or is written or spoken about. In Borges' terms, now you know what the word stands for in an experiential way, not just a categorial way. Now the word means something personal and embodied to you. This experiential base is what you use to create what we called in the last chapter "situational meanings," the meanings for words that apply in, and vary across, different contexts of use (Barsalou 2008; Bergen 2012; Gee 2004, 2017).

The word is now a sensuous construction for you. It can readily call to your mind not just a category but a bevy of sensual experiences. The word, when you relate to it not just as a category but as a sensuous construction, is more general than any specific experience of a durian, but less general and abstract than a category (a label) that can be used for categorial reasoning, for example: "All fruits have seeds, so durian most have seeds." Categorial meanings and reasoning certainly have an important place in life, but words as sensuous constructions do, too, since they are the stuff of situated communication in social interactions where we interact in—in partially create—shared contexts.

Example 1: Boxer

Now we will look at two examples of learning design that uses sensuous constructions, that is images or symbols that take on general meanings that are closely tied to sensation and action and never lose that tie and become just categorical labels. In this section we will deal with Boxer and in the next with Dragon Box.

The well-known science educator, Andrea diSessa (2000), early in his career, developed a way to teach algebra that used what we are calling sensuous constructions (a term he did not use). He successfully taught the algebra behind Galileo's principles of motion (principles related to Newton's laws) to children in sixth grade and beyond using a specific computer programming language called Boxer that was midway between general and specific (see also Gee 2008; Zhang 2022).

The students type into a computer a set of discrete steps in the Boxer programing language. For example, the first command in a program meant to represent uniform motion might tell the computer to set the speed of a moving object at one meter per second. The second step might tell the computer to move the object. And a third step might tell the computer to repeat the second step over and over. Once the program starts running, the student will see a graphical object move one meter each second repeatedly, a form of uniform motion. The student will also see the relationships between the steps in the programming language (symbols) and actual events happening on the screen (ones that resemble real-world movement). They will eventually realize that the program is a model (just like the neural connections in the head) of aspects of the world.

Next, the students can elaborate the model in various ways. For example, they might add a fourth step that tells the computer to add a value a to the speed of the moving object after each movement the object has taken. Let us say, for convenience, that a adds one more meter per second at each step. Now, after the first movement on the screen (when the object has moved at the speed of one meter per second), the computer will set the speed of the object at two meters per second (adding one meter), and, then, on the next movement, the object will move at the speed of two meters per second. After this, the computer will add another meter per second to the speed, and on the next movement the object will move at the speed of three meters per second. This will repeat forever, unless the student has added a step that tells the computer when to stop repeating the movements. This process is modeling the concept of acceleration. Of course, you can set *a* to be a negative number instead of a positive one and watch what happens to the moving object over time instead. Indeed, you can try anything you want—explore (SEEK)—and see what happens.

The student can keep elaborating the program and watch what happens at every stage. In this process, the student, with the guidance of a good teacher, can discover a good deal about Galileo's principles of motion through his or her actions in writing the program, watching what happens, and changing the program. The student is seeing, in an embodied way, tied to action, how a representational system that is less abstract than algebra or calculus (namely, the computer programming language, which is actually composed of a set of boxes) "cashes out" in terms of motion in a virtual world on the computer screen.

An algebraic representation of Galileo's principles is more general – basically, a set of numbers and variables that does not directly tie to actions or movements as material things. As diSessa points out, algebra doesn't distinguish effectively "among motion ($d = rt$), converting meters to inches ($i = 39.37 \times$ m), defining coordinates of a straight line ($y = mx$), or a host of other conceptually varied situations" (diSessa 2000, pp. 32–33). They all just look alike. He goes on to point out that "[d]istinguishing these contexts is critical in learning, although it is probably nearly irrelevant in fluid, routine work for experts," (p. 33) who of course have already had many embodied experiences using algebra for a variety of different purposes of their own.

Once learners have experienced the meanings of Galileo's principles about motion in a situated and embodied way, they have understood one of the situated meanings for the algebraic equations that capture these principles at a more abstract level. Now these equations are beginning to take on a real meaning in terms of embodied understandings. As learners see algebra spelled out in additional specific material situations, they will come to master it in an active and critical way not just a set of symbols to be repeated in a passive and rote manner on tests. As diSessa (2000) puts it:

> Programming turns analysis into experience and allows a connection between analytic forms and their experiential implications that algebra and even calculus can't touch. (p. 34)

Abstract systems originally got their meanings through such embodied experiences for those who really understand them. Abstraction (at least in many important cases) rises gradually out of the ground of situated meaning and practice and returns there from time to time, or it is meaningless to most human beings.

The end result of working with Boxer is that students are able to internalize some procedures in ways that allow them to operate on automatic pilot, without conscious awareness (embodied associations). This frees up simulation powers, that require effort and time (slow associating), to be used for further development, discovery, and invention.

Example 2: Dragon Box

As another example we will turn now to a video game designed to teach algebra. Look at the two images below:

(1) $a = x + 2 + -2 + b + -b$

(2)

Figure 4. Dragon Box play screen.

(1) is in the language of algebraic equations. (2) is a picture made up of smaller pictures. If you know how to interpret each image, you know that they "say (much) the same thing." Image 2 is from a game for children as young as 5, a game called Dragon Box 5+ meant to teach the beginnings of algebra.

At the beginning of Dragon Box 5+, the game uses several different kinds of cards. Some are like dice (with dots on them) and some have pictures of different creatures on them. Each card—dice or creatures—has two sides, a day side and a night side. The card with a picture of a box on it is the Dragon Box. The goal of the game is to get the Dragon Box all alone on one side of the gameboard by using a few simple rules.

One rule is this: if you move a day card onto its night card, the two cards disappear. Once you do this on the game screen above, you are left with the dragon box on one side, alone, and the (day) picture of a creature in a shell on the other. Since the dragon box is alone on one side, you have won this round of the game. You get extra points if, when the Dragon Box is alone, you have left nothing on the screen that could have been removed. In Dragon Box this amounts to discovering that the answer to the original puzzle (pictured above) is "shell creature = dragon box" (where "=" in Dragon Box is represented by the line down the middle of the game board).

To solve the algebraic equation in (1) we can use the mathematical rule that the addition of any positive number (the equivalent of a Dragon Box day card) and negative number (the equivalent of a Dragon Box night card) equals 0 (the equivalent of disappearing in Dragon Box). So, we get "a = x" (or "x = a" by equivalent rules in both algebra and Dragon Box). This solution to the equation is the algebraic equivalent to the answer "shell creature = dragon box" in Dragon Box.

Within a few hours of play, Dragon Box moves players from pictures to full-blown algebraic equations, some of them quite complicated (see 3 below). The player has learned that the algebraic symbols and the pictorial symbols are like different words in different languages that translate to the same meaning or concept, where meaning here means recipes for doing not just knowing.

(3)

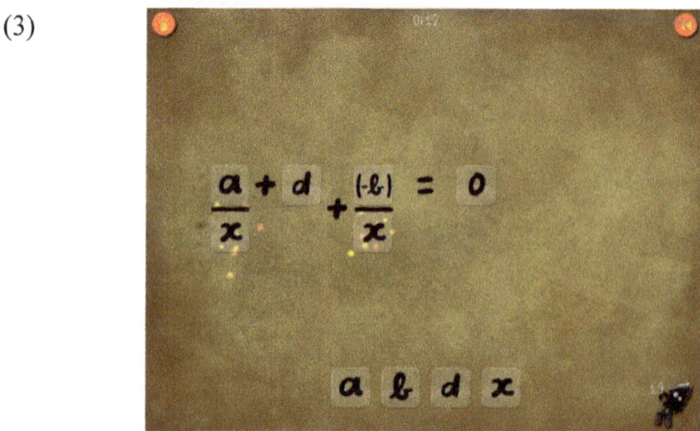

Figure 5. Dragon Box play screen after a few hours of play.

In the game the dice and creature pictures—and the rules for manipulating them—are a concrete imagistic way to see the meaning (the "semantics") of algebraic symbols and rules. In the first parts of Dragon Box, rules become movements and algebraic symbols become images that are meaningful outside of the realm of numbers and mathematics. At a deeper level, Dragon Box is teaching players that solving equations is a form of pattern recognition and pattern manipulation, a basic set of skills we use in many parts of our lives.

Dragon Box is teaching, but, of course, it is not a human teacher. While it is digital, it need not be. It could be played as a card game in physical space (just like popular games like *Magic the Gathering* and *Yu-Gi-Oh!* that are played both ways).

Lessons Learned

Both Boxer and Dragon Box start with a simplified version of algebraic language and one that can be manipulated physically in the world by the learner. That is, both offer the learner a physical version of algebra that can be sensed and acted on much as we do things in the world. And both offer a version of algebra that does not look like the "real thing" and, thus, may not trigger fears and stereotypes learners bring with them to instruction.

Both Boxer and Dragon Box let the learner manipulate a simplified version of algebra and then almost immediately see what happens in a virtual world (on a screen). The learner clearly sees the correlation between a change they have made (in the Boxer programming language or in the Dragon Box game) and a change in a world they can sense. Thus, change in a representational system is coupled with change in the world. The learner begins to form associations between the two, which is what it means to learn a representational system and to learn it in a way that you see it as a way to act on the world.

Two other crucial elements enter in this coupling of change in representational system and change in world in these approaches to teaching and learning. The human web of associations, based on experience, is a prediction engine. Humans learn best when they have a goal to accomplish (a problem), one which they care about, in a situation where they can predict what will happen and then act, get a result, and see if their prediction was right or wrong.

Second, humans need to know how to assess the results of their actions. They need to know, when they have acted, whether the result they have gotten is good, bad, or somewhere in between and whether they should stop or go on. The standards of such judgements very often reside within social identities. For example, in algebra, it is not good enough to solve an equation, but leave unnecessary elements in it, even though this does not affect the "truth" of the equation. Learners need to learn what we can call an "appreciative system," a system of values by which one knows what is a good or bad result and when it is appropriate to stop and settle for what you have achieved and when it is not. Different social identities engage in different sorts of work or play (or both) and therefore have different sorts of appreciative systems.

Both Boxer and Dragon Box can trigger learner's predictions about what will happen and allow them to test these predictions. If their prediction is wrong, both Boxer and Dragon Box allow them to try again and guide them with "rules" about what is a good result and when it is fine to stop and call it a success and when not. One way Dragon Box does this is to assign stars to an answer. Three stars means your answer is technically right, but not the shortest, least redundant version of the equation you could have reached. For that, you need to get four stars.

So, in the end, the learner forms associations among predictions, changes in representations, changes in the world, and an assessment or appreciation of the results within the value system of a particular social identity (here an identity of someone who uses algebra as part of their problem-solving efforts in the world). In the act, learners learn to make better predictions, to automatize some skills, and to be able to simulate (do math in their minds) in order to learn new things and engage in discovery.

Of course, in the case of Boxer and Dragon Box, learners have learned a somewhat different language than actual algebra as a representational system. To go further in "language acquisition" here they need to learn to translate between the system they have learned and "real" algebraic representations. But this is relatively easy because they have already learned to meld prediction, change in representation, change in world, and appraisal of results and that same process will work for the more formal representations of algebra.

In Dragon Box, learners start with symbols and pictures that have no apparent tie to algebra but which are, nonetheless, recipes to do algebra. As they learn, the game transitions them gradually to algebraic symbols. Eventually they get a mixture of Dragon Box images and algebraic symbols. Then they get all algebraic symbols, but still in the tiles they have learned to move around and manipulate. Finally, they just get algebraic symbols and see them as recipes for action and making change in the world. They have learned a new language. The four screenshots from Dragon Box below show this progression.

(4)

Figure 6. The progression of the play
(https://itslearning.com/global/news/dragonbox/)

CHAPTER 15

AOT: BUILDING A SENSUOUS CONSTRUCTION

In this chapter, we will look at how AOT designs a sensuous construction and uses it to allow viewers to think about, reflect on—and, also, sense and feel—important ideas, the sorts of ideas that should constitute a curriculum in the humanities. Here ideas are communicated not as words or pictures but as sensuous constructions. Sensuous constructions allow viewers a good deal of latitude to use their own creative interpretive powers to fill out their own version of the meaning of the sensuous construction. However, viewers do this—if the designers do their work well—within the foundations the designers have set.

We will look in detail at how AOT turns a simple red scarf into a sensuous construction that accrues more and more meaning across AOT. The red scarf appears across many episodes in AOT, accruing meaning and triggering feelings and emotions in viewers as the story unfolds. Below we look at a number of different episodes. Across these episodes, the red scarf becomes part of a story in which it is the central character.

The Beginning of a Lifelong Bond
(E6 The World the Girl Saw)

The red scarf marks the beginning of Eren and Mikasa's life-long relationship, a relationship central to AOT. It first appears in a deeply tragic event. One day, Dr. Jaeger, Eren's father, brought Eren along on one of his regular visits to checkup on Mikasa's mother, who was pregnant with her second child. Shockingly, he found her and Mikasa's father dead in their home, the victims of a violent murder. Mikasa, a young child, was missing. Dr. Jaeger ordered Eren to wait for him outside the house and hurried off to find the military police. However, Eren makes up his mind to leave and try to find Mikasa on his own.

Eren finds a house in the forest where Mikasa is being held captive. Despite being only nine years old, he sneaks into the house and hides in a side room where he finds a knife. He rushes out of the room and uses the knife—in a white-hot rage—to kill two of the murderers, but gets caught by the third. Despite her great fear, Mikasa picks up the knife Eren has dropped and stabs the last murderer in the back.

When Eren's father finds Eren and Mikasa together, he scolds Eren for disobeying him and Eren responds, in tears, that he had just wanted to save Mikasa as quickly as possible. Mikasa asks Dr. Jaeger: "Which way should I go to get home from here? It's cold, I don't have anywhere to go home to." Hearing this, Eren walks up to her, takes off his red scarf, and wraps it around Mikasa's head, saying: "You can have this. It's warm, isn't it?". Mikasa responds: "It's warm." This is a the first of many associations the scarf will pick up.

Eren's father tells Mikasa that she should come and live with them. Hearing his father's words, Eren looks at Mikasa and says: "Come home, let's go back. Let's go back to our home." Mikasa responds with tears: "Okay, let's go home." This tragic event formed a belief in Mikasa that would affect her life thereafter: "A cruel world, in which only the victor survives. But in this world, I have somewhere to go home to. Eren, as long as I have you, I can do anything".

The red scarf is the sign of a bond born in tragedy between Mikasa and Eren. It is also a sign of rebirth for Mikasa. She gains a new family and a new identity. Eren becomes her purpose in life and she longs to eternally support him. And she will do so throughout all of AOT until the end of AOT where her bond to Eren is sorely tested.

In AOT there are two Erens (two sides to Eren, two persona in Eren). One Eren is the Eren born of the red scarf, bonded to and guided by Mikasa, a young woman who turns out to be stronger and more thoughtful than Eren. This Eren is a person strongly committed to his relationship with Mikasa and their friend Armin and to their common search for a life together outside the confines of the walls that enclose them in the poorest part of Paradis Island.

The other Eren—who will appear later, but there are already signs of him when he is a child—is an Eren committed to the cause of liberating all the people on Paradis Island. He plans to do this by destroying not just the walls that surround them, but their corrupt government inside the walls and all the humans who live outside these walls in other countries, people that hate the people on Paradis Island. This Eren is a grand, but totalitarian, liberator committed to a revolution at home and destruction abroad that will create a utopia for the people of Paradis (whether they want it or not). This Eren will break (or seem to) his bond with Mikasa.

When the Red Scarf Falls (E26 Beast Titan)

Mikasa, Eren, and their close friend, Armin, eventually join the Survey Corps to fight the Titans. It is here that Eren discovers his own Titan powers. In Episode 26, we see a flashback to when Eren was a boy. He runs up to mother who is hanging washing to dry on a clothesline. He has dirt and bruises on his face showing he has been (again) injured in a fight with other boys. The following encounter ensues:

> **Mother**: Oh Eren.
> Did you get into *another* fight?
> **Eren**: Those jerks started it! They made fun of me!
> **Mother**: So, I assume Mikasa had to come to your rescue again?
> [*Mikasa, quite uninjured, having indeed rescued Eren, comes up wearing her scarf and silently begins to help the mother hang the clothes.*]
> **Mother**: No matter how cruel someone is or how much you hate them,
> you can't always charge at them head-on!
> You're a man!
> Show some restraint!
> You need to be there for Mikasa, too!

When this flashback ends, we see Eren, in the future, in bed recovering from the injuries he has gotten from an epic battle he has had, in his Titan form, with the Female Titan, one of the Survey Corps' fiercest enemies. Mikasa sits on a bench next to his bed. She is asleep, holding the red scarf on her lap. Eren gets up to look out a window and sees the scarf fall from Mikasa's hand to the floor. He picks it up, wakes her, and gives it to her, saying: "That thing's seen better days. I'll get you a new one, if I see any in our supplies". As he speaks, Mikasa silently caresses the scarf.

Here Eren fails to see the specific scarf he gave Mikasa as associated with her care for and bond with him. He sees the scarf as something general that can be replaced, yet keep the same meaning. What Mikasa sees as a sensuous construction (meanings associated with the scarf that remain embedded in sensation and feeling) he sees as a simple category, a replaceable piece of clothing.

There is a long history, in reality and literature, of people who cannot read "signs" appropriately in context, cannot see the embodied meanings of things, but only their types and categories, as Eren has done here. Such people can be dangerous. They may, for example, see and react to a person not as a specific unique being but as a category (a caste, a class, a gender, an ethnicity, a culture, or as "them" versus "us").

Eren will eventually, unlike Mikasa and his friend Armin, see the people outside of Paradis Island not as diverse and specific beings, each with their own feelings, hopes, desires, and rights, but as lesser foreigners, as "them" to the people of Paradis as the true humans. Shockingly, he will eventually see Mikasa as a category (an Ackerman, her family name and ethnic group) and not as a specific person. In history, it has always been easier for humans to demean and sometimes even kill others they see as categories and not as specific distinctive individual beings.

In the context of the flashback that we saw before this scene, where Mikasa has once again saved headstrong but weak Eren from bullies, we see Mikasa, as she always is, wearing the red scarf. It is, for her and viewers of AOT, a sign of her calm strength, strength she received on the day Eren tried to rescue her and gave her the scarf. It is the sign of Mikasa's purpose in life, protecting Eren. As AOT goes on, Eren's battles are no longer with children. After he discovers his Titan powers, they are eventually with all of humanity outside Paradis Island which he will, in his usual all or nothing headstrong way, seek to destroy. When this happens, Eren will need rescuing from himself and Mikasa will seek to do just that.

Hiding behind the Scarf (E33 The Hunters)

In a battle with the Armored Titan and the Colossal Titan, Eren loses and is badly injured. Unable to use his Titan form, he is captured and taken away by the two Titans. Armin tells Mikasa that, since they lack a way to pursue them, all they can do is wait for reinforcements from the Survey Corps. Hearing Armin's words, Mikasa becomes concerned and depressed. She finds her red scarf on the ground, picks it up, and wraps it around her neck and lower face. As she wraps the scarf around herself, she and Armin have the conversation below. They remember that even as a child Eren was always running off:

Mikasa: Hey, Armin. Why? Why does Eren always go somewhere far away from us?

Armin: Yeah, now that you mention it, Eren has always run off on his own, leaving us behind. I guess that's just the way things are meant to happen, for Eren at least.

Mikasa: But all I want is to be at his side. [*With tears*]

Figure 7. Mikasa in red scarf with tears (WIT Studio)

While they are waiting for the reinforcements, Hannes, the garrison soldier who has watched over Eren, Mikasa, and Armin since they were children, walks up to Mikasa and Armin and reminds them of Eren's tenacity and determination in any fight. Mikasa grabs the upper edge of her scarf (picture above) as Hannes talks:

Hannes: Ever since the good old days, you two have been there to clean up the mess of that brat.

That's what I would call a lousy relationship, Sheesh.

It's a different time and different place,

but you kids are doing the same thing you always have.

Am I right?

Armin: The neighborhood bullies and Titans are a little bit different in size.

Hannes: True… The thing is, that brat isn't even that good at fighting.

But no matter if he's up against three or five, he'll charge in all the same.

By the time Mikasa or soldiers showed up, he'd be beaten into a pulp every time.

But you know…

I've never seen him win a fight before,

but I've never seen him get beat and give up either.

> Sometimes he's so tenacious that even I think it's scary.
> No matter how many times he's knocked over, he gets back up.
> That's the kinda guy he is.
> You think he'll get taken away without putting up a fight?
> Nope. He'll keep resisting as long as he has strength.
> Even more so when he's up against just two.
> He'll give 'em hell no matter who he's up against.
> Until you or I show up to help.
> That's how Eren's always been.
> [*Mikasa widens her eyes and looks at Hannes with agreement.*]
> **Hannes**: I loved those good old days
> If you asked Eren, he'd say those days were nothing more than a false peace.
> But for me, I'm more than happy to be a drunk, useless soldier.
> If it means getting back those plain, ordinary days…
> …I'll do whatever I have to.
> No matter how long it takes to get there.
> I'm coming too.
> Without you three together again, I can't bring back the good old days.
> [*Armin nods a strong assent and Mikasa lowers her scarf and nods assent as well. Then she lowers her scarf completely and, with Armin and Hannes, she strenuously eats rations to prepare for battle.*]

Here, as elsewhere in AOT, the red scarf registers Mikasa's emotions. It can be a sign of her fears and weaknesses or of her resolve and strength. Here she first holds the scarf tight around her face as if to protect herself from her fear that she may lose Eren and her inability to go save him. Then she lowers it when her belief in Eren is reinforced by Hannes. Now the scarf can again be a source of power and not something to hide behind. The scarf is both a shield to hide behind and a sword to empower her. It is true of many humans, including many who have accomplished a great deal in life, that their weaknesses (for Mikasa this is her bond to Eren) is also their strength (for Mikasa this bond is what powers her training and skills as a warrior).

Hannes brings out an important contrast between Eren and Mikasa, a contrast that is also an historically important one between different social and political viewpoints (Sowell 1996). Hannes wants to fight to attain a "normal" life, a mundane life centered on relationships among everyday people accepting the everyday compromises, weaknesses, and imperfections of human beings and their ever-fraught institutions. Such people believe things are never perfect, you can easily make them worse, and making them a lot better (let along perfect), given the nature of humans, is nearly impossible and can lead to dire unforeseen consequences. This is essentially a conservative viewpoint: We need to conserve what we have, imperfect as it is, and change it carefully, since it is easier to do even worse. Furthermore, the purpose of life is relationships in a community, not institutions or governments.

But there are others—and this is one part of Eren—that cannot accept mundane daily life and all of its constraints and imperfections. They cannot accept humanity as it is and just seek to make things incrementally better. Rather, they seek a wholesale transformation of society where people can achieve a utopia and transcend the weaknesses of humanity and its flawed institutions. For Eren, this utopia is a state of freedom from constraints for the people of Paradis, though at the cost of the lives of those outside Paradis's walls and those who oppose him inside Paradis. Historically utopias have most often ended up totalitarian regimes that enforce one order—one vision of perfection—on all. In the act—whether with Mao, Stalin, Hitler, Mussolini, or others in history—often a great many people have had to die to bring about a utopia that never actually arrives (Hiruta 2021).

The young Eren, the Eren of the red scarf, had wanted to venture outside the walls with his friends to live free of walls and institutional constraints with them in an idealized state of nature. The liberator Eren wants to destroy the walls, reform the government wholesale, and remove all of his foes—inside or outside Paradis—in one fell swoop to create a utopia.

The red scarf is a domestic item associated with Mikasa's daily life as Eren's adopted sister and protector living in a small circle of family and friends. It is also associated with her strength in this role but also, later, her strength in her role as the Survey Corps strongest and best fighter, committed to fighting alongside and protecting Eren, a role that entangles her with Eren's violent search for Utopia.

"You Wrapped This Scarf around Me" (E37 Scream)

Eventually, the Survey Corps, with Mikasa and Armin participating, successfully rescue Eren. However, in the act, they get trapped by Titans who surround them in the wild. Then Eren and Mikasa see a Titan walk toward them, a Titan who happens to be the very Titan who killed Eren's mother. Hannes comes to help Eren and Mikasa. Eren tries to turn into his Titan form to revenge his mother, but fails to do so, because his body has not recovered from his previous battle with the Armored Titan. In the end, Eren watches Hannes get eaten by the Titan. Eren becomes maniacal in his grief and feels powerless. He screams to himself: "Mom, I still can't do anything…at all." Mikasa realizes, surrounded by Titans as they are, this might be their last moment on earth. She starts to confess to Eren her feelings for him:

> **Mikasa**: Eren, listen. I need to tell you something. You've always been by my side. Thank you. You showed me how to live with purpose. Thank you. And you…You wrapped this scarf around me. Thank you.
> **Eren**: I'll wrap that around you as many times as you want. Now and forever… as much as you want.

Figure 8. Mikasa recalls when Eren first wrapped red scarf around her (WIT Studio)

This is the red scarf Eren, the person Mikasa saw and devoted herself to when she received the red scarf. After this scene, the red scarf itself and the bond between Eren and Mikasa will begin to tatter and fray. Eren's promise here will be sorely tested. The red scarf event gave rise to Mikasa as we know her and to Eren as the person the scarf bonds her to. But there are two Erens, as we have seen, not just in terms of his human and Titan self, but in terms of the familiar Eren, defined by his friends and relationships, and the crusading totalitarian Eren, defined by a sacred cause.

The Estrangement (E73 Savagery)

Long after the wars with the Titans began, Eren and his friends discovered secrets no one else in Paradis knew. They found, in the basement of Eren's old home, secret diaries from Eren's father. These diaries tell them that there are other countries outside the walls of Paradis and that these countries are filled with people who hate the people on Paradis Island and wish for their destruction. The Eldians on Paradis are, unbeknownst to themselves, the descendants of a great Empire that had conquered much of the world. When their Empire was defeated, their last king fled to the Island and, using his Founding Titan powers, wiped clean the memory of his people so they would be unaware that in their history they had used Titans to kill so many people.

As the AOT story continues, Eren, Mikasa, and Armin venture, with the Survey Corps, further beyond the walls of Paradis and they see for themselves that the people of Paradis are in grave peril from those outside the walls, including from a country called Marley. Marley, the power that had defeated the Eldian empire, has created and placed the mindless Titans outside the walls of Paradis Island to keep the Eldians trapped behind them. Marley has become an imperial power itself, but is fighting other countries that have developed new and better weapons. Marley now wants to conquer Paradis Island and take its natural resources to fuel their war efforts and their search for better technologies for warfare.

Learning all this, Eren comes to believe that, in order to let the Eldians on Paradis live freely without deadly hatred from the outside world, he must, by using his Founding Titan power, kill everyone else in the world starting with Marley. This will, at last, put an end to warfare. His extreme belief attracts a lot of Eldian followers who form their own group, the "Jaegerists," and engage in a civil war to take over the government of Paradis.

Armin and Mikasa think Eren cannot really believe what he is saying and that he must have been manipulated by others. They meet with him to find out his true beliefs, though they are not sure he any longer trusts them and they know Eren now has the power to imprison them. Eren tells them he is not being manipulated, that whatever he does, it comes out of his own free will. He claims it is Mikasa and Armin who have been manipulated and who, unlike him, have no free will:

> **Eren**: The things I do and choices I make are all decided by my own free will.
> …
> **Mikasa**: No, you're being manipulated! You wouldn't get kids and innocents involved, even if they were enemies! Plus, I know you care about us more than anyone! Don't you?
> [*Mikasa has her scarf wrapped around her neck in this whole scene. Now she gestures to her scarf and continues:*]
> The reason you saved me in the cabin, the reason you gave me this scarf, is because you're kind …

Then Eren says something deeply hurtful to Mikasa. It is certainly out of character for Eren in terms of all we have seen of his relationship with Mikasa. Mikasa's father was an Ackerman. The Ackermans are a traditional bloodline of warriors who were born—even programmed—to protect the old kings of the original Eldia. However, they are now a persecuted clan because they were not willing to accept the original Paradisian king's decision to wipe clean the peoples' memories. Eren uses Mikasa's Ackerman identity to deny that she has free will and claims she was acting on an uncontrollable instinct in terms of her loyalty to him:

> **Eren**: The Ackermans were intentionally designed to protect Eldia's King. Back then [in the cabin where Mikasa was being held captive], faced with a life-or-death situation, you heard my order: "Fight." In that moment, instincts awoke from within you. By mistake, you thought I was the host you had to protect.
> **Mikasa**: No.
> **Eren**: No? No, what?
> **Mikasa**: It wasn't a mistake.
> [*At this point, Mikasa starts to recall the first time Eren wraps the scarf around her.*]
> **Mikasa**: It's because it was you, Eren! I became strong because of you!
> …
> **Eren**: Your family was made to forget who they are and live only to forget. In other words, slave.
> **Armin**: Enough, Eren!
> **Eren**: Do you know who I hate more than anyone? Those who aren't free. Just like livestock.
> **Armin**: Eren!
> **Eren**: Just seeing you has always pissed me off so much, and now I finally know why. I can't stand the sight of a slave who obeys orders without question. Ever since I was little, Mikasa, I've hated you.

Armin attacks Eren after he has hurt Mikasa and Eren has them both imprisoned. The two friends wonder whether Eren is lying, perhaps to protect them from involvement in the internal civil war he has helped to create and the violence he intends to unleash on the world. They cannot believe this is the Eren they have known and loved and who has loved them.

As Mikasa wraps the scarf tightly around herself, Eren disowns the bond the scarf stands for. Eren is obsessed with freedom in the sense of a lack of constraints of any kind. He believes that destroying the rest of humanity is the only way the humans of Paradis can be truly free and live without walls and without the corrupt government he and the Jaegerists have overthrown. He claims Mikasa's support for and loyalty to him are not freely chosen, but the results of her biology as an Ackerman. She is constrained to act as she does. He no longer sees her as a specific person, but now as a category, an Ackerman, and only that category now defines her. Eren is claiming that it is not the Eren of the red scarf she loves and protects, it is Eren as royalty (though he is not a member of the royal family, he attains his great powers through contact with them). He is claiming that the bond of the scarf is false, even Mikasa's initial act in saving Eren was not freely chosen.

Eren claims he freely chose his new path, yet he too is the product of biology and history. When Eren says he hates Mikasa he has already inherited the Attack Titan which gives him the power to see his own future (but not change it). Knowing his future, he sees it is pre-determined and not feely chosen in any simple sense. This is, in fact, the plight of all humans: we have no idea how much of our decisions are the result of our biology; our unconscious feelings, associations, and beliefs; our past experiences; and a future determined by a great many things other than ourselves. Free choice is a very vexed issue for humans, philosophically, morally, and even in terms of how our brains and bodies actually work. Freedom and choice are very important themes in AOT. The red scarf intersects with the theme of freedom because it is also a sign of how hard it is to really know why we have chosen what we have and what was the role of fate in it all.

Armin holds out the belief that Eren is lying to push him and Mikasa away so that they will not be caught up in the upheaval of government and the world Eren is leading. Is Eren seeking to save Mikasa even as he and his followers have killed those in Paradis who opposed their new regime and will kill those outside the walls who stand in his way? Is his personal familiar bond to Mikasa here transcending his totalitarian world-transforming identity? Is he, in the end, loyal to the red scarf? Or is he now an entirely different person?

Judgement (E76)

Eren tells the Jaegerists to put Mikasa and Armin in an underground prison. Soon after, Marley initiates a powerful surprise attack on Paradis in reprisal for an Eldian attack. As Eren fends off Marley, Armin and Mikasa are discussing whether they should help him.

> **Armin**: What do you think, Mikasa? Do you want to help Eren?
> **Mikasa**: I want to. But like Eren said, it's probably because of that…
> Because I'm an Ackermann. This isn't my own will.

As Mikasa talks, the camera gradually shifts attention from her face, panning in several shots down her body to focus at last on her right hand grasping the end of the red scarf as it is about to drop.

Figure 9. Mikasa holds tight red scarf (MAPPA Studio)

This is the beginning of the end for the red scarf. Eren has torn apart the lived meanings of the red scarf and rendered it a suspect sign, a false sign, a sign not of a freely chosen bond but of the subservience of a servant or slave. Will the red scarf still give Mikasa the powers she needs to fight, overcome, and conquer her fear and protect Eren, even if this means putting an end to Eren the liberator and conqueror?

Sneak Attack (E77)

After the discussion above, Mikasa and Armin, decide to help Eren. As Mikasa and Armin climb up the stairs from the dungeon, Mikasa asks Armin why Eren tried to push them away by telling them they have no free will.

> **Mikasa**: If Eren's hiding his intentions, why did he push us away? Why would Eren say that he hates me?
> **Armin**: He had to come up with a lie. Once this is all over, we can ask him. [*Armin is here saying that Eren must be lying, but they cannot know why Eren is lying unless they help him win the battle with Marley.*]

When Mikasa says, "Why would Eren say he hates me," the camera puts emphasis on the red scarf.

While Mikasa is gearing up for the battle with Marley's army in the prep room, she carefully folds her scarf and puts it down. Louise—a girl who was saved by Mikasa from a Titan when she was young and has seen Mikasa as a role model ever since—notices Mikasa is not taking the red scarf with her. She asks Mikasa: "You're leaving your scarf behind?" Mikasa gives the scarf another look and answers firmly, "I am." Then she leaves the room, leaving Louise staring at the red scarf she has left behind.

Before this scene, Mikasa is seen wearing the red scarf a good deal of the time, even in battles. After this, she does not wear it again.

Armin and Mikasa can only find out Eren's true intentions if they help him to survive yet again and then can ask him again what he is really up to. Mikasa has always acted on her bond with Eren and the powers the red scarf has given her. All her later choices are a product of the choice she made when Eren wrapped the scarf around her. All her loyalties have been to "her" Eren, the Eren of the red scarf, the Eren who is embedded in a familiar "plain and ordinary" relationship with her and Armin. They were not to the Eren committed to a sacred cause that overrides any notion of people as individual mundane weak humans whose feeling and identities are not in the end categorial, but specific and relational in multiple ways.

The Missing Scarf (E82 Sunset)

Paradis eventually defeats Marley and Eren attains a key power he needs to fulfill his promise to kill the rest of humanity. He now has the power to start the Rumbling where an army of massive Titans controlled by Eren will march across the world destroying everything in their path. Armin and Mikasa are at a loss at what to do. Yet, even in a moment like this, what concerns Mikasa most remains Eren. Mikasa asks Armin what will happen to Eren. Hearing the name "Eren," Armin who is overwhelmed, finally loses his cool and yells at Mikasa: "I don't know! What can we do anyway?!" Then he leaves the room and Mikasa is alone. Mikasa now realizes her scarf is gone.

Even as Eren goes off to do something neither Mikasa nor Armin approves of and even as he is not the Eren they have known, Mikasa cannot stop worrying about him, about what will happen to him, as she has done since he and she were children. But now the scarf is gone and she must wonder whether her Eren is gone as well. What are her responsibilities now? What choices should she make now, when she cannot be guided by the pact of the red scarf? Will these choices be "freely" chosen?

Pride (E83)

Mikasa recalls that Louise might be the one who took her scarf. She finds Louise in the field hospital. Louise is lying on a bed with the red scarf around her neck. Mikasa asks her to give her the scarf back:

> **Mikasa**: I found you.
> **Louise**: I'm glad. Did you come looking for me? Or for this scarf?
> **Mikasa**: I knew you would have it.
> **Louise**: I'm sorry. I thought it'd bring me closer to you. I have Thunder Spear shrapnel in me that they can't remove. It's a pity I won't be able to see the free world that Eren Jaeger creates. It wasn't much, but I had the chance to speak with him about you. He talked about wanting to throw the scarf out. So, rather than throw it out, I thought I'd just…
> **Mikasa**: Give it back.

Mikasa is in a shock when she hears Eren wants the scarf thrown out. Despite that, she takes the scarf back. In the rest of the season, she is no longer seen with the red scarf. She has kept it, but put it away.

Mikasa finds out that Eren has disowned the scarf and this seems to solidify for her the case that he meant what he said when he said he hated her. Ironically, since Eren claims she is forced to act to aid him because of her Ackerman blood—and always has been—she now takes the scarf back, but hides it inside her clothing, and goes out to oppose Eren. In opposing Eren she shows that she is indeed free, more than just an Ackerman.

"Thank You for Wrapping This Scarf around Me" (The Manga, Volume 34)

The AOT anime has, at the point we are writing this, one more half-season to run. The red scarf does, however, appear again in the ending of the AOT manga. As the Rumbling continues (causing the destruction of those outside Paradis), those opposed to it realize that the only way to stop it is to kill Eren. Mikasa painfully accepts this proposal. While Eren and his army of Titans is advancing to lands outside Paradis, he uses his Titan power to summon Mikasa to an imaginary world of his own creation. Here Mikasa and he live peacefully in isolation. In the end, however, Eren tells Mikasa to forget him after he dies. Once Mikasa is sent back to reality, she takes out the scarf inside her shirt and tightly ties it around herself. Meanwhile, she responds to Eren's request (though he is not there): "I'm sorry. I can't do that" (forget him). From this moment on, Mikasa never takes the scarf off again. Eventually Mikasa kills Eren and the Rumbling stops.

Years after Eren's death, Mikasa goes to visit Eren's grave. She sits next to the gravestone recalling young Eren's sleeping face. She cannot control her tears, murmuring "I miss you so much." At that moment, a Parasitic Jaeger—a large bird (yes, Eren's last name is Jaeger)—flies down and wraps the scarf more tightly around her using its beak. Jaegers are migrant birds who travel across the seas, so they have been seen as a symbol of freedom. Mikasa is shocked to see the bird doing this to her. Then she smiles with tears, staring at the bird flying back to the sky, and says: "Thank you for wrapping this scarf around me, Eren." (Note: these are the same words she uttered in Episode 37).

The Red Scarf as a Sensuous Construction

The red scarf picks up meanings—meanings attached to it—as it journeys through AOT. It is always an object with its own sensuous properties, but it has a myriad of meanings clinging to it, so it is also a sign pointing to those meanings, much as a word does. It is on its way to being abstract and it is already more abstract than a brute thing, but it never loses its bearings in sensation and its grounding in the material world and the multiple specific contexts that have formed its meanings.

Words can be purely categorial. "Cat" can mean "feline," "democracy" can mean "representative government." These are what we call system or structural meanings. They are part of grammar (which is a system of "rules"). But words can also be like the red scarf. Though they do not have relevant sensory features as the red scarf does (it is soft but strong and can offer one warmth and protection), they can accrue different meanings in different specific experiential contexts, meanings which, in turn, can be used to understand future contexts in ways we have understood past ones. And they can continue to accrue new contextual meanings, as well, in novel contexts. We call these situational meanings. They make a word something like the red scarf, a sensuous construction.

Designers let things like the red scarf become sensuous constructions because it allows them to avoid words which may be already too fraught with other meanings from other contexts. They can then build their own special purpose signs, just as if they had created a brand-new word with its situational meanings. This process also allows them to bypass grammar and specific languages. The accrued meanings of a sensuous construction are at least in part, open to speakers of any language. They just need their shared human sensory systems and their shared human knowledge of the world we all, in a great many respects, share.

The red scarf accumulates meanings in different contexts that resonate with themes—many of which we have discussed above—that are important historically, philosophically, socially, and morally. It, thus, helps make AOT a site that can generate important reflections and discussions that are, in the deepest sense, educational.

CHAPTER 16

VAGUENESS

In this chapter we will look at a distinction that plays a big role in speaking, writing, and education. This is the distinction between clarity (or explicitness) and vagueness. We tend to see—especially in formal education—clarity as an unmitigated good and vagueness as bad. However, clarity and vagueness have different uses. They can each be good or bad in different contexts. And, vagueness—when it is used in the right way—can be the more participatory, life-enhancing, and creative part of the binary. Used well, vagueness leaves others with more options and power than does clarity.

We need to note, for readers trained to think of vagueness as a property of the poor speaker or writer, that we are not celebrating all forms of vagueness or a lack of total clarity. We are celebrating only some forms of vagueness. But these are essential to communication, sociality, and creativity.

A Sweet Spot

Vagueness shares with empathy, intuition, feelings and emotions, and the other things we have discussed so far, the property that it seems removed from the things we most value in school: analysis, reasoning, clarity, objectivity, facts, and rules. Just as intuition seems to some an enemy of reasoning—when it is actually its guide and partner—vagueness seems an enemy of clear reasoning and learning when it is often their precondition.

No communication in language can say everything in words (Gee 2004; Hanks 1996; Halliday 1978). It would take far too long to say everything we meant explicitly; communication would be too slow. Communication in language always requires hearers or readers to fill in some of the meaning from context and shared knowledge.

However, there is a continuum at work here. While no communication is fully explicit, some ways to communicate are more explicit than others. When communication is towards the explicit side, the speaker or writer is doing most of the work of meaning making, trying to say or write what they mean as clearly as they can. When it is towards the vague side, the hearer or reader is doing more of the work of meaning making, trying to interpret what the speaker or writer might mean but has not explicitly said.

Communication that is too explicit, that tries to leave little to the hearer's or reader's imagination, can be rude because it can presume to tell hearers and readers what they already know and can easily fill in by themselves. And it can be a form of distrust, assuming the hearer or reader cannot be trusted to understand the message without having the point belabored. Communication that is too vague can also be rude, because it leaves too much up to the hearer or reader and can cause confusion about why the speaker or writer is even bothering to speak or write.

For different communicational purposes and situations, the sweet spot on the continuum between too explicit and too vague is in different places in the middle. We will see in this chapter that, in language, vagueness of the right sort is a form of inclusion, mutuality, and immersion in each other's worlds.

Vagueness can also be an important source of learning. If I tell or show you what I want you to learn so completely and directly that I leave little room for your own thinking, you can just memorize what I have said with little commitment to it. You may well soon forget it. If I recruit you own thinking and processing, you will integrate the learning better with what you already know and remember it better in the future (Chi & Wylie 2014; Jason 2017). A certain degree of vagueness requires more active mental processing by the hearer or reader and this leads to deeper learning and longer retention. This mental processing means the hearer or reader will more deeply connect what it is being said or written to their prior knowledge captured in their web of associations.

In Defense of Vagueness

"Vague" is usually a derogatory term. This is partly because vagueness can happen because of incompetence or oversight. But we are talking in this chapter about what we will call "strategic vagueness" where vagueness is done artfully and on purpose (Keefe & Smith 1995). We will see in the next chapter that such vagueness is central to art.

At a deep level, vagueness has long troubled philosophers. An influential strand of work in Western philosophy defines meaning in terms of set membership where any given entity is either in the set or not (Cresswell 2006; Sigmund 2017). So, the category "fish" is defined as any and all things that are in the set of fish. A thing is either a fish or it isn't. Categories are taken to have strict boundaries.

This conception of meaning has long been formalized in terms of modern formal logic (van Benthem & Ter Meulen 2010). In this conception, if it was vague what counted as a fish—if there were borderline cases—then we would not know what a fish is and, and most problematically for logic, we would not be able to ascertain whether "this is a fish" is true or false. And true and false are the only two categories in standard logic.

This conception of meaning is, however, unable to deal with the reality that most words in human language are vague, not a matter of clear yes and no decisions. There are borderline cases. How thin, bald, smart, or tall does someone have to be to be thin, bald, smart, or tall? If a seven-foot person is clearly tall, is a six-footer tall? What about a 5' 9" person? There is no sharp line to be drawn and there is no definitive set of tall people that can be set up.

Many people assume that vagueness is just a property of vernacular ("everyday") language, not more formal varieties of language like academic writing. However, academic writing does use vagueness strategically, as Greg Myers (1996) points out in his article "Strategic Vagueness in Academic Writing":

> … academic writing takes place within social institutions that require negotiation of complex boundaries: between departments, between disciplines, between academic and applied goals, between academic and popular audiences. From this perspective we can understand some vagueness as strategic, enabling the terms and interests of one group to be translated into those of another group. For instance, a vague name for an approach may allow one to include apparently conflicting authors within it. (p. 3)

The word "fish" in biology, though often used differently than in everyday language, is still vague in the sense of its meaning being subject to context, purposes, goals, and social agreements that may change in other contexts. In biology, if we use genetics, we get a different set of things as fish than we do if we use morphology (structure and appearance) (Miller 2020). Lung fish are fish morphologically, but not genetically. Furthermore, since evolution is gradual there is no definitive way to decide where the first "real" fish arose than there is to say where tallness "really" begins or ends.

Myers argues (p. 12) that scientists need to remain open to further developments. For example, a certain vagueness as to how they state their claims allows their claims to be compared to results in other studies from somewhat different conditions. Or, a certain vagueness between results and implications can allow room for the text to be assimilated to future developments. Thus, interestingly, a good command of how to use vagueness strategically, both in vernacular and academic speech and writing, is an important for native and non-native speakers of a language.

The point of this discussion of vagueness is that meaning making, whether in language or some other form, is always situated in shared experience, both the shared experience of communicating in a specific context and shared past experiences. Meaning making requires participation, negotiation, imagination, and proactivity. And what we have said about language here is true for all designed experiences like painting, dance, music, poetry, architecture, media, and teaching. All involve situated meaning making in context often in participatory and collaborative ways.

Du Fu

Now we will discuss a specific example of how strategic vagueness works in a designed experience like poetry. We will use as our example a poem by the great Chinese poet, Du Fu (Hawkes 1967; Rexroth 1956) written in Mandarin.

Mandarin is a language that marks syntactic (grammatical) relationships less overtly than English. Linguists have argued that Mandarin is more discourse focused than syntactically focused (Erbaugh 2019; Li & Thompson 1981). When a language lowers the focus on overtly marking syntactic relationships, it allows the words and phrases of an utterance to play with each other and associate in different ways with each other, even to create some tensions, before things are resolved, if they are. Chinese poetry takes this discourse focus even further than vernacular language.

Below is a part of poem by Du Fu 杜甫 called "Spring Scene." Du Fu is considered by many as China's greatest poet. Spring Scene, composed in 757, reflects Du Fu's experience of the turmoil and destruction caused by the An Lushan Rebellion, a conflict between the Tang dynasty and various regional powers. Du Fu is struck by the destruction humans have wrought on each other and their towns and cities amidst the continued survival and even flourishing of nature.

Christopher Tong, in his paper "Nonhuman Poetics (By Way of Wang Guo-wei)" (2015) offers a word-for-word English rendering of part of the poem below:

> State ruined mountains-rivers survive
> City spring grass trees thick
>
> Moved by times flowers sprinkle tears
> Hating separation birds startle heart

Tong offers various translations of the poem that are meant to capture different syntactic possibilities and thus different interpretations. His interest is in how art treats the relationship between humans and the non-human world and how it could come to present a more equal, less human centric, balance between the two. The time we are living in is sometimes called the Anthropocene—the sixth great extinction of life on earth, this time caused by humans. At such a time, it is surely worth thinking about the relationship between humans and other living things and how they can live in harmony or balance before most of them are extinct.

We will not use Tang's translations here, but, rather, use our own English versions that we hope capture more directly the differing relationships between humans and nonhumans the poem can convey. This is fairly easy to do in English because of its syntactic overtness. We will take just one line of the poem: "Moved by the times the flowers sprinkle tears." Below are five possible translations of this line. In each of these "translations" (interpretations) we see a different relationship between the distressed human poet and the flourishing flowers in the field.

1. In my deep sorrow, even the flowers seem to weep.
2. In my deep sorrow, the flowers bring tears to my eyes.
3. In deep sorrow, we weep side by side, the flowers and I.
4. The flowers weep at my deep sorrow.
5. In deep sorrow, the bright flowers weep.

In (1) the poet's emotions cause him to impose sorrow on the flowers so they reflect his emotions. This is a human centric world in which the world is a product of human sensation and emotion.

In (2) it is still how the poet senses—is affected by—the flowers that brings him to tears, as in (1), but now the flowers act on the human to make him feel this way; he does not just impose his mood on the flowers.

In (3) the poet feels distraught and the flowers cry (side by side). They are independent of each other but "in synch" with each other, in harmony with each other.

In (4) the flowers cry because of (are themselves distressed by) the poet's distress. Again, they are in harmony, but here the harmony is not just side by side, but caused by the flowers' response.

In (5) the flowers cry because of (are distressed by) the human war, perhaps by the effects human war has on the harmony between nature and humans. This is a flower centric view, save only for the personification of human emotions in flowers.

Each "reading" gets less and less human centric. Is there, though, any reading that could express the equal standing and necessary harmony between humans and flowers without personifying the flowers? Perhaps, that is a new task for art in the Anthropocene.

Du Fu's poem is a very important first step on this task and has much to teach us. The poet uses the powers of Mandarin to let words jostle and play, creating frictions and sparks without any necessary resolution, perhaps suggesting that it is the frictions and sparks—the holding of determinacy at bay—the living with disharmony long enough to imagine harmony without certainty—that might, in the end, bring us to at least a partial resolution that will illuminate a path forward. Poetry and art are much better than academics at this, but academics better catch up, and soon, to make truth, and not lies, the stuff of poetry. A harmony between academics and art may be necessary to our survival as well.

William Carlos Williams

Du Fu's poem is strategically vague and thus allows multiple juxtapositions and interpretations that jostle together and can be compared and contrasted and even added to by the reader's imagination. Mandarin, and Chinese poetry in particular, is good at this. But much the same thing is done in lots of other poetry across various cultures. For example, below is a poem by William Carlos Williams, one of the poets who was central to the Imagist movement in American poetry.

The Red Wheelbarrow

so much depends
upon

a red wheel
barrow

glazed with rain
water

beside the white
chickens

At one level, this poem powerfully creates a specific set of sensations in one's imagination. Yet the poem is also vague—some have even called it cryptic. The reader must fill in *what* depends on a red wheel barrow glazed with rain water beside the white chickens.

People who are unfamiliar with the design features of imagist poetry and how they are meant to guide one's sensual experience of the poem sometimes interpret the poem as about the importance of manual labor, farming, or the relation between humans and nature. But such interpretations do not consider that it is not just a wheelbarrow, or rain water, or chickens on which so much depends—things than can remind us of labor, farming, or nature—it is the full range of images the poem tries to get you to create in your imagination on which so much depends.

The poem asks you to first imagine a red wheel. Then imagine a barrow, which switches the red from the wheel to the wheelbarrow, a new whole. Then you are asked to imagine the red wheelbarrow glazed with rain (painted with rain). Only then are you asked to imagine water and, thus, just as wheel became wheelbarrow, rain becomes rainwater, a new whole. Finally, you are asked to imagine something specific ("the") and white, but you know not what this specific thing is, so you live a second with just the feeling or imagination of the color white as a thing in its own right. Then you are asked to imagine chickens and, again, we get white transferred to white chickens, a new whole. As in sensation in life, things come apart and recombine as a dynamic process of sensing in time.

The poem is not made of words *per se*—signs—but of images that the reader must create. The poem is about sensation and the importance of the flow of sensations in time and the juxtapositions of sensations in space. It is trying to guide readers to find relevance in experiences in new ways, ways that attend to flow and juxtaposition of parts and wholes, where atmosphere decomposes into more discrete sensations that still remain, as they emerge, elements of atmosphere. The poem is about a way of being in the world, a way of paying attention, a way of using and building imagination, a way of using sensation and experience to build your mind and couple body and world.

This poem has frustrated many a student when it is taught in school (Teicher 2006). Many students' first response is to say it isn't a poem, that they have no idea what it means, that it is about farming or communism (because the wheelbarrow is red). This is because school often teaches poems as claims or statements, not as sounds and images.

The words in an imagist poem are not there as categories or concepts, but as guides for forming images and sensations in one's imagination and it is these images and sensations that are supposed to guide interpretation, not the words as items in a dictionary. Even "so much depends" is not a claim, but a suggestion that the reader treat the imaginative experience the poem leads to as important (relevant)—the basis of learning new ways to experience the world.

Students are taught to find "the meaning" of a text, to find its "deeper meaning." In poems as texts, they are often taught to search for "hidden meanings," as they are in religious texts. William Carols Williams's poem does not have a deep meaning, a hidden meaning, or really any meaning as claims at all. The meaning of the poem is the images and their flow and juxtaposition that the poem guides but does not determine. The poem suggests that sensation is its own meaning, not a symbol of some other "deeper" meaning. Just as Wittgenstein suggested that the meaning of a word is the uses we make of it in actual situations, so William Carlos Williams is suggesting that the meaning of a sensation or experience is how it feels *in situ*, what it does to us.

Vagueness in Prose

Vagueness can serve creativity, participation, and reflection not just in poetry. Wittgenstein, one of the most important modern philosophers, wrote his famous *Philosophical Investigations* in short paragraphs. His prose encourages readers to reflect on, and fill in meanings for, his rather bare statements. One such famous statement is: "If a lion could speak, we could not understand him"

(Wittgenstein 1953, p.223). This remark has triggered a great deal of discussion since Wittgenstein wrote it. Wittgenstein does not tell the reader explicitly what it means. He wants the reader, in the context of what else he has said in the *Investigations*, to process it, reflect on it, and explicate it in his or her own mind.

Wittgenstein, on our reading of the remark, is making a point we made when discussing language in Chapter 13. If the lion spoke English, of course we would understand what he said grammatically and literally. What we would have trouble understanding is how the lion contextualizes the meanings of his words in his experience in the world and not ours. The lion has what Wittgenstein calls a different "form of life" than humans—he lives in what we earlier called a different *umwelt* (experiential world). What would "love," "child," "death," "ethics," or "good" mean to a lion? If we were to have a real conversation with the lion, we would have to share his form of life or have him share ours, something hard to do when lions and humans sense the world in such different ways. Wittgenstein's remark, for us, makes us wonder, in the face of the hatred, violence, and conspiracy theories prevalent in American politics today, whether there are some humans who barely share a "form of life." Can they contextualize words in similar enough ways to really converse?

Christ in the New Testament often talks in parables. These are short vignettes that carry a moral meaning, but listeners must reflect on the parable—and contextualize it in their own lives—to fully appreciate its meaning. The great and revered philosopher and essayist Michel de Montaigne often wrote in ways that also required his readers to add their own meanings to his remarks based on their own experiences. For example, when he writes "If you press me to say why I loved him, I can say no more than because he was he, and I was I" (Bakewell 2010, loc 1561) readers may well at first find the remark cryptic and, then, on reflection, find it truthful and insightful in terms of their own experiences, experiences they now look at in a new way.

Of course, vagueness, in inviting listeners and readers to participate in meaning making, risks being misunderstood or being interpreted in ways we might not at all like. However, we cannot change people's minds by telling them what to believe, only by getting them to think new thoughts for themselves. Even more explicit prose needs to leave space for readers to reflect and put things in their own words.

Vagueness in Nature

The brain is a prediction engine (Eagleman 2020; Seligman, Railton, Baumeister & Sripada 2016). When you pick up your old ceramic coffee cup your brain predicts what your fingers will feel on the cup. If the prediction is correct, you will not be consciously aware you have made any predictions. And you will learn nothing new. You will go on as usual. There is no invitation to actively engage. You take the coffee cup in your grasp entirely for granted.

However, if the cup has a new crack in it and a finger falls on it, the brain's predictions will be wrong and you will immediately notice the crack, precisely because it contradicts your brain's predictions. This contradiction will be felt as a surprise, a form of learning. It is also an invitation to actively engage, for example to wonder how it happened, whether the cup will break further, or whether the coffee will leak out. Is the cup useless or has it now just got more character, the way an aging face sometimes does? Now you no longer take the coffee cup and your grasp on it for granted.

The first situation—when your unconscious predictions are correct—means you just accept things as they are. The second situation, where you are surprised, means you must wonder about things, figure things out, engage in interpretation, engage the world at hand with your imagination.

This second situation is vague in the way a poem often is. In William Carlos Williams poem discussed above, you must ask yourself why so much depends on a red wheelbarrow, because he does not tell you. In the act, you co-author the poem. So, too, when the coffee cup contradicts your expectations, you must ask yourself what has happened here and why and, in the act, not just accept the context you are in, but actively co-construct it. Is this a danger, a loss, or a new identity for my old coffee cup?

So, at one level, vagueness is surprise when your expectations (predictions) about the world fail and what you have heretofore taken for granted has to be dealt with anew. This brain principle has its analogue in art, in the way in which art can make things we have come to take for granted strange again. Art can make us see old things in new ways (and, thus, surprise us) and, in the act, re-program our brain.

Vagueness as surprise and making strange is also connected to the role of context in sensation and language. The more meaning a speaker leaves to assumptions and inferences to be made by the hearer, based on how the hearer construes their shared context, the more the hearer participates in and co-constructs the ongoing communication. Delacroix says the same thing about painting:

> Perhaps the only reason why the sketch for a work gives so much pleasure is that each beholder can finish it as he chooses (Wellington 1995, p. 183).

> ... imagination, a faculty that enjoys vagueness, expands freely, and embraces vast objects at the slightest hint (Wellington 1995, p. 216).

So, vagueness of the sort we are describing here is a way of creating surprise, context, making strange, sacrificing accuracy, all in the name of inviting engagement and participation in sensation, art, and communication (Keefe & Smith 1996). We will call this productive vagueness. Obviously, a lack of clarity done only in the service of creating confusion, deception, or due to ignorance is not the same thing. Productive vagueness creates what we will call a Zone of Engagement and Participation ("ZEP"). The ZEP is related to and inspired by Vygotsky's "ZPD"— Zone of Proximal Development (Vygotsky 1978). Teachers and designers who want to create a life-enhancing ZPD need first to create a ZEP. The ZPD involves the imposition, by "masters," of values, forms of interpretation, and practices on "apprentices." Without allowing for a ZEP—a realm of proactive and creative participation and freedom for the apprentice—the ZPD can become "colonizing." With a functioning ZEP, it becomes real teaching at its best.

Productive vagueness is what propels the human mind and body into action and engagement. Good learning experiences must be vague in part—there must be aspects that unsettle our expectations, our taken for granted certainties—so that we are forced to imaginatively engage and add new meanings—new associations—to our minds, the map of the world that is our brain.

When humans enter new experiences where they have limited knowledge of their surroundings, most information available to them is ambiguous, incomplete, even mysterious or threatening. This sets the human mind and body into an attentional, engaged, action-focused stance, puts them into the ZEP.

Vagueness as we are describing it here can be a state of surprise that seduces the human mind and body to enter the scene, whether it be in nature, in art, or in communication, and figure out its "composition," its patterns and connections and how they may relate to the self. Our imagination is energized to form new associations, to fill in the gaps that have arisen in our taken for granted world.

Our school system too often insists on "cold accuracy" ("facts") as the learning objective. Students are thereby pushed out of the ZEP, not into it. Facts are of little use on their own. They only have meaning and effect when we know how they hang together, what unifies them. Just as a great painter invites viewers to see the details of his or her painting as a coherent unity that gives rise to emotion, so, a great teacher invites students to see facts, information, and data as a coherent whole that gives rise to emotion, especially caring.

Vagueness in Complex Systems

Daniel Christian Wahl in his book *Designing Regenerative Cultures* (2016) has this to say about what he learned from his mentor Brian Goodwin, a founding member of the Santa Fe Institute for Complexity Studies:

> Brian taught me that any system that is constituted of three or more interacting variables is more appropriately described by non-linear mathematics and should be considered a complex dynamic system. One of the defining properties of complex dynamic systems is that they are fundamentally unpredictable and uncontrollable (beyond controlled laboratory conditions). Uncertainty and ambiguity are therefore fundamental characteristics of our lives and the natural world, including human culture, society and our economic systems (p. 41).

Complex systems are lived realities of vagueness. We must face uncertainty and ambiguity and, as with all productive vagueness, this leads to our active engagement and participation. Thus, Goodwin went on to say:

> We are not supposedly 'objective' observers outside these systems, trying to manipulate them more effectively; we are always participants. He suggested that the insights of complexity science invite us to shift our attitude and goal to our appropriate participation in these systems, as subjective, co-creative agents. Our goal should be to better understand the underlying dynamics in order to facilitate the emergence of positive or desirable properties – emerging through the qualities of relationships in the system… (p. 41)

As Wahl says, "complexity means befriending uncertainty and ambiguity" (p. 32), that is, being able and willing to enter the ZEP. Vagueness is both at the heart of the world as a complex system composed of complex systems and is the only hope we have of dealing with the systems that are now running out of control because of human greed, ignorance, and arrogance.

The brain is a web of associations (encoded in connections among neurons) that is our model of the world. This model is used by the brain to continuously make predictions, consciously and quite often unconsciously. It is the failure of these predictions that lead to surprise and uncertainty that is a form of productive vagueness. Entering the ZEP can then lead to changes in our model of the world. Being wrong is often more useful than being right.

CHAPTER 17

DELACROIX AND VAGUENESS

In this chapter we turn to a painter who has a great deal to tell us about the power of vagueness done right. Eugène Delacroix (April 26, 1798 – August 13, 1863) was one of the earliest and most important Romantic painters. He deeply influenced the later Impressionists by his dynamic brushstrokes and how he worked with color within the overall composition of his paintings (Allard & Fabre 2018; Jobert 2018). His disdain for realism and the stress he put on paintings as evocative of emotion and imagination—as well as his ideas about art as teaching people new ways to see the world—have a kinship with the Imagists, as well.

Connections and Harmony

Delacroix, for years, kept journals of his thoughts and daily life (Wellington 1995). The journals are, at one level, a fascinating intimate look into the everyday life of a unique artist in the 19th Century and, at another level, they explicate Delacroix's ideas about art and the world. These ideas stress vagueness and the imagination. Delacroix's ideas about painting as an art form are centered on the power of the sketch and the dilemmas of the final work, which should never be fully finished. Below is a sketch and the final painting of Delacroix's famous painting "Liberty Leading the People":

Figure 10. Sketch for The 28th of July: Liberty Leading the People (https://en.thevalue.com/articles/christie-london-delacroix-liberty-leading-the-people)

Figure 11. Eugène Delacroix The 28th of July: Liberty
Leading the People, 1830. (Louvre Museum)

We will develop Delacroix's ideas about art here using a good deal of his actual words from his journals. Delacroix argues that what we see are not things but things in relationships to each other:

> When we look at the objects around us, whether in a landscape or an interior, we notice that between each of them there is a kind of connection produced by the surrounding envelope of air and the various reflections which, as it were, cause each separate object to be part of a general harmony. (p. 371)

These connections—this harmony—are ensembles of sensation where, like a musical ensemble, the whole is more than sum of the parts. But what makes the ensemble interesting and relevant to the beholder? Delacroix tells us that "In painting … proper justice is done … to what the soul finds inwardly moving in objects that are known through the senses alone (pp. 6-7). So, the ensemble is interesting to the extent that it moves the beholder's soul, whether in the world or in art. The term "soul" here is interesting. Many cultures have taken the soul to be the "breath of life", the vital force that distinguishes living things from non-living ones.

But, then, why do we need painting, or any other art for that matter? Why is sensation and experience in the world not enough? The answer is that artists design experiences for us that teach us how to sense and care—find things relevant—in new ways. The artist does not need to discover new ideas. Delacroix argues that what inspires an artist is not new ideas "but their obsession with the idea that what has already been said is still not enough" (p. 41):

> You who know that there is always something new, show it to others in the
> things they have hitherto failed to appreciate. Make them feel that they have
> never before heard the song of the nightingale, or been aware of the vastness
> of the sea. (p. 43)

This point is similar to the notions of "defamiliarization" or "making strange"—"ostranenie" in Russian—developed by the Russian Formalist Victor Shklovsky in his 1917 essay "Art as Device" (Shklovsky 1965). Shklovsky argued that the purpose of art is to make us sense anew things we have come to take for granted. To see them again as strange and, thereby, come to sense them and feel about them in new ways and even question our prior taken-for-granted knowledge (familiarity).

Delacroix sees the figures and objects in a painting, which seem to the viewer to be actual things, as a "solid bridge to support [the viewer's] imagination as it probes the deep, mysterious emotions of which these forms are, so to speak, the hieroglyph" (p. 213). Sensation in the world is always about melding what we sense in the outer world with the feelings and emotions these sensations give rise to in our inner world as they excite our imagination. Good artists see "nature in their own way" (p. 42) and help others, through their art, a form of designed experience, sense the world in a new way that enhances their imaginations and amplifies their emotions.

The artist seeks to design a new sensual experience and connect it to new feelings and emotions and, in turn, help the viewer to bring these new sensibilities back to experience in the world and the formation of his or her web of associations. The artist helps build our minds (our web of associations, our model of the world) anew.

Delacroix's Theory

How can art do this? Delacroix explicates how painting, in his view, does it and then compares this with how other art forms do it. His theory of painting is based on an ingenious comparison of the artist's initial sketch and the final painting. He points out that a sketch for a work—the initial rough drawing from which the painting eventually comes--gives us pleasure because "each beholder can finish it as he chooses" (p. 183). This is because the sketch is vaguer than the final painting and, thus, leaves more room for the active work of imagination on the part of the beholder:

> Here we come back, as always, to the question of which I have spoken before: the finished work compared with the sketch—the great edifice when only the large guiding lines are visible and before the finishing and coordinating of the various parts has given it a more settled appearance and therefore limited the effect on our imagination, a faculty that enjoys vagueness, expands freely, and embraces vast objects at the slightest hint. (p. 216)

For Delacroix the "first and most important thing in painting is the contour" (p. 28), the overall gestalt or ensemble of the painting's elements. The sketch is the highest expression of the artist's idea not just because it suppresses less relevant details, but because it subordinates the details to "the great sweeping lines that come before everything else in making the impression" (p. 239).

Delacroix is not saying that the details or elements of the sketch or final painting don't matter—indeed, he argues that such details "make up the composition and are the very warp and weft of the picture itself" (p. 239). Rather, he is arguing that details have to emerge out of the overall composition—the harmony of elements in relation to each other—and do so in a way that never leaves them isolated from the set of relationships from which they have emerged and to which they return as the beholder sustains his or her sensual attention to a painting.

Given the power of the sketch, then, why bother finishing the painting? As the painter adds more details to the painting—rendering it less vague—the painter risks losing the proactive work the beholder does in filling in aspects of the sketch based on his or her imagination. The painter risks dominating the beholder's imagination in the way didactic teaching often does and, in the act, leaving the beholder unmotivated to proactively process the painting:

> … an artist does not spoil a picture by finishing it, but when he abandons the vagueness of the sketch he reveals his personality more fully, thereby displaying the full scope of his talent, but also its limitations. (p. 183)

The art of the final painting is a test of the artist's skill. The artist must suppress certain details and enhance others—while still leaving a degree of vagueness (so the goal is not "realism")—in the service of a gestalt that subordinates the details but in ways that enhance them as members of an ensemble and not as isolated units. It is a very difficult balancing act in which the artist seeks to fill out the sketch with his own imagination while still leaving room for the creative operation of the viewer's imagination.

To that end, Delacroix talks about the need "to make sacrifices," which he calls "the first of all principles" (p. 425). By sacrifices Delacroix means leaving some things out, not seeking accuracy as if it was the ultimate truth. He means putting in and enhancing only elements that make the composition alive as an ensemble, a whole from which an effect emerges in the viewer that connects sensation and imagination in a compelling new way:

> In the works of the Dutch and Flemish masters ... you notice ... this art of concealing sacrifices made for the delight of the imagination - a faculty that quickly grasps an artist's meaning and understands even what he does not make it manifest. (p. 398)

Delacroix tells us he formerly had been "haunted by this passion for accuracy that most people mistake for truth" (p. 210). He learned that "absolute truth can give an impression contrary to truth, or at least contrary to that relative truth at which art must aim" (pp. 280-281). Truth in art is relative because it is always relative to the perspective—the unique way of sensing the world, the new aspects the artist finds in old things and ideas—of the artist. Delacroix suggests, as well, that whatever truth we find in sensation and experience in the world is relative to our perspectives, to our webs of association—our capacity for imagination and emotion—that we bring to our new experiences based on our past experiences, some of which may well have been designed experiences such as one of Delacroix's sketches or final paintings.

Delacroix's views on relative truth remind us what the great physicist of quantum mechanics, Werner Heisenberg (1958) had to say about absolute and relative truth: "What we observe is not nature itself, but nature exposed to our method of questioning" (p. 58).

Delacroix also has interesting things to say about how different art forms work. For example, in music or literature there is no sketch as there often is in painting. On the other hand, he argues that "nothing can compare with the emotion which music inspires. ... For its eternal honour we ought to reverse Figaro's remark, 'Whatever we cannot sing, we speak'." (p. 287). Instead of the vagueness of a sketch carried over into a final painting that retains enough vagueness to inspire imaginative participation while expressing a yet fuller view of the artist's own imagination, music dispenses all together with images or signs (like words)—with what we might call "content." Music designs sensations that speak directly to the hearer's emotions and imagination. How this works is a topic I will take up later.

In writing, whether prose or poetry, Delacroix argues that there needs to be "a chain of argument, an entirety, arising out of the birth of one idea from another"

(p. 235). This "entirety" is the equivalent of the painter's overall composition, the whole that has properties—and an effect—that is not the sum of its parts, but is the active set of relationships into which they enter.

Here is what Delacroix has to say about reading versus viewing a painting:

> Reading any book that is not entirely frivolous means having to work; it causes a certain amount of fatigue. The author seems to wrestle against criticism. He argues, and one can argue with him in return.
>
> The works of painters and sculptors, on the other hand, are all of one piece, like the works of nature. The author does not appear in them, is not in touch with us like the writer or orator. He offers, as it were, a tangible reality, yet one that is full of mystery. He does not need to lure us into giving him our attention, for the good passages in his work can be seen at once. (pp. 277-278)

Delacroix is here stressing writing as conversation between people—which means that writing must be vague enough to allow for the reader's mind to fill in some of the details imaginatively and to fuel a response. The art in writing is, as we saw earlier, to use words in a way that leads the reader to give them situational meanings that create new associations and emotions (and a response). Writing is painting with signs, with abstractions that become rendered as specific realities in the reader's imagination. In this sense, one might say that good writing is always a sketch, never a finished product.

CHAPTER 18

FREE WILL

The issues we have discussed in this book raise concerns central to philosophy, history, and psychology. Yet, too, these concerns are crucial to humans as they live their everyday lives. They are concerns where research and lived reality come together. Too often academics and everyday life are separated to the detriment of both.

When we see how much of what humans feel, think, and do stems from unconscious and social forces that they have little control over, problems arise over what it means to say humans have free will, that they are responsible for all their choices. When we realize that humans are social animals, but often chafe against (sometimes violently) social, institutional, and governmental constraints, problems arise about what "freedom" is and means. Humans have long faced the problem that some people's freedom is bought at the price of others.

The work from research on neuroscience, evolutionary biology, and embodied theories of learning we have used in this book speaks to concerns humans have dealt with since they became human. We will deal with one such concern in this chapter: The problem of free will. In the face of the many unconscious processes leading to human feeling, decision, and action and the many social forces acting on humans beyond their control, how responsible are humans for the choices they make? Do they make such choices "freely" and what does this mean?

The issue of free will is real and important in human life and society. There are a great many other issues like it, issues like war and peace; civil disobedience; religion and government; justice and mercy; individuality and culture; cultural diversity; the meaning of life, sickness, suffering, and death; and the nature of beauty, morality, and the good life. Such issues have fueled intellectual debate across the ages. And they have impacted on—and been part of debates among—everyday people in their everyday lives for ages, as they attempt to survive, let alone flourish in the world.

Such issues were traditionally taken to be part of education in the broad sense, in the sense that Socrates meant when he praised living an examined life. They are not so taken, for the most part, today. Today, many people think living an examined life—reflecting on the sorts of issues we have mentioned—as the preserve of an academic elite who they view as largely irrelevant. And, in turn, many celebrate those who live their everyday lives with little reflective examination of such issues as does the well-known neo-conservative writer Norman Podhoretz (1999):

> Such, I think, is the situation with most people. They go from day to day, trying to earn a living and to raise their kids as best they can in accordance with the morals, customs, and traditions they have inherited from their own parents or have absorbed almost unknowingly from the culture around them. The ideas that underlie their way of life are mostly taken for granted and remain unexamined—luckily for them, since the biggest lie ever propagated by a philosopher was Socrates' self-aggrandizing assertion that the unexamined life is not worth living. (p. 80)

We disagree. We, like Podhoretz (ironically), have chosen to lead examined lives. We do not believe Socrates was lying. We believe that those who fail to lead examined lives, especially in complex, fast-changing, dangerous times like those we live in today, imperil others even if they believe with Podhoretz that they do not imperil themselves (but, in our view, they do).

It must be said, though, that many of the schools we have today are perfectly fit for those who think leading an examined life is an elitist lie. These schools are full of claimed "facts" offered without any deep background, context, or examination, "facts" forgotten by students not long after they are assessed. On the other hand, it is an interesting question as to what a school for leading an examined life would look like, especially in schools as politicized as those in the United States.

Now, it is interesting that some good media today, including some popular culture media, engages its audience with issues key to a real education and leading an examined life. Not all viewers take up this invitation, but many do as they enter affinity spaces (Gee 2018) on the internet and engage in reflection, explication, critique, debate, and arguments about their own views. AOT engages its viewers with just such issues. It grounds these in sensation, images, actions, and drama, but always in ways that allow viewers to accumulate, through these sensations, actions, and drama, enough thinking and reflection to examine their lives, their societies, and their histories. The internet is chock full of the thoughts, reflections, and debates viewers have been led to by AOT. And these viewers bring these thoughts, reflections, and debates back to their viewing and reviewing AOT—and other media—as they begin to view and think about media more like designers and producers than consumers (Zhang 2022). And, we think this is all to the good for them, for us, and for society.

In this chapter we will look at the issue of free will, an issue central to any reflection—academic or in everyday life—on human life in society and history. Here we will first discuss this issue academically. Then, in the next chapter, we will turn to look at how AOT deals with the issue of free will. AOT, as popular media, can create a bridge between academic discussions and everyday life reflections on issues like free will and many others.

What we have said in this book about the nature of living things and humans in particular makes the issue of free will complex, problematic, and in need of thought and reflection. We will reflect on this issue analytically here and, in the next chapter, we will look at how AOT deals with it dramatically.

It is common in academic writing to state one's views categorically rather than to continue to point out that our claims are what we believe and are not true just because we claim them. And we do this in this book. Of course, in reality, academic claims are social. They are based on arguments and evidence others have offered, not just ourselves. However, just as AOT viewers are free to reflect on and debate how AOT deals with important issues like free will, freedom, religion, and government, our readers are free to reflect on and debate our claims and should do so. The difference is that, in the case of AOT, readers can and regularly do reflect and debate on social media sites that do not require them to be an academic—to have credentials—to participate. AOT—and other media like it—is a form of public pedagogy in a way that academics rarely is.

The Issue of Free Will

The idea of freedom has fueled philosophical, political, and religious debates for thousands of years, debates which have never really been settled. There are two major problems associated with freedom. One is the problem of free will (Gazzaniga & Steven 2004; O'Connor 2022). Do humans have free will? Are the choices they make freely made? Do they bear full responsibility for them? Whatever the answer to this question is, it is clear that society and courts of law are, in most cases, based on the belief that humans have free will and bear responsibility for their choices.

The other major problem about freedom is the problem of constraint. Many people believe that human beings have an inherent right not to be coerced by others, individuals, institutions, or societies to act against their own wishes or interests. The key issue here, though, is how free (unconstrained) should humans be left. Obviously, one human's desire to act can constrain or even take away another human's freedom to act. To live in a community and a society, all humans must accept some degree of constraints on their freedom. Of course, though, through history, powerful individuals and states have often gone too far in forcing people to do what they want them to do for their own interests (Hiruta 2021).

The two freedom problems are related, of course. People are not making free choices if they are forced by others to act in ways they do not wish. However, the problem of free will is really about whether people have free will when no one is forcing them to act and when their actions have good or bad consequences. Do they, then, deserve credit for the good and blame for the bad?

Choice and Free Will

Anyone would agree that if someone is forced to do something "against their will" they are not free to choose. When we are not forced to do things, we humans believe we are free to choose. When we choose, we think we "willed it," though the notion of "will" is a hard concept philosophically and neurologically speaking. It is not clear what and where the will is.

It turns out that forces we are unaware of often incline humans to act and these inclinations, in some sense, force us to act as we do. Human action (as all animal action) is a product of complex environmental and social interactions, most of which we have no conscious awareness of and which even science is often confounded by. Only a small part of our brain is conscious and most of what goes on in our brain and body leading to our feelings, beliefs, and actions is not open to conscious awareness (Gazzaniga 2011, 2018). Yet the small—and poorly informed—conscious part of our brain (sometimes called "the Interpreter," Gazzaniga 2011) confidently confabulates and firmly believes that we have made free and informed choices.

When I choose to have coffee in the morning, I have no real knowledge of how much this choice was "forced" by habit and the chemical state of my organs at the time. At a deeper level, choices are driven by feelings. If we have no feelings about something—say, for example, which of three hats to wear—then we have no basis on which to choose. Feelings, however, arise before cognition and guide it and evaluate its choices (Damasio, A. & Carvalho 2011; Damasio 2018). And the sources of our feelings are very often beyond our conscious awareness.

When I choose who, among several choices, to befriend, I may have all sorts of conscious ideas about what made me choose one person over another. However, I have little knowledge of all the unconscious forces, forces based on my past experiences, my web of associations, and the internal conditions of my body and brain, that have given rise, in a specific situation at a specific time, to feelings that affected my choice (guided the choice and will assess it based on how my feelings are affected as I get to know the person).

When we say that we chose something, we mean that the conscious rational part of us chose it. We thought it over, however quickly, and made a decision. Yet, in many cases, our past experiences, the context we are in, the social influences operating on us, and the current state of our biology guide our choice. And what we think of as rational deciding is often a story we tell ourselves to make the best sense, based on limited knowledge, of what is happening (Gazzaniga 2011, 2018).

Now, while there are reams of work in philosophy and theology on free will, at a practical level the concept does not matter much except when we think about right or wrong. If I choose a blue hat over a red one not much rides on whether this was a rational choice I made or a product of my past experience combined with my current state. What matters when we talk about choice— what the problem of free will is really about—is when we make choices that can be right or wrong and whether and how much responsibility we bear for the results of those choices.

This idea—that free will exists in the sense that humans bear responsibility for the results of their choices (deserve credit for good and blame for bad)—is not one most humans or society can easily give up. And, yet, here, too, when someone has done something harmful to others, it may well be the case that forces outside of their conscious control played a much bigger role than "will" (rational choice).

In reality, "free choice" is a prosocial notion necessary for the existence of society (and law) and not an empirical reality at the level of "nature." Without people accepting that they make free choices and are responsible for the outcomes of those choices (within limits), society could not exist, nor could collective action.

We may accept that, in a sense, what people do is the product of complex interactions that go well beyond "will," but still demand that society apportion reward and blame (and punishment) to keep us safe and society functioning.

Language Games: What Does Free Will Amount To?

Wittgenstein, the most influential philosopher of the 20th Century, argued that words are best understood as names for what he called "language games" (Wittgenstein 1953). A language game is a way a given social group uses a word or set of words to organize and carry out specific practices in the world. It is a way of "moving on" in the act of living, surviving, and, hopefully, flourishing. Words are not pictures, descriptions, or representations of the world, but are "pieces" in a social game. This is a much better way to look at words like "choice" and "free will" than debate their realities philosophically or scientifically.

Take the word "democracy" as an example. At an abstract structural level (the level of grammar), it means something like "representative government." But, in actual situations of use, we have to make decisions about what, here and now, the term will mean or, better yet, do. Take a situation where people can vote only if they own land, something that used to be true in England and America. Is this a democracy? There is no answer to this question apart from what people, as a social group, decide. What they decide are the "rules of the game," a game that involves both how we use words and how we behave. People who do not want to play by the rules can make their own rules, though they thereby form their own "discourse community." People can fight over the rules or separate over them.

The same thing is true of the words "free will" and "choice." Catholics argue that seven years old is the "age of reason." At seven and beyond, children are guilty of their sins and must confess them and avoid them or pay the spiritual price. Others do not see seven-year-olds this way. Some societies treat people with low IQs as criminally responsible for their deeds, others do not. Some groups see ignorance as an excuse for making a bad or illegal choice, others do not.

Is a drug addict responsible for his or her misdeeds done while drugged or only the original choice to become addicted? Was that original happening a free choice? What about if the drug addict was the victim of serious childhood trauma? Since we can rarely know the full outcome of our choices, how responsible are we for those outcomes? What can it mean to say we chose those outcomes, many of which might be unintended or even unwished for? What about the cases where we have no good idea about how to act but must act anyway?

Different social groups and different societies create—and pass on as habits—different ways to organize how they talk about choices and free will and how they behave in regard to these notions. They create, play, and sometimes revise (or abandon) different language games as they "play" with these words.

You do not have to believe free will is "real" to engage in language games involving words like "choice," "free will," and "responsibility." After all, almost everyone is in these language games whether they like it or not. Balls and strikes aren't "real" outside the game of baseball, but they have real effects for those who play the game.

But now we face an important paradox. If choice and free will are ways with words to accomplish things socially and different groups can create and operate by different language games, how does a social group or society choose the rules of the game, the sorts of games they will play with words like "choice" and "free will"? Such a "choice" is not made by any one individual and a great many people playing the games aren't aware that they are playing a game. They often think their words describe or represent a reality even though different groups use different words or the same words in different ways.

Of course, how we play language games is not so much the product of choices as it is social forces stemming in complex ways from a myriad of interactions among people and institutions in history. Nonetheless, at the level of philosophy, theology, or science we can argue over what would be "best" for people or societies in terms of language games and their concomitant social practices, though we have to specify what we mean by "best."

Existentialism

Many humans have long been aware that the idea that we make free choices and live with their consequences is a stress inducing thing in a complex world where we often have little control over things. Different philosophical schools and different religions have spoken to this issue in different ways. We will consider two of them here. In this section we will discuss Jean Paul Sartre's form of existential philosophy and in the next a more social view of the dilemmas humans face in dealing with freedom.

Many people are aware they are making choices in a world so vast and complex—and with a self so formed by forces (biological, social, cultural, historical, and political) beyond their knowledge and control—that they feel adrift. No philosopher spoke to this feeling more strongly that the existentialist philosopher Jean Paul Sartre (Aronson 1980, 2004; Reynolds & Renaudie 2022). Sartre said, faced with this profound dilemma, it is, nonetheless, up to humans to choose the principles on the basis of which they will live their lives.

Humans are "condemned" to freedom, according to Sartre. With every specific choice we make, we commit to the principles that are implicit in our choices. To be "authentic," in Sartre's terms, is to live up to those principles, come what may. Even choosing not to choose is a choice. Authenticity is to recognize that making choices, despite all the complexities involved in the very idea, is inescapable.

Sartre argues that this plight leads humans to feel anguish, a form of solitude in the face of having to decide and live with the principles inherent in our personal decisions. This is how humans create of themselves a consistent principled person. For Sartre, we live in a form of solitude because each of us is an island of our own creation in the face of anguish and the complexity of life. Values—the principles by which we live—are a human creation, not facts built into the nature of things. They are not "objective;" they are created by a "free and lonely self" as Iris Murdoch put it.

Clare Mac Cumhaill and Rachel Wiseman (2022, p. 150) say the following about Sartre in their book *Metaphysical Animals*:

> Rather than seeking to align ourselves to some external measure of goodness and value, each of us, individually, is the source of an image of the human as we believe it should be. When each individual chooses for himself, Sartre explained, 'he chooses for all men.' In choosing he 'creates himself as he wills to be,' and so endorses 'an image of man such as he believes he ought to be.' We must therefore always ask ourselves: would I through my choices legislate for all mankind?

We will see in the next section, that, from Aristotle on, many philosophers have argued that the ways humans ought to behave—what is right and wrong—is to be found in the "form of life" of humans as a biological species, in human nature. However, Sartre argues that "existence" comes before" essence."

Essence is what we are in terms of our nature as humans, existence is the choices we make. We do not act out of our nature, we create ourselves. This is, Sartre argued, "the first principle of existentialism" that "man is nothing else but that which he makes of himself" (Sartre 1946, p. 349). Individual humans create values through their own choices and actions, each creates their own set of principles, their own ethics, which he or she takes to be applicable to all in the sense that this is their "image of man"—of humans—as they take them to be.

Sartre was writing during and after World War II and the fall of France to the Nazis. Existentialism of this sort has always appealed to those living in and through crisis. In such circumstances, we humans have a profound desire to create new meanings and new views of ourselves and those around us, and to believe that free choice exists and can give rise to transformation, if only of ourselves.

The philosopher and novelist Iris Murdoch (1970), who admired Sartre but later in life disagreed with him, argued that ultimately his view of humans, though courageous and inspiring, was flawed. Benjamin Lipscomb in his book *The Women Are Up to Something* (2022, p. 125) explains Murdoch's view this way:

> We are not as solitary and self-possessed as his [Sartre's] early writings suggested. Rather, we are (as she would put it later) "egocentric system[s] of quasi-mechanical energy, largely determined by [our] own individual history[ies], whose natural attachments are sexual, ambiguous, and hard for the subject to understand or control." Philosophical ethics, she thought, must theorize the "fat relentless ego" and determine what techniques might enable us to overcome it. But already she knew that the way out of a controlling obsession is not to courageously assert your freedom. Changing your life is more like steering a ship or building a habit than like taking a single, fateful step. It is hard, but in a different way.

Human Flourishing

Sartre looks at each individual as if he or she is facing the world alone. But humans are social animals. This is both a good and bad thing. Humans are often so influenced by their social groups that they believe things in order to go along with the group, not because they have any real evidence for them. On the other hand, work on collective intelligence has shown that groups of people (Malone 2018; Sunstein & Hastie 2015), if organized in the right way, can act more intelligently than individuals or groups organized in the wrong ways.

Collectively intelligent groups have the following features:

1. They are composed of people with diverse life experiences, people who have learned different things from their experiences
2. Each person inputs their opinions freely; no one holds back

3.   People in the group listen to each other and seek to take each other's per-
     spectives
4.   Who speaks and what is decided is not influenced (or influenced as little as
     possible) by status and power

Even though each person in a collectively intelligent group is, like all of us, prone to error, biases, and a lack of knowledge faced with the complexity of the world and of themselves, collective intelligence works. It works because, in such groups, people have different biases and weaknesses and, to an extent, these biases and weaknesses cancel each other out and what remains is about as good as we humans can do in reaching truth. This is how science at its best works and it is how humans can engage in collective projects that enhance their individual minds.

When we think about collective intelligence, we can imagine groups coming together to decide the basis for ethical decisions. Each person in the group may well have a different religion and some may have none, so a specific religion or religion in general cannot decide the matter if people are to live with diverse others. What can decide the matter though may be something many religions support and that many non-religious people will accept as well. So, what could this be? It is something Aristotle offered us as an answer long ago, an answer that modern scientific work on humans as kinds of creatures supports.

Ethics and Flourishing

The words "morality" and "ethics" are used in overlapping ways. They both have to do with "right and wrong" and "good and bad." Some people associate morality more with personal or religious values and ethics with standards set by communities and institutions. We will just use the word "ethics," but readers can replace the word with "morality" if they like.

Many people have believed that what is right and wrong is determined by their religion. Others, realizing that different people and different religions dif-fer over what they think is right and wrong, believe that ethical claims are just opinions and are not related to any facts or empirical claims. Still others have believed that ethical claims are facts, that certain things are objectively wrong and right, though they differ over what the empirical basis is for these claims. One basis some have appealed to is a human inborn sense of right and wrong, a sense that all humans share when they are free of forces that seek to control or coerce them to do otherwise.

Aristotle essentially gave a biological answer to the question as to what is right and wrong, good and bad (Lipscomb 2020, p. 167). Aristotle argued that each type of animal has its own characteristic nature, its own way of being in the world in ways that allow it to survive and, at best, flourish. So, we can say that what is good for humans is what allows them to flourish as individuals and social groups given the sort of creatures they are. We can also argue that humans are not going to flourish if other living beings on earth cease to exist and, so, human flourishing requires other life to flourish as well.

We saw at the beginning of this book that we can measure how much any creature is flourishing by measuring their allostatic load, that is the amount of damage, if any, that stress is doing to their organs, including their brains. If humans are to flourish, then we must create conditions where the human form of life, set by the conditions of human evolution and biology, can thrive.

In history, some human groups have sought flourishing at the cost of other groups. This obviously is not conducive to human flourishing as a whole. Diminishing others' flourishing as the cost of our own will, in the end, bring us back to a "state of nature"—where the strong dominate the weak—in which even our own flourishing is imperiled and eventually diminished. Aristotle wanted to work out the set of traits that enable humans to live vibrant lives, to flourish. He realized that to do this required drawing on work on biology, psychology, anthropology, human development, and, too, we now realize, work on evolution.

Of course, others do not have to agree that the basis of right and wrong is human flourishing, though, in a sense, this is what religions have always argued even if they have held different perspectives on the nature of such flourishing. However, we can say this: if other people believe that your flourishing is not a relevant consideration (though there may be other considerations at play as well) of what it is right or wrong for them to do, you should cease to deal with them as a matter of self-interest. This is, we can say, a basic principle for any "ethical contract" among humans who consent to live together. Religions and other systems of ideas can add to this principle, but to deny it as a basic principle is to enter a state of warfare, the struggle of each against the other.

There are religions that have argued that people's flourishing in this life does not matter because an after-life exists where people will be happy. These views, in history, have often been used as arguments that people lower on the social

hierarchy or oppressed by those in power ought to accept their positions do-
cilely because their rewards will come later. In its denial of the basic principle,
however, it is dangerous for those who believe they have but one life. The same
is true of leaders who have argued that dying for the noble cause of the dominance of a given nation will bring one subsequent glory. This is not to say that
there are not causes worth dying for, but only to say that these causes ought to
be about enhancing flourishing for humanity as a whole and life on earth, not
diminishing it.

The idea that flourishing is the basis of ethics is a start to conversations about
ethics, not the end of them. Once humans are flourishing, we can argue over
how to best organize society and our language games in society. The basic principle of ethics has, at least, been upheld. If few are flourishing, allostatic needs
kick in at the level of brute survival and people are ill equipped for thinking and
collaborating in collectively intelligent ways.

CHAPTER 19

AOT ON FREEDOM

In the last chapter we discussed free will in academic terms. AOT deals with the issue of free will, as well, but embeds the issue in images and other sensations and in actions and dramatic storytelling. Over the course of many episodes, AOT uses these images, sensations, actions, and its storytelling to encourage questioning and reflection at the individual level and on social media of different types at the social level. At the social level, this amounts to a public public pedagogy where viewers engage in discussion, debate, and teaching that can be, at their best, exemplars of education in the broad sense.

Example: To Bite, or Not to Bite

We are now going to look at one set of events in AOT about making choices. These events constitute one coherent story but are spread out across several episodes in AOT. We will first lay out some background for the events, then we give a transcript of the verbal parts of the events, and, finally, discuss the implications of how AOT deals with choice.

Levi Ackerman

Captain Levi Ackerman, though short in stature, is the strongest solider in the Survey Corps, the only part of the military that ventures outside the walls to fight Titans. Soon after he was drafted into the Survey Corps by Commander Erwin Smith, a man who became his longtime friend, he lost two close friends in a battle with Titans. He had felt his friends were not yet ready for battle and, so, he discouraged them from joining the fight. His friends told him not to make the decision for them and to have faith in them. Levi relented and, to his deep regret, they were both killed. After the battle, seeing Levi's sorrow and regret, Commander Erwin says to Levi:

> Stop. Don't regret it. A regretful memory will dull your next decision. Then, you'll probably try to leave it up to someone else. All that awaits you then is death. Nobody knows what the outcome will be. A decision first has meaning when it's the basis for the following decision. (Attack on Titan Original Animation DVD: No Regrets)

For Levi, these words point to a painful truth about the fundamental nature of human existence—one Sartre focused on—that humans often must live with the anguish that comes from the results of their choices and yet accept those results and move on to make new choices.

Erwin Smith

After the Survey Corps and the government of Paradis Island discover that Eren can turn into an intelligent Titan, they fear that he may use his Titans powers—which he has not yet learned to control fully—against them. Some argue that they should kill him. However, Commander of the Survey Corps Erwin Smith believes Eren could be a super weapon for Paradis. Erwin suggests that they test Eren to see if he can learn to control his Titan form and fight safely on their side.

Erwin tasks Levi with choosing four elite soldiers to form a Special Operations Squad to guard and protect Eren and to experiment on his Titan powers. Levi's squad will take Eren out with the Survey Corps on their next expedition. If he can help with their mission, he will become a trusted member of the Survey Corps and, perhaps, become the salvation of Paradis with his Titan powers.

As these events are unfolding, Commander Erwin Smith has come to believe that the Survey Corps has a traitor in their midst. One of his soldiers, he believes, is—like Eren—a human who can turn into an intelligent Titan and is working in the interest of some unknown enemy. Actually, unbeknownst to Erwin, the Survey Corps harbors several traitors. Each of these are Marleyan spies that have infiltrated the Survey Corps and each is a human who can turn into an intelligent Titan. They are an advance team meant to check out Paradis Island and the Survey Corps in preparation for a Marleyan invasion of the island.

Through a process we cannot fully describe here, as it involves multiple details in many episodes of AOT, Erwin has hypothesized that the traitor is someone who can turn into a Titan. Furthermore, Erwin assumes the traitor will pursue Eren and be a source of grave danger to him. It is crucial in the scenes we will discuss below about choice that Erwin has reached his assumptions not by definitive evidence and a well-worked out logic, but by intuition. He is, as is said, "going with his gut."

The key question for the soldiers Erwin will lead into battle will be whether they can trust his intuition about the traitor in their midst and the military plan it has given rise to when he gives them orders based on it. He is, after all, a massively well experienced, courageous, and competent leader, but he could be wrong and he cannot fully explicate the logic behind his intuition and the plan to which it gives rise.

Based on his intuition, Erwin plans to carry out a secret mission on the next Survey Corps expedition outside the walls, the one where he will also take Eren out as part of Levi's squad. On this expedition, he will bring along a new weapon that can be used to trap Titans. He suspects the traitor who can turn into a Titan will appear and pursue Eren. He will use Eren to lure the Titan into the trap. Once the Titan is captured, he will be able to find out which of his soldiers is inside the Titan. Because he does not want to alert the traitor to his plans, and does not know who it is, he is not able to share what he knows with any others except for a very few of his fellow soldiers he is certain are not the traitor, one of whom is Levi. Thus, as his plan unfolds, most of the troops will be confused as to why they are doing as they are.

Before the expedition, Erwin trains the Scouts on a new formation, one that he hopes will work for his plan. They will be spread out on their horses across a great distance in a semicircular formation. Scouts across the formation will use flare signals to warn of any approaching Titans. Eren and the rest of the Levi Squad will be at the center rear of the formation, the most secure position. Most of the troops will assume this is a typical expedition outside the walls to assess the Titan situation.

Soon after the expedition begins, a massive and powerful Female Titan, leading a horde of unintelligent Titans, appears at the right flank of the formation, slaughtering many soldiers. Thanks to smoke signals from flare guns, Erwin becomes aware of the chaos on his right flank and believes it is probably being caused by the Titan he is trying to draw out. When he reaches the borders of a great forest, he gives the order that only the soldiers escorting the wagon carrying the special weapon and Levi Squad are to enter the forest. All the other Survey Corps forces are to go around on either side of the forest and stay on the edges outside it. This causes a good deal of confusion among the soldiers about what is going on. After all, they have lost their commander and are left to face the horde of Titans that are coming from the right flank. Meanwhile they have no idea what is going to happen inside the forest.

As Erwin suspected would happen, the Female Titan eventually rushes into forest after Eren. She has discovered Eren's position though an interaction with one of her fellow traitors in the Survey Corps who has figured out where Eren has been placed in the formation. As she comes up to and chases Levi's squad, Levi's soldiers—seeing her path of destruction—ask Levi to let them engage her in battle. Levi, knowing the goal is to lead her into a trap, refuses and tells everyone to continue moving forward. Eren does not understand why the best Titan killers in the Survey Corps are being ordered to keep going and, in the process, abandoning their comrades from the escort troops being attacked and killed by the Female Titan.

Levi successfully leads the Female Titan into the trap where she is captured as a myriad of metal rods, fired by the new weapon, fix her to the ground. Levi tells his team to move on by themselves in the forest while he and Erwin deal with the Female Titan and try to get whoever is inside the Titan to come out. As they seek to attack the Female Titan, she lets out a deafening scream that draws hordes of unintelligent Titans to her from outside the forest. They surround her and begin to eat her Titan form, In the chaos the traitor inside (Annie) escapes with her Omni-Directional Mobility Gear, the gear that allows Survey Corps soldiers to fight in the air and not just on the ground. She will now blend in with all the other troops and yet be able to attack them or even turn back into a Titan. She eventually finds Eren and his squad mates and begins to attack them in her attempt to take Eren.

We will now look at these events scene by scene. We will be looking at what words are said or thought, but readers must keep in mind that these words transpire amidst fast action with many cuts back and forth from different perspectives and with quick flashbacks to earlier scenes to illuminate what characters are saying or thinking. We are watching Eren have to make choices on the fly in the midst of chaos with limited knowledge about what is going on. Repeatedly, he must choose between trusting others and their more extensive knowledge and experience as soldiers or to trust himself, limited though his knowledge and experience is in comparison to theirs.

The scenes discussed below extend across three episodes in AOT (E19 "Bite", E20 "Erwin Smith", and E21 "Crushing Blow"). Together these scenes last around 5 minutes.

**Transcript [We have adjusted the English translation
in places and abridged in places.]**

Part 1 (E19 Bite)

As they were ordered to, Levi's squad, with Eren among them, is riding at top speed into the forest on horseback. The Female Titan enters the forest and begins to attack the soldiers escorting the wagon carrying the Titan weapon. She is killing them right and left. The soldiers in Levi's squad want to attack the Female Titan, but Levi commands them to charge forward and let their comrades keep battling the Female Titan alone, in all probability to die. He does this because he knows, unlike his squad, that their real task is to lure the Female Titan into a trap laid further on in the forest. Eren cannot understand why the best Titan-killers in Survey Corps are refusing to help the soldiers.

In the transcripts below, sometimes characters are speaking and sometimes the words tell us what they are thinking. Petra, Oluo, Gunther, and Eldo are the members of Levi Squad along with Eren.

> **Petra**: Captain, your orders?!
> **Oluo**: Let's get the Titan.
> It's dangerous…
> We should kill it!
> **Eldo**: At this rate, it *will* catch up with us!
> We should kill it here…
> Right, Captain!
> **Eren**: Captain, your orders!
> **Levi**: Everyone, cover your ears.
> [*Levi fires a noise grenade to signal to Erwin, who is waiting with some of his soldiers at the trap, that the Titan is coming.*]
> **Eren**: A noise grenade?
> **Levi**: [*turns behind to speak to his team as they gallop on their horses*]
> What is your job?
> Is it to let yourself be swayed by whatever you're feeling at the moment?
> No, it's not.
> Our squad's job is to keep the brat [Eren] from getting a single scratch on him.
> Even it costs our lives.
> We keep going on our horses, got it?
> **Petra**: Roger!
> **Eren**: Keep going? For how long?
> And it's right on top of us.
> If we don't help them, they'll all be wiped out!
> **Gunther**: Eren, eyes on the road!

Eldo: Keep your pace up…
Stay at top speed!
Eren: Why?!
If Squad Levi doesn't defeat it, who will?
Another one's dead…
And maybe we could've saved him!
One's still fighting…
We could still make it!
Petra: Eren, eyes back on the road! Keep going!
Eren: Are you telling me to look away?
To abandon my comrades and run?!
Petra: Yes, that's right!
Obey the Captain's orders!
Eren: I don't understand why we're leaving them to die!
Or why he won't explain!
Oluo: That's because the Captain decided the reason should not be explained.
You just don't understand because you're still green!
If you get it, then shut up and obey!
Eren: Well…
I can fight on my own. [*Eren looks at his hand—Eren can become a Titan by biting his hand*]
Why am I relying on others?
I can just fight on my own. [*Eren starts to bite himself*]
Petra: What are you doing, Eren?
You're only allowed to do that [*become a Titan*] if your life is in danger.
You promised us! [*Eren stops, but then starts to bite again*]
Eren!
Levi: You aren't wrong. [*Levi is speaking to Eren, but looking forward, riding at the head of the team; it seems as if he is talking to himself*]
If you want to, do it.
I can tell he [*Eren*] is a real monster.
And it has nothing to do with his Titan power.
No matter what power you use to suppress him,
no matter what cage you put him in,
he will never submit to anyone.
Flashback to Eren in an earlier scene shouting in a rage: I just want to slaughter the Titans.
Eren, the difference between your decision and ours is experience.
But you don't have to rely on that.
Choose.
Believe in yourself.
Or believe in the Survey Corps and me.
I don't know…
I never have.
I can believe in my own abilities
Or the choices of companions I trust.
But no one ever knows how it will turn out.

So, choose for yourself whichever decision you'll regret least.

Eren puts his hand down, looks up and rides on, and then looks back at the Female Titan pursuing them and attacking the soldiers trying to stop her. He starts to bite his hand again.

Petra: Eren!

Have faith!

[*Eren hesitates... he can't make up his mind.*]

Eren recalls his previous days with Levi Squad and the loyalty they showed to him.

Petra: Have faith in us!

Levi: Eren!

You're taking too long! Decide!

Eren: I will go forward!

Eren looks pained but accepting of his decision, but then he sees the Female Titan kill a soldier who yells "Let me go!" as he is in the Titan's grasp. Eren closes his eyes and looks down and says:

Eren: I'm sorry!

[*The Female Titan runs after Levi Squad as they flee.*]

Oluo: Target [the Female Titan] is accelerating!

Levi: Go!

We will outrun it.

Eren: It's impossible to outrun it…

If we keep running away, it'll stomp us all flat!

We might all die,

But everyone chose to go on,

Even if it meant abandoning our comrades.

Captain Levi has been looking forward this whole time.

And the rest of this squad believe in him,

And put all their trust in him.

I'll believe in them, too…

Like they believed in me!

The Female Titan runs into the trap as the squad rides past her and escapes.

Gunther: Well, Eren? see that?

We caught that Titan!

Oluo: That is the power of the Survey Corps!

Don't underestimate us, fool.

Well, do you get it now?

Eren: Yes! [*With a satisfied look on his face*]

Part 2 (E20 Erwin Smith)

Jean and Armin (Armin and Mikasa are Eren's two best friends) are up in a tree on the edge of the forest as Titans try to climb up to get them. They are among the troops who were told to stay outside the forest and are unaware of what the plan is and what is going on in the forest. They are waiting for orders to retreat.

When the Female Titan originally attacked the right flank of the formation, Jean and Armin were two of the soldiers she attacked, so they know she is there some place. The Female Titan, unbeknownst to everyone, is Annie, a fellow solider and a friend of Armin's.

AOT here continually cuts between this conversation between Jean and Armin outside the forest and a conversation among the members of Levi's squad inside the forest. The two conversations flow into one another seamlessly and compose one coherent conversation. The two conversations can be read continuously as if the two groups are in the same conversation.

Jean and Armin Conversation

Jean: Armin…
It sounds like something is going on deeper in the forest.
I think I have some idea what. [*He is making a guess*]
They lured that Female Titan all the way here in order to capture it.
More precisely…
To capture whoever is inside of it.
That was Commander Erwin's goal…

Levi Squad Conversation

[*Eren and the rest of Levi Squad are further in the forest having gone ahead as Levi ordered them.*]
Eren: That was his plan from the very start!
Right!
I can see why he wouldn't have told the new troops.
But why wouldn't he tell you when you've all been with the Survey Corps for so long?
Oluo: Shut up!
Petra: Are you saying the Commander and the Captain don't trust us?
Eren: But that's what this means…
Oluo: Petra, rip out his teeth!
Swap the front and back teeth when you shove 'em back in!
Eldo: No, Eren's right.
I think there was a reason the Commander couldn't trust us.
Gunther: Like what?
Eldo: There's only one reason he wouldn't trust his fellow soldiers.
There's someone who can become a Titan, a spy in the Survey Corps.

Jean and Armin Conversation

[*Cuts back to Jean and Armin in the tree.*]
Jean: You think so, too, right?
It has to be one of us.
Armin: Yes, I think so.

Levi Squad Conversation

[*Cuts back to Levi squad.*]
Gunther: A spy?
Is that possible?
Eldo: At any rate, the Commander is certain.
I'd imagine the only soldiers who were told of the plan were those who've
stayed alive for the past five years [*because they were there before the spy
arrived*]
Gunther: I see…
So that's it.
Oluo: Must be.
Understand, Eren?
That's why.
Petra: Yeah, if that's the reason, I understand.
He's assuming that five years ago, when the first wall fell,
a spy infiltrated our ranks…
And that's how he narrowed down the possibilities.
…
Eren: If this succeeds [*capturing the Female Titan*], I can get closer to the truth
of this world.
But…Too many died, regardless.
Eldo: Do you think the Commander was wrong?

Jean and Armin Conversation

[*Cuts back to Jean and Armin.*]
Jean: I can't say he was right.
If we'd known there was a Titan informed of our operations,
we would've dealt with this in a different way.
Your team's squad leader and the others would've, too.
Armin: No, it wasn't wrong.
Jean: What wasn't wrong?
How many do you think died for no reason?
Armin: Jean, after the fact, it's easy to say, "We should've done something else."
However, no one knows how things will turn out.
And even so, you have to make a choice.

You must.
The lives of a hundred fellow soldiers…
Or the lives of all the humans within the walls…
The Commander made his choice.
He chose to let those hundred die.

Levi Squad Conversation

[*Cuts back to Levi Squad.*]
Eldo: Eren, you don't know it yet,
but you will soon.
The reason that Erwin Smith is entrusted with humanity's hope, the Survey Corps.
Petra: Just look at how much Captain Levi trusts him!
Oluo: If you live that long…

Jean and Armin Conversation

[*Cuts back to Jean and Armin.*]
Armin: I haven't lived that long,
But I'm certain of one thing.
If there's anyone who can bring change,
It will be someone willing to sacrifice what they care for.
It will be someone who can throw aside their humanity, in order to defeat monsters.
Someone who can't sacrifice anything can't ever change anything!

Part 3 (E20 Erwin Smith)

Inside the forest, Erwin and Levi are trying to secure the Female Titan in the trap and find out who is inside. They are attacking her to make the person inside give up and come out. Eventually, however, she screams a deafening scream that brings a great many unintelligent Titans from outside the forest to her. They cover her and eat her Titan form so she can escape from inside her Titan form without being seen. The person is Annie and she has her Survey Corps uniform and mobility gear that will allow her to blend in with the troops and attack them as she wants. She will also be able to turn into a Titan again. The Titans she has called are rampaging and Erwin orders a retreat. His plan has been a failure.

The smoke signals that order a retreat are spotted by Levi's squad. They prepare to leave, wrongly thinking the Female Titan has been captured and the identity of the traitor inside the Titan has been discovered.

Levi Squad Conversation

[*The squad is further along in the forest and does not know the captured Female Titan has escaped in her human form.*]
Gunther: Looks like it's over.
Back to the horses! Prepare to retreat!
Oluo: You heard the man!
Let's go see what the bastard inside looks like.
Eren: Will we really find out who it is?
Petra: It's thanks to you.
Eren: I didn't really do anything.
Petra: You had faith in us.
This is the result of your choice to trust us back then.
Making the right choice isn't easy.
[*Someone wearing the uniform of the Survey Corps fires a smoke signal. Gunther sees it from afar and thinks it is Captain Levi. It is actually Annie in her human form wearing the Survey Corps gear.*]
Gunther: Oh, I'm sure that's the signal from Captain Levi.
We'll rendezvous with the Captain!
Cut the chatter till we get back.
[*Gunther fires another smoke signal to respond to the one he has seen and heads toward Annie, thinking it is Levi.*]
Gunther: Captain Levi?
No, it's not!
Who are you!
[*Annie quickly kills Gunther with her blades.*]
Eren: G-Gunther!
What? Why?

Part 4 (E21 Crushing Blow)

This part continues from Part 3 above where Annie in her human form has killed Gunther. Eren, Oluo, and Eldo have left their horses to approach Annie behind Gunther. After they see Annie kill him, they need to flee. Annie turns into her Female Titan form and pursues them.

Eren: Gunther!
Oluo: Eren, don't stop!
Onward!
Eren: But Gunther…
Oluo: Damn it, what do we do?
Eldo, where should we go?
Eldo: There isn't time to reach the horses!

Head for HQ, as fast as you can!
Oluo: Is it just the Female Titan or are there others?
Petra: Damn you...
How dare you?!
Come at me!
I'll defeat you, even if it kills me!
Eren: The Female Titan?
Impossible...Why?
Didn't we catch it?!
Eldo: I knew it...
It's coming!
The Female Titan!
Eren: Damn you...
How dare you!
This time, I will defeat it! [*Eren starts to bite his hand*]
Eldo: No.
The three of us will kill the Female Titan.
You will continue to head straight for HQ at top speed!
Eren: I'll fight, too!
Eldo: No...
This is the best move...
Your power is too risky!
Oluo: What? Do you doubt us?
Petra: Do you, Eren?
Do you find it that hard to trust us?
[*Eren puts down his hand and turns his body forward.*]
Eren: I believe my squad will be victorious.
Good luck!
[*Eldo, Petra, and Oluo start to battle with the Female Titan. They successfully take away its vision. Eren has been watching this whole time.*]
Eren: They're so strong.
The Female Titan is totally on the defensive.
How can they launch co-op attacks like that without even speaking to each other?
I bet it's only possible because they believe in one another.
They've overcome many hardships that way.
That's why they're so strong, even right after losing Gunther.
I'll go forward...
If I go forward and believe in them, without turning back, then... I'm sure that's the right answer.
I finally understand!
[*Flash back to Levi's words: "I don't know...I never have. I can believe in my own abilities or the choices of companions I trust. But no one ever knows how it will turn out."*]
[*Eren looks back and sees the Female Titan bite Eldo in half. Eren immediately turns back and starts crying and screaming.*]
Petra: Eldo!

H-How!
It can't possibly see!
It hasn't even been thirty seconds… [*since they blinded it.*]
Only one eye?
It prioritized one eye to accelerate the healing…
Is that even possible?
Oluo: Petra!
We need to regroup!
Petra, now!
The Female Titan stomps Petra to death. Eren cries and screams even more.
Oluo: Hey…
Die!
How?
My blade can't pierce it…
The Female Titan gives Oluo a jump kick and kills him too. Eren is stunned by what's happening.
Eren: I…
I will…
I'll kill it!
Eren finally transforms into his Titan.
Eren: [*Thoughts Eren is having as he, as a Titan, battles the Female Titan:*]
I made the wrong choice…
I wanted to believe in my companions…
Because of that, everyone died!
If I had believed in myself from the start and fought…
If I'd only killed it at the beginning!
Back then, if I'd turned into a Titan…
No…
If I'd fought even before that…
Captain Levi would have been there, too.
We would have won.
Maybe we could've captured it.
[*Flashback to Levi's saying: "You aren't wrong. If you want to, do it."*]
I…
I made a choice.
And it killed everyone.
It's my fault they died.
But despite all that…
It's still your [*the Female Titan's*] fault!
[*Eren howls at the Female Titan.*]

Despite an epic battle, Eren loses and the Female Titan rips him out of his Titan and takes him captive. She has achieved her goal of capturing Eren.

Part 5 (E24 Mercy)

Eren's Titan loses to the Female Titan in the battle. The Female Titan bites Eren out of his Titan body and runs away with him. The whole purpose of Levi's squad was to protect Eren and now he has been captured. Levi and Mikasa have to go after the Female Titan and rescue Eren. After everything is over and they are back inside the walls, Eren and Levi have the conversation below:

> **Eren**: I'm sorry.
> Back then, if I hadn't made the wrong choice…
> This never would've happened.
> **Levi**: I told you…
> No one ever knows how things will turn out.

Analysis

We start with Levi saying facetiously: "What is your job? To let yourself be swayed by whatever you're feeling at the moment?" His soldiers serve in an army and, thus, are supposed to follow orders. This is a classic example of social constraints on human freedom in the service of society. We are all forced to do things because duties, rules, roles, and institutions tell us we must. In some cases, we may have chosen to join an institution like the army, but after that our degrees of freedom are constrained. Levi is effectively telling Eren and his fellow squad mates that they need to trust the military and its leaders (including himself) to make good decisions and not rely on their emotions or individual judgement. He is telling them that they need to choose not to choose beyond choosing to obey.

Levi orders the squad to flee and not fight the Female Titan. One squad member, Petra, tells Eren to obey Levi's orders. In response, Eren says: "I don't understand why we're leaving them to die! Or why he won't explain!" Eren wants to understand in some rational well-reasoned way, but in the midst of battle and working inside an institution with many layers of policy, planning, and goals any such explanation is often impossible. And, too, any such explanation itself would itself have to be trusted.

In this situation the problem is deeper yet because Levi is privy to a secret plan Erwin has made based on intuition. Even if he wanted to, Erwin could not fully explain in logically analytic terms his intuition that there is a Titan traitor in their midst in pursuit of Eren. He does not have all the evidence and much of his belief is based only on feeling and insight, not logic.

When Levi sees Eren's hesitation and indecision about following orders, he says: "No matter what power you use to suppress him, no matter what cage you put him in, he will never submit to anyone." Here, Levi brings up another major issue with choice. People act based on who they are. Eren is a person who hates to be constrained. Since he was a child, he has wanted to be free, acted on impulse, and resisted subjugation to others. Levi is suggesting that people's choices flow from who they are—their nature—not their reasoning. So, perhaps, in the end, it is pointless to reason with Eren.

Levi then gives Eren a short speech that seems to be as much about himself as about Eren (remember the earlier episode where Levi lost his two dearest friends when he made the decision to allow them to enter the battle with him because they asked him to trust them):

> Eren, the difference between your decision and ours is experience. But you don't have to rely on that.
> Choose.
> Believe in yourself.
> Or believe in the Survey Corps and me.
> I don't know…
> I never have.
> I can believe in my own abilities
> Or the choices of companions I trust.
> But no one ever knows how it will turn out.
> So, choose for yourself whichever decision you'll regret least.

Levi admits he doesn't know what choice to make. He realizes that when we make a choice we can rely on our own experience and desires, or we can rely on the longer and deeper experience of others, or we can trust authority and our role (here the Survey Corps). Levi suggests a critical criterion for choosing: Since no one knows how any choice will turn out, we should reflect on the possibilities—the possible good and bad outcomes—and choose the outcome that will bring us the least regret. This is a Sartre-like view: Choose, based on principles you want to live by as a person, and then accept the results, come what may. In the act, you create yourself as a person of a certain type.

When the Female Titan is captured, AOT artfully switches between two conversations taking place at different places. One is between Jean and Armin outside the forest and the other is among the Levi Squad members inside the forest. All these soldiers have not been informed of Erwin's secret plan and have been operating on trust until now. Armin was earlier attacked by the Female Titan and Levi Squad has witnessed that she fell into Ewin's trap. They now are all coming to realize that all that has happened was Erwin's plan from the beginning. Their remarks—which fits seamlessly together—focus on how to assess Erwin's plan, his choice to keep most of the troops in the dark, and the resulting deaths of many soldiers. In this conversation, Petra (who will, not too long after this, be killed by the Female Titan after she escapes the trap) says (making her best guess about what must be going on): "He's [Erwin] assuming that five years ago, when the first wall fell, a spy infiltrated our ranks...And that's how he narrowed down the possibilities." She is aware that Erwin was acting on intuition based on his past experiences and his well-practiced skills as a leader, not on full knowledge and purely rational logic. Erwin has gambled the lives of his soldiers on his intuition, his "gut feeling."

In these conversations, Armin gives an extended speech that resonates with what Levi has said earlier. His speech is directed at Jean's claim that Erwin's choice was wrong. Jean says: "I can't say he was right. If we'd known there was a Titan informed of our operations, we would've dealt with this in a different way." Armin replies:

> Jean, after the fact, it's easy to say, "We should've done something else."
> However,
> No one knows how things will turn out.
> And even so, you have to make a choice.
> You must.
> The lives of a hundred fellow soldiers...
> Or the lives of all the humans within the walls...
> The Commander made his choice.
> He chose to let those hundred die.
> ...
> If there's anyone who can bring change,
> It will be someone willing to sacrifice what they care for.
> It will be someone who can throw aside their humanity, in order to defeat monsters.
> Someone who can't sacrifice anything can't ever change anything!

Armin is pointing to a fact that has played a major role in history. When one is fighting monsters, they often must become monsters themselves. They must sacrifice even what is dearest to them, even their humanity. This is a sort of dark Sartrean position. Rather than creating our own humanity through living with our choices, we give up that humanity and become something else for the greater good.

After the Female Titan escapes and attacks Levi Squad, the squad tells Eren to hold back and let them fight the Titan. After all, their job is to protect him. In the beginning, when they successfully blind the Titan, Eren is amazed by their teamwork: "How can they launch co-op attacks like that without even speaking to each other? I bet it's only possible because they believe in one another. They've overcome many hardships that way." Here Eren brings up the role of collective intelligence in choice. The members of Levi Squad have been handpicked to be a team that brings different skills to the task but are able, through trust and practice, to integrate these skills in a way that makes the team more powerful than any one member in it. This has been called a "cross-functional team" and is a form of collective intelligence (Parker 2002). Eren is reflecting on the possibility that, perhaps, it is not individuals who should be the source of choices but intelligent teams or groups that can pool much more experience and much more diverse experiences when they choose and act.

In the end, though, the Titan recovers and kills the members of Levi's squad. Eren finally chooses to turn into a Titan and battle the Female Titan. This choice, of course, jeopardizes the Survey Corps' whole goal of protecting Eren so he can learn to control his Titan powers and become the salvation of Paradis Island, its super-weapon. To Eren, it now looks like this was the right choice all along—to trust himself:

> **Eren**: [*Thoughts Eren is having as he, as a Titan, battles the Female Titan*]
> I made the wrong choice…
> I wanted to believe in my companions…
> Because of that, everyone died!
> If I had believed in myself from the start and fought…
> If I'd only killed it at the beginning!
> Back then,
> if I'd turned into a Titan…
> No…
> If I'd fought even before that…
> Captain Levi was there, too.
> We would have won.
> Maybe we could've captured it.
> I…
> I made a choice.
> And it killed everyone.
> It's my fault they died.

Yet, in the end, Eren loses and is carried away by the Female Titan. He has to be rescued, at great risk, by Levi and Mikasa. Perhaps, he would have won if he had made the choice earlier—as he says, earlier Levi was there (and he is the best fighter in the Survey Corps). Who knows? As Levi said earlier and as he says once again after everything is over and they are back at their base inside the Walls: "No one ever knows how things will turn out." Indeed, this is a remark we have also heard Commander Erwin Smith and Armin make.

These scenes constitute a meditation on choice, one carried out not just in words but in actions, drama, and emotions. Core dilemmas around the notion of choice are dealt with by being acted out: the role of rational reasoning versus intuition; whether to trust others who have more experience than us; how far to follow our social roles and obligations; how much to trust leadership and institutions; what it means to choose under pressure; how choices most often involve uncertainty and a lack of access to much we need to know; and how to deal with the outcomes of our choices, including unintended consequences. Free will, in the sense of choosing freely and being morally responsible for the consequences of our actions, appears very vexed indeed. Of course, we do not always choose under such tight time constraints and under such pressure and stress, but we very often must choose in circumstances equally complex.

There is a term "fog of war" which means all the aspects of a battlefield about which we are in the dark, about which we have no good information. AOT is suggesting, in these scenes, that when we must choose, especially in consequential situations, there is a "fog of choice," much like the fog of war. In his great novel *War and Peace*, Tolstoy asks how much generals giving orders in battle actually has to do with the final outcome of the battle, which seems more determined by a myriad of interacting happenings on the ground. We, too, can ask how much we actually have to do with the outcomes of our choices in our lives.

AOT offers no answers to the many questions about choice to which it gives rise. It offers questions and dramatic happenings as examples to think about. Interestingly, an anime video game—*Xenoblade Chronicles III*—offers an insight that does not appear in AOT except in its reference to the effectiveness of well-practiced teams. The insight is: Pick your friends carefully.

In *Xenoblade III*, a team of young warriors, men and women, fight together. They have become friends, but started as enemies from very different backgrounds. The game story suggests that the best way to make choices is to pick your friends well and carefully and then work out what constitutes the right thing to do by living and acting collaboratively with them. This is a sort of social version of Sartre. We make choices based on our mutually shared experiences with our friends in life and, in the act, create ourselves as part of "team." This approach, however, requires we have the opportunity to pick who we will befriend from diverse people, ones who can allow us to learn and grow beyond our own limitations.

CHAPTER 20

THE IS AND THE AS

This book was inspired by relatively new work in neuroscience, evolutionary biology, animal studies, learning science, and work on the nature of humans as distinctive types of living beings. This work is showing us what sort of creature we humans are. It is rich with implications for education, therapy, healthcare, and for ameliorating—or, at least, understanding—some of our social divisions and broken institutions.

Like all new and cross-disciplinary work, there are controversies and new discoveries that make any summary vulnerable to future corrections. We have not offered such a summary. What we have offered is our view of the important implications of this work. These implications, we believe, transcend the controversies in the research because they reside at a higher, more big-picture, level than those controversies (e.g., the controversy over whether the mid-brain has its own form of consciousness in regard to basic emotions).

The Two Systems

The work that has inspired us puts three connected components of a human being at the foreground of human experience and learning. These three components comprise a system. This system includes 1) the affective part of being human: feelings, emotions, empathy, and intuition (Barnett 2017; Damasio 2018; Damasio, A. & Carvalho 2013; Immordino-Yang & Damasio 2007); 2) the embodied and reciprocal relationship between humans and their environment (Capra & Luisi 2014; Clark 1997; Gee 2020; Paul 2021); and 3) the unconscious and automatic workings of our inner and outer senses and brain as an association engine (Barnett 2020; Eagleman 2020; Seligman, Railton, Baumeister & Sripada 2016).

This system has no agreed-upon name. It is centered, for the most part, in the right side of the brain (McGilchrist 2019, 2021). It is a system that differs from the sorts of conscious analytical and logical reasoning that is associated with the left brain (and with school). When you ask Google for an antonym for "analytical" you get words like: disorganized, illogical, irrational, incoherent, and chaotic. But the opposite of "analytic" is not always "disorganized." Sometimes the opposite of "analytic" is "intuitive" and intuition is at the heart and soul of the system we seeking to name.

So, what can we call this system that is deprioritized in schools and society, but is, nonetheless, crucial to understanding the human brain and body, human learning, and what sorts of creatures humans actually are? Let's call it the "Intuitive System" (the IS for short), keeping in mind that this is a shortcut that stands for all three components.

Foregrounding the importance of the Intuitive System, by no means, is meant to demean the system that is currently foregrounded in schooling and education more generally, a system that uses conscious analytical, logical, and linear reasoning. We can call this system the Analytic System (AS for short). This system is, for the most part, centered in the left side of the brain. The argument is not that one system is better than the other. Rather, the argument is that the AS works best when it is guided by, partners with, and helps feed back into the IS.

The AS is best used as a tool to carry out, improve, and validate insights from the IS. Just as the human body is enhanced by using tools, but must remain in charge of the tool, the IS can be aided and improved by the AS, but must be in charge of it, guide it and integrate its detailed results back into a bigger whole. This is to say, then, that feelings, emotions, intuition, and empathy must trigger and guide detailed analytic reasoning and problem solving based on insights gained from experience and a sense for the bigger picture.

This viewpoint begins to close the yawning gap between science (usually seen as the realm of the AS) and art (usually seen as the realm of the IS) in today's world, a gap that has not always been there in history. Both science and art can be forms of discovery and learning. and both, in their best work, use the IS and can feed and improve this system in humans. And, of course, both science and art also involve, in their proper place, analysis, logic, and reasoning, but, we hope, in the service of survival and flourishing. In fact, science at its best is art and art at its best is a form of inquiry and discovery that helps us understand ourselves and the world better.

The two systems—the IS and the AS—are two different powers that operate best together and can each be dangerous when acting alone. The IS involves the ability to consider many possibilities, to make connections, to find patterns and regularities, to integrate parts into wholes and to appreciate wholes as more than the sum of their parts. This power considers things in and across contexts and appreciates nuances and complexities. It focuses on specific properties of things and processes and not just generalizations about them and the categories they fall into. It is the source of intuition.

The IS is not verbal in the sense that it is not adept at words. Indeed, it is impossible to put many of its musings and insights into words in any way that truly captures them. Try putting into words how to tie a shoe, something you often do with little or no conscious awareness.

The IS is adept at images and metaphors (finding commonalities in things and processes that otherwise appear quite different). This power appears also to be crucial for human beings' sense of and feelings about social connections and the foundation of their ability to engage in empathy, perhaps because is so strongly committed to making connections of all sorts.

Our other power—the AS—operates at the level of conscious awareness and focused effort. We are consciously aware of what we are thinking and doing when using this power. It takes more mental effort to use it. This power focuses on specific problems (often handed to it by the other power). It is adept at analysis, step by step procedures, decomposing wholes into units and parts, decontextualizing, abstracting, generalizing, and categorizing, all in the name of solving problems without being overwhelmed by complexities and nuances that show only the forest but not the trees.

The AS is not only adept at words, but it was likely created much beyond the capacity it has in other animals by the evolution of human language, a system unlike anything any other animal has. Language, at the level of structure (grammar)—though not at the level of situationally contextualized meanings—is inherently categorical. It orders things (nouns) and processes (verbs), as well as their attributes and states (adjectives and adverbs).

The IS and the AS meet in the human power to simulate, that is, the power to form and view images, patterns, and scenarios in the "theater of our mind." We can use our simulation powers to imagine and fantasize and imagination and fantasy are fed by the IS. We can also use our simulation powers to manipulate images, patterns, and symbols (including words) to engage in analysis, logical problem solving, and the construction of reasoned sequential arguments. The problems we engage with in this analytical way are often given to us by intuition or insights stemming from the IS.

Simulation as imagination and fantasy and simulation as analysis and symbol manipulation can and should feed each other. We saw this when we discussed sensuous constructions and situational meanings for words. A sensuous construction like a painting in a bird guide book or the red scarf in AOT combines sensuous images formed in experience with more general meanings extracted from those experiences. A painting in a bird book means a specific bird species (a type, a generality, a category, an abstraction) but still is embedded in sensation. So, too, with situational meanings for words. A phrase like "one-click democracy" both calls to mind experiences we have had with the internet and social media and contextualizes a category ("democracy"). In both cases, the IS and the AS are cooperating. Sensation and feeling are combined with generality and categorial analysis.

At their best, the two systems work as a team. When the IS discovers something, unconsciously or through the sort of awareness that constitutes feeling, it can hand it over to the AS for analysis, reasoning, and validation. Unfortunately, perhaps, when the IS hands over its discoveries and gives the AS tasks to do, it does not share how it reached its results (Gazzaniga 2011, 2018). The AS cannot know how the IS has processed things to reach its insights. Much of this processing is hidden, unopen to consciousness ("encapsulated" in the terms of some neuroscientists). So, the AS has to "guess" (seek outside evidence for or even confabulate about) how and why the IS reached its insights. Once the AS has done its work and has solved a problem analytically and methodically, it returns (or should return) its results to the IS, so the IS can re-integrate the AS's solution into its big-picture perspective and the patterns, contexts, and nuances the IS constantly processes (mulls over).

We have developed a picture of two systems—the IS and the AS—joined to the capacity to simulate. The IS can feed "data" to simulation and simulation can engage in "cinematic" activities like remembering, daydreaming, fanaticizing, or scenario planning. Simulation can also be used to solve problems analytically step by step, often, but not always, by using words and symbols (it can use images and patterns as well). This usually takes a good deal of conscious effort ("work") and can be a slow process.

Humans can, of course, think and solve problems entirely in terms of language or other symbol systems if need be. Such thinking is a form of simulation that manipulates not images but symbols alone (words are symbols). Manipulating symbols is a quite different enterprise than manipulating images and is not a strongly developed capacity in any other animal than humans, thanks to our possession of human language. Language (and the manipulation of symbols) has allowed humans to take the AS capacity much further than other animals.

The human ability to formulate or imagine (simulate) infinite possibilities has been, for us humans, a double-edged sword. It is the source of creativity, but it has always allowed us to dream up gods, spirits, and life after death and worry endlessly about them and sometimes fight wars over them. The human ability to carry out symbolic manipulations in our minds—and eventually on paper—has also been a double-edged sword. It has given us profound technical knowledge to solve hard problems and the skills to invent powerful tools and technologies. But, then, we have too often used them to destroy others and the world we live in. The IS and the AS were gifts with strings attached. There are times other animals may be fortunate they do not have them in the ways we humans do, especially since we have used them to dominate all of life on earth and, perhaps, if we are not careful, may well bring much of life on earth to an end, a process we have already started.

Final Words to Educators

Much education in school addresses just the AS and its analytical problem-solving abilities. It does not usually sufficiently address the IS and its powers of intuition and insight and how they need to be fed by building up the association network that is our brain, a brain that is always operating. This network is built not just by words and symbols, or even primarily by words and symbols. It is built by sensations in the world and media that, once they become a part of our brain, allow the IS to discover rich and useful associations, relationships, and patterns that can underwrite insight, intuition, and creativity, and, too, good questions and good problems to send to the AS for more focused, analytical work.

What motivated this book was the paradox that educators regularly claim that humans learn from experience yet ignore sensation, feelings, and emotions, the "stuff" from which experience is composed. As we have said, new work on how the human brain and body work; on the human *umwelt* (the world as our human senses present it to us); and on the evolution of humans as distinctive kinds of creatures with great strengths and glaring weaknesses offers deep insights to what is central to human learning, survival, and flourishing. This work, on our reading, argues that things like sensation, feeling, empathy, intuition, and belonging—come before the sorts of analytical and logical reasoning that school focuses on. They "come before" in the sense that analytic and logical reasoning does not work well for individuals and society if these other things are not given priority and are not well in place as we teach for analytic and logical skills.

These things that "come before"—things that constitute the basic nature of humans as distinctive sorts of creatures—we have discussed one by one in this book. They are listed below. Here, then, are the questions we want to end this book on. Look through this list and answer the following questions: How many of these things have priority and importance in schools today? How many have priority and importance in society and its institutions? The answer, we think, is none or few. And that, we argue, is a problem that explains a lot of our other problems such as how we are dealing with climate change, rampant political polarization, environmental degradation, civilizational conflicts, and many others.

1. Empathy
2. Intuition
3. Balance, Homeostasis, Allostasis
4. Atmosphere, Immersion, and Contextualization
5. Tension and Release
6. Feelings & Emotions
7. Personhood and Character(s)
8. Landscapes and Grounding in Nature: Coherence, Legibility, Complexity, Mystery
9. Images and Simulation: The Ideal; The Extended Body; The Extended Social Body (Imagined Communities); Spirts and Spirituality
10. Action, Caring, and Attention
11. Situational Meanings in Language
12. Sensuous Constructions
13. Strategic Vagueness

REFERENCES

Allard, S. & Fabre, C. (2018). Delacroix. Metropolitan Museum of Art.

Anderson, B. (1983). Imagined communities: Reflections on the origin and spread of nationalism. Verso Books.

Aronson, Ronald (1980). Jean-Paul Sartre – Philosophy in the World. NLB

Aronson, Ronald (2004). Camus & Sartre: The Story of a friendship and the quarrel That ended it. University of Chicago Press.

Asch, S. E. (1951). Effects of group pressure upon the modification and distortion of judgments. In H. Guetzkow, Ed., Groups, leadership and men; research in human relations. Carnegie Press, pp. 177–190.

Atzil S., Gao W., Fradkin I., & Barrett L. F. (2018). Growing a social brain. Nat Hum Behav, 2(9):624-636.

Bakewell, S. (2010). How to live or a life of Montaigne in one question and twenty attempts at an answer. Random.

Barenboim, D. (2009). Music quickens time. Verso.

Barnett, L. F. (2017). How emotions are made: The secret life of the brain. Houghton Mifflin Harcourt.

Barnett, L. F. (2020). Seven and a half lessons about the brain. Houghton-Mifflin Harcourt.

Barsalou, L.W. (2008). Situating concepts. In P. Robbins & M. Aydede, Eds., Cambridge handbook of situated cognition (pp. 236-263). Cambridge University Press.

Bentley, M. (2013). Atmosphere in games—part 1—atmosphere introduced. Game Developer. https://www.gamedeveloper.com/design/atmosphere-in-games---part-1---atmosphere-introduced

Bereiter, C., & Scardamalia, M. (1993). Surpassing ourselves: An inquiry into the nature and implications of expertise. Open Court.

Bergen, B. K. (2012). Louder than words: The new science of how the mind makes meaning. Basic Books.

Berwick, R. C. & Chomsky, N. (2016). Why only us? Language and evolution. MIT Press.

Borges, J. L. (2000). The craft of verse. Harvard University Press.

Bourdieu, Pierre (1991). Language and symbolic power. Harvard University Press.

Bransford, J. D. & Johnson, M. K. (1972). Contextual prerequisites for understanding: Some investigations of comprehension and recall. Journal of Verbal Learning and Verbal Behavior 11.6: 117-726.

Brockmeier, J. & Carbaugh, D. (2001). Narrative and identity: Studies in autobiography, self and culture. John Benjamins.

Brooks, D. (2011). The social animal: The hidden sources of love, character, and achievement. Random House.

Burke Harris, N. B. (2018). The deepest well: Healing the long-term effects of childhood adversity. Houghton Mifflin Harcourt.

Capra, F. & Luisi, P. L. (2014). A systems view of life: A unifying vision. Cambridge University Press.

Chabris, C. & Simons, D. (2009). The invisible gorilla: How our intuitions deceive us. Crown.

Chaloupka, G. (1993). Journey in time: The 50.000-year story of the Australian Aboriginal rock art of Arnhem land. Reed.

Chi, M. T. H., & Wylie, R. (2014). The ICAP framework: Linking cognitive engagement to active learning outcomes. Educational Psychologist, 49.4: 219-243.

Chomsky, N. (2016). What kind of creatures are we? Columbia University Press.

Churchland, P. S. (2013). Touching a nerve: The self as brain. Norton.

Clark, A. (1997) Being there: Putting brain, body, and world together again. MIT Press.

Clottes, J. (2016). What is Paleolithic art? Cave paintings and the dawn of human creativity. University of Chicago Press.

Corn, D. (2022). American psychosis: A historical investigation of how the Republican party went crazy. Twelve.

Cosmides, L. (1989). The logic of social exchange: Has natural selection shaped how humans reason? Studies with the Wasson Selection task. Cognition, 31.3: 187-276.

Cresswell, M. (2006). Formal semantics. In M. Devitt & R. Hanley, Ed., The Blackwell guide to the philosophy of language. Wiley-Blackwell.

Csikszentmihalyi (2009). Flow and the foundations of positive psychology: The collected works of Milhaly Csikszentmihalyi. Springer.

Curtis, G. (2006). The cave painters: Probing the mysteries of the world's first artists. Anchor Books.

Damasio, A. (2018). The strange order of things: Life, feeling, and the making of cultures. Pantheon Books.

Damasio, A. & Carvalho, G. (2013). The nature of feelings: Evolutionary and neurobiological orientations. Nature Reviews Neuroscience, 14, 143-52.

David, B. (2017). Cave art. Thames & Hudson.

Davies, P. C. (2019). The demon in the machine: How hidden worlds of information are solving the mystery of life. D. Appleton.

Desdemaines-Hugon, C. (2010). Stepping stones: A journey through the ice age caves of the Dordogne. Yale University Press.

Duranti, A. & Goodwin, C., Eds. (1992). Rethinking context: Language as an interactive phenomenon. Cambridge University Press.

diSessa, A. A. (2000). Changing minds: Computers, learning, and literacy. MIT Press.

Douven, I. (2021). Abduction, The Stanford Encyclopedia of Philosophy (Summer 2021 Edition), Edward N. Zalta (ed.), URL = https://plato.stanford.edu/archives/sum2021/entries/abduction/

Eagleman, D. (2020). Livewired: The inside story of the ever-changing brain. Pantheon Books.

Einstein, A. (1954). Ideas and opinions. Three Rivers Press.

Erbaugh, M. S. (2019). How the Chinese language encourages the paradigm shift toward discourse in linguistics: Pressure from 'the three zeros'. Chinese Language and Discourse, 10.1: 84-112

Frye, D. (2018). Walls: A history of civilization in blood and brick. Faber & Faber.

Garfield, J. (2022). Losing ourselves: Learning to live without a self. Princeton University Press.

Gazzaniga, M. S. (2011). Who's in charge: Free will and the science of the brain. HarperCollins.

Gazzaniga, M. S. (2018). The consciousness instinct: Unraveling the mystery of how the brain makes the mind. Farrar, Straus and Giroux.

Gazzaniga, M. & Steven, M.S. (2004). Free will in the 21st Century: A discussion of neuroscience and law, in Garland, B., Ed., Neuroscience and the Law: Brain, Mind and the Scales of Justice, Dana Press, pp. 51–70.

Gee, J. P. (2004). Situated language and learning: A critique of traditional schooling. Routledge.

Gee J. P. (2008). Game-like learning: An example of situated learning and implications for opportunity to learn. In P. A. Moss, D. C. Pullin, J. P. Gee, E. H. Haertel, L. J. Young, Eds., Assessment, equity, and opportunity to learn. Cambridge University Press, pp. 200-221

Gee, J. P. (2015). Social linguistics and literacies: Ideology in Discourses. Fourth Edition. Taylor & Francis. Fifth Edition.

Gee, J. P. (2017). Teaching, learning, literacy in our high-risk high-tech world: A framework for becoming human. Teachers College Press.

Gee, J. P. (2018). Affinity spaces: How young people live and learn on line and out of school. Phi Delta Kappan 99.6: 8-13.

Gee, J. P. (2020). What is a human? Language, mind, and culture. Palgrave/Macmillan.

Geil, D. and Moshman, M. (1998). Collaborative reasoning: Evidence for collective rationality. Thinking & Reasoning 4.3: 231–48.

Glenberg, A. M. (1997). What is memory for? Behavioral and Brain Sciences, 20.1: 1–55.

Glenberg, A. M. (2011). How reading comprehension is embodied and why that matters. International Electronic Journal of Elementary Education 4.1: 5-18.

Glenberg, A. M., & Gallese, V. (2012). Action-based language: A theory of language acquisition, comprehension, and production. Cortex, 48.7: 905-922.

Goldman, A. I. (2006). Simulating minds. Oxford University Press.

Gopnik, A. (1993). How we read our own minds: The illusion of first-person knowledge of intentionality. Behavioral and Brain Sciences 16.1: 1–14.

Grandin, T. (2022). Visual thinking: The hidden gifts of people who think in pictures, patterns, and abstractions. Riverhead Books.

Graziano, M. S. (2013). Consciousness and the social brain. Oxford University Press.

Halliday, M.A.K. (1978). Language as a social semiotic. Edward Arnold.

Hanks, W. F. (1995). Language and communicative practices. Westview.

Hartig, T. (2008), Green space, psychological restoration, and health inequality, Lancet 372(9650), 1614–1615.

Hawkes, D. (1967). A little primer of Tu Fu. Clarendon Press.

Hickok, G. (2014). The myth of mirror neurons: The real neuroscience of communication and cognition. Norton.

Higham, T. (2021). The world before us: The new science behind our human origins. Yale University Press.

Hiruta, K. (2021). Hannah Arendt & Isaiah Berlin: Freedom, politics, and humanity. Princeton University Press.

Hoffman, D. (2019). The case against reality: Why evolution hid the truth from our eyes. Norton.

Immordino-Yang M. H. and Damasio A. (2007). We feel, therefore, we learn: The relevance of affective and social neuroscience to education. Mind, Brain, and Education 1.1:3–10.

Jackson, M. O. (2019). The human network: How your social position determines your power, beliefs, and behavior. Pantheon.

Jason, Z. (2017). Bored out of their minds. Harvard Ed Magazine, Winter.

Jobert, B. (2018). Delacroix: New and expanded edition. Princeton.

Kahneman, D. (2011). Thinking fast and slow. Farrar, Straus and Giroux.

Kaplan, R. & Kaplan, S. (1989). The experience of nature: A psychological perspective. Cambridge University Press.

Kauffman, S. A. (2019). A world beyond physics: The emergence and evolution of life. Oxford University Press.

Keefe, R. and Smith, P. Eds. (1996) Vagueness: A reader. MIT Press.

Kline, A. K. (2014). How to learn about teaching: An evolutionary framework for the study of teaching behavior in humans and other animals. Behavioral and Brain Sciences 38: 1-71.

Kozhevnikov, M. & Shepherd, J. (2005). Spatial versus object visualizers: A new characterization of visual cognitive style. Memory and Cognition 33.4: 710-26.

Lawlor, R. (1991). Voices of the first day: Awakening in the Aboriginal dreamtime. Inner Traditions.

LeDoux, J. (2019). The deep history of ourselves: The four-billion-year story of how we got conscious brains. Viking.

Levinson, S. (1983). Pragmatics. Cambridge University Press.

Levinson, S. (1995). Three levels of meaning. In F. Palmer. Ed., Grammar and meaning: Essays in honour of Sir John Lyons (pp. 90-115). Cambridge University Press.

Li, Charles N.; Thompson, Sandra A. (1981). Mandarin Chinese: A functional reference grammar. University of California Press.

Lieberman, M. D. (2013). Social: Why our brains are wired to connect. Crown.

Lipscomb, B. J. B. (2022). The women are up to something: How Elisabeth Anscombe, Phillipa Foot, Mary Midgley, and Iris Murdoch revolutionized ethics. Oxford University Press.

Lorblanchet, M. & Bahn, P. (2017). The first artists: In search of the world's oldest art. Thames & Hudson.

Lloyd, S. A. & Sreedhar, S. (2022). Hobbes's moral and political philosophy, The Stanford Encyclopedia of Philosophy (Fall 2022 Edition), E. N. Zalta & U. Nodelman (eds.), https://plato.stanford.edu/archives/fall2022/entries/hobbes-moral/

Mac Cumhaill & Wiseman, R. (2022). Metaphysical animals: How four women brought philosophy back to life. Doubleday.

Madigan, T. (2011). Singer & Santayana on love. Philosophy Now 85: 18-20.

Malone, T. W. (2018). Superminds: The surprising power of people and computers thinking together. Little, Brown and Company.

McEwen B. S. (2006). Protective and damaging effects of stress mediators: central role of the brain. Dialogues Clin Neurosci 8.4: 367-81.

McGilchrist, I. (2009). The master and his emissary: The divided brain and the making of the Western world. Yale University Press

McGilchrist, I. (2019). Ways of attending: How our divided brain constructs the world. Routledge.

McGilchrist, I. (2021). The matter with things: Our brain, our delusions, and the Unmaking of the world. Perspectiva Press.

McRaney, D. (2022). How minds change: The surprising science of belief, opinion, and persuasion. Portfolio.

Mesquita, B. (2022). Between us: How cultures create emotions. Norton.

Mínguez-López, X. (2014). Folktales and other references in Toriyama's Dragon Ball. Animation: An Interdisciplinary Journal 9.1: 27-46.

Miller, A. M. (2017). Grounding: Hype or healing? US News: Wellness.

https://health.usnews.com/wellness/articles/2017-11-03/grounding-hype-or-healing

Miller, L. (2020). Why fish don't exist: A story of loss, love, and the hidden order of life. Simon & Schuster.

Mlodinow, L. (2022). Emotional: How our emotions shape out thinking. Pantheon.

Moss, M. (2013). Salt, sugar, fat: How the food giants hooked us. Random House.

Murdoch, I. (1970). On "God" and "good." In The Sovereignty of Good. Routledge.

Myers, G. (1996). Strategic vagueness in academic writing. In By E. Ventola & A. Mauraen, Eds., Academic writing. John Benjamins, pp. 3-18.

O'Connor, T. and Franklin, C. (2022). Free will, The Stanford Encyclopedia of Philosophy (Winter 2022 Edition), Edward N. Zalta & Uri Nodelman (eds.), URL = https://plato.stanford.edu/archives/win2022/entries/freewill/'

Pallasmaa, J. (2012). The eyes of the skin: Architecture and the senses. Third Edition. Wiley.

Pallasmaa, J. (2014). Space, place, atmosphere. Emotion and peripheral perception in architectural experience. Lebenswelt 4.1: 230-245.

Panksepp, J. & Biven, I. (2012). The archaeology of mind: Neuroevolutionary origins of human emotions. Norton.

Panksepp, J. (1998). Affective neuroscience: The foundations of human and animal emotions. Oxford University Press.

Parker, G. (2002). Cross-functional teams: Working with allies, enemies, and other strangers. Jossey-Bass.

Paul, A. M. (2021). The extended mind: The power of thinking outside the brain. Mariner Books.

Perry, B. D. & Szalavitz, M. (2006). The boy who was raised as a dog and other stories from a clinical psychologist's notebook: What traumatized children ca teach us about loss. Love, and healing. Basic Books.

Pickett, K. & Wilkinson, R. (2009). The spirit level: Why greater equality makes societies strong. Bloomsbury Press.

Pinker, S. (2015). The village effect: How face-to-face contact can make us healthier and happier. Vintage Canada.

Podhoretz, N. (1999). Ex-friends: Falling out with Allen Ginsberg, Lionel & Diana Trilling, Lillian Hellman, Hannah Arendt, and Norman Mailer. The Free Press.

Poincare, H. (1914). Science and method. Nelson & Sons.

Ramachandran, V. S. (2000). Mirror neurons and imitation learning as the force behind "the great leap forward" in human evolution. Edge.org. https://www.edge.org/conversation/vilayanur_ramachandran-mirror-neurons-and-imitation-learning-as-the-driving-force

Reynolds, J. and Renaudie, J-P. (2022). Jean-Paul Sartre, The Stanford Encyclopedia of Philosophy (Summer 2022 Edition), Edward N. Zalta (ed.), URL = https://plato.stanford.edu/archives/sum2022/entries/sartre/

Reynolds, A. S. (2021). Science is based on metaphor. IAI News. Issue 96. 24th May. https://iai.tv/articles/all-science-is-based-in-metaphor-auid-1809

Rexforth, K. (1956). One hundred poems from the Chinese. New Directions.

Roe, J. J., Thompson, C. W., Aspinall, P. A., Brewer, M. L., Duff, E. I., Miller, D., Mitchell, R. & Clow, A. (2013). Green space and stress: Evidence from cortisol measures in deprived urban communities, International Journal of Environmental Research and Public Health 10.9: 4086–4103.

Safina, C. (2020). Becoming wild: How animal cultures raise families, create beauty, and achieve peace. Henry Holt.

Sartre, J-P (1946). Existentialism is a humanism. In W. Kaufman, Ed., Existentialism from Dostoyevsky to Sartre. Penguin, 1991, pp. 345-69.

Sapolsky, R. M. (1994). Why zebras don't get ulcers. Henry Holt.

Sapolsky, R. M. (2001). A primate's memoir. Scriber.

Sapolsky, R. M. (2017). Behave: The biology of humans at our best and worst. Penguin.

Seligman, M. E. P., Railton, P., Baumeister, R. F., & Sripada, C. (2016). Homo prospectus. Oxford University Press.

Sfard, Anna (1994). Reification as the birth of metaphor. For the learning of mathematics 14 (1): 44-55.

Shklovsky, V. (1965). Art as technique. In L. T. Lemon & M. J. Reis, Eds., Russian Formalist criticism: Four essays. University of Nebraska Press, pp. 3-24.

Sidky, H. (2017). The origins of shamanism, spirit beliefs, and religiosity: A cognitive anthropological approach. Lexington Books.

Sigmund, K. (2017). Exact thinking in demented times: The Vienna Circle and the epic quest for the foundations of science. Basic Books.

Smagorinsky, P. & Taxel, J. (2005). The discourse of character education - Culture wars in the classroom. Psychology Press.

Smith, T. W. (2015). The book of human emotions: From ambiguphobia to umpty—154 words from around the world for how we feel. Little, Brown and Company.

Solms, M. (2021). The hidden spring: A journey to the source of consciousness. Norton.

Steele, C. M. & Aronson, J. (1995). A threat in the air: How stereotypes shape the intellectual identities and performance of women and African Americans, Journal of Personality and Social Psychology, 69.5: 797–811.

Steele, C. M. & Aronson, J. (1998). Stereotype threat and the test performance of academically successful African-Americans. In C. Jencks and M. Phillips, Eds., The Black–White test score gap. Washington, DC: Brookings Institution Press, pp. 401-427.

Storr, W. (2021). The status game: On human life and how to play it. William Collins.

Stuart-Smith, (2020). The well-gardened mind: The restorative power of nature. Scribner.

Sunstein, C. R. (1999). The law of group polarization. John M. Olin Law & Economics Working Paper No. 91. University of Chicago Law School.

Sunstein, C. R. & Hastie R. (2015). Wiser: Getting beyond groupthink to make groups smarter. Cambridge, MA: Harvard Business Review Press.

Swaab, D. F. (2014). A neurobiography of the brain, from the womb to Alzheimer's. Spiegel & Grau.

Taylor, S. (2015). Understanding empathy: Shallow and deep empathy. https://www.psychologytoday.com/us/blog/out-thedarkness/201509/understanding-empathy

Teicher, C. M. (2006). William Carlos Williams: "The Red Wheelbarrow": Just what does depend on that old wheelbarrow, anyway? Poetry Foundation.

https://www.poetryfoundation.org/articles/68731/william-carlos-williams-the-red-wheelbarrow

Tomasello, M. (2014). A natural history of human thinking. Harvard University Press.

Tomasello, M. (2019). Becoming human: A theory of ontogeny. Harvard University Press.

Tong, C, K. (2015). Nonhuman poetics (By way of Wang Guowei). Chinese Literature: Essays, Articles, Reviews (CLEAR) 37: 5-28.

Truong, Rachel, Attack on Frost Giant: How Shingeki no Kyojin examines the Nordic cycle of fate (2018). Undergraduate Honors Theses.56. https://digital.sandiego.edu/honors_theses/56

Ursini, F., (2017) Themes, focalization and the flow of information: The case of Shingeki no Kyojin. The Comics Grid: Journal of Comics Scholarship 7, 2.

van Benthem, J. & Ter Meulen, A, (2010). Handbook of logic and language (2nd ed.). Elsevier.

Vergano, D. (2014). Cave Paintings in Indonesia Redraw Picture of Earliest Art: The dating discovery recasts ancient cave art as a continent-spanning human practice. National. https://www.nationalgeographic.com/science/article/141008-cave-art-sulawesi-hand-science

von Uexküll, J. (1934/2010). A foray into the worlds of animals and humans with a theory of meaning. University of Minnesota Press.

Vygotsky, L. S. (1978). *Mind in society: The development of higher psychological processes*. Cambridge. Harvard University Press.

Wahl, C. (2016). Designing regenerative cultures. Triarchy Press.

Warner, M. (2013). Pandora's lunchbox: How processed food took over the American meal. Scribner.

Wason, P. (1966). Reasoning. In B. M. Foss, Ed., New horizons in psychology. Harmondsworth, UK: Penguin, pp. 135-151.

Wason, P. (1968). Reasoning about a rule. Quarterly Journal of Experimental Psychology 20.3: 273–281.

Wellington, H. (1995). Journal of Eugène Delacroix. Third Edition. Phaidon Press.

Wilkinson, R. & Pickett, K. (2019). The inner level: How more equal societies reduce stress, restore sanity and improve everyone's well-being. Penguin.

Wittgenstein, L. (1953). Philosophical investigations. Blackwell Publishing.

Young, S. N. (2008). The neurobiology of human social behavior: an important but neglected topic. Journal of Psychiatry and Neuroscience, 33.5: 391-392.

Yukari, F. (2013). Women in Naruto, Women reading Naruto. In Berndt, J. &

Kümmerling-Meibauer, B., Eds. Manga's Cultural Crossroads. Routledge, pp. 172-191.

Zagorin, Perez (2009). Hobbes and the Law of Nature. Princeton University Press.

Zhang, Q. A. (2022). Sensation, experience, and being alive: Foundations of cognition, learning, and flourishing. Doctoral Dissertation, Arizona State University.

Zimmer, C. (2021). Life's edge: The search for what it means to be alive. Dutton.